Cold Comfort

My Love Affair with

In 1936 the least-known area of Canada was the west coast of Baffin Island, part of which was still unexplored. Graham Rowley first went to the Arctic as the archaeologist of a small British expedition to map and investigate this uncharted area. *Cold Comfort* is the personal account of his experiences in the north before the Second World War and his remembrances of a bygone age in arctic history.

Rowley documents an era of arctic exploration fast passing from living memory, capturing the traditional way of life in the north before the dramatic changes of the last half century. This was the last expedition in the Canadian north to depend on traditional techniques, and he recounts how members of the expedition lived as the Inuit did and travelled by dog team over unexplored land. He describes the isolation, the extraordinary vicissitudes of travel in a sometimes savage environment, and the generosity and kindness of the Inuit.

Apart from completing the map of Baffin Island's coastline and finding new islands, Rowley was able to locate and excavate the first pure Dorset site, near Igloolik, establishing the Dorset culture beyond doubt. The carvings and artifacts found there, several of which are reproduced in this book, remain among the most beautiful that have been recovered.

Based on his own diary and the diaries of other members of the expedition, Rowley's captivating story presents the perceptions of a young man faced with a completely alien, yet fascinating, environment and culture. *Cold Comfort* will appeal to a wide audience as well as to those concerned with the Arctic in general. It is an invaluable source to those who specialize in the archaeology, anthropology, geography, and history of northern Canada.

GRAHAM W. ROWLEY, after retiring from government service, was a research professor of northern and native studies at Carleton University. He continues to excavate in the Arctic, and is still known to the Inuit as *Makkuktunnaaq* (or more simply *Makotenaq*), "the young man."

McGill-Queen's Native and Northern Series
Bruce G. Trigger, Editor

Cold Comfort
My Love Affair with the Arctic

Graham W. Rowley

McGill-Queen's University Press

Montreal & Kingston • London • Ithaca

© McGill-Queen's University Press 1996
ISBN 0-7735-1393-0 (cloth)
ISBN 0-7735-1823-1 (paper)

Legal deposit second quarter 1996
Bibliothèque nationale du Québec

Printed in Canada on acid-free paper
First paperback edition 1998

McGill-Queen's University Press
acknowledges the support of the
Canada Council of the Arts for
its publishing program.

Canadian Cataloguing in Publication Data

Rowley, Graham
Cold comfort: my love affair with the Arctic
(McGill-Queen's native and northern series ; 13)
Includes index.
ISBN 0-7735-1393-0 (bnd)
ISBN 0-7735-1823-1 (pbk)
1. Rowley, Graham – Journeys – Northwest
Territories – Baffin Island.   2. Baffin Island (N.W.T.) –
Discovery and exploration – British.   3. Baffin Island
(N.W.T.) – Description and travel.   I. Title.   II. Series.
FC4167.2.R69   1996   917.19′5042   C96-900122-3
F1060.9.R69   1996

To Diana, my other love affair,
who learned to share this one

Contents

Maps

Preface

Some time ago I agreed to give a talk on the Arctic. When I saw the notice of the meeting, I found I was to speak on "My Love Affair with the Arctic." The title was a surprise to me but it served to focus my thoughts. A few months later I decided to write down what I could remember having said, adding what I had not said, either because I had forgotten or because I thought it would make the talk too long. I refreshed my memory by re-reading my old diary and the diaries of those who were with me in the north.

The interesting parts of a love affair are how it starts and how it ends. The middle tends to be repetitive and of concern only to those directly involved. As this love affair has not ended, my account covers how it began. The subsequent fifty-five years, so far, must be left for another time.

I had the good fortune to go to the Canadian north on a small arctic expedition in the years immediately before the Second World War. I did not realize at the time that what was for me the beginning of a personal discovery of the north was, in a wider context, the end of an era in polar exploration. We had to live in the ways the Inuit had evolved, and to travel by dog team in land that was still unexplored. There was the excitement of the unknown and of finding what lay over the next hill.

This is my personal account of those years, but it is also to some extent the story of an arctic expedition. I was a member of the British Canadian Arctic Expedition until our different scientific interests and the separation this involved made it simpler for some to work independently. The geographical discoveries made by its members are now part of the map of Canada, their collections are in museums, and their scientific work has appeared in scientific journals. The expedition was completed after the outbreak of the Second World War, and its story was never told. All its members were serving in the armed forces within a few weeks of returning to the south. They who could have written it – and those who might have been interested in reading about it – were preoccupied with more immediate matters. As this was the last expedition in the Canadian north to depend on traditional techniques, and also made significant geographical discoveries, its story forms a legitimate part of the history of the Arctic.

Since the Second World War, changes to the map of Canada have been made from air photography. Geologists, archaeologists, and other scientists have reached their destinations by airplane and helicopter in a few hours, rather than by traditional means in months. They have been able to bring much of the south with them, replacing the satisfactions the north provides. They have lost more than they gained, and I do not envy them.

The spelling of Inuit words is always a problem for an author. I have retained the customary spelling for those words, such as igloo and komatik, that have become part of the English language. Where the Canadian Permanent Committee on Geographical Names has adopted a name for a feature I have used that name and spelling in the text and on the maps, except where a different name was then current in the north. I have often omitted the English generic with Inuit names, because it is frequently repetitious and confusing. For Inuit place-names I have tried to follow the orthography recommended by the Inuit Language Commission. I have also followed its orthography for Inuit personal names unless the individual or his family used a different spelling.

I have in most cases used Inuk (singular) and Inuit (plural) when referring to the Eskimos living in Canada. I have sometimes retained Eskimo as an adjective when it seemed more natural. It was a word that had earned respect and admiration throughout the north, and suggestions that it was in any way derogatory would in those days have been considered ridiculous.

I am greatly indebted to many friends, both Inuit and white, who encouraged me to write this account and helped me to complete it.

Acknowledgments

Many people have helped me in many ways to complete this book. Most of them have read, commented on, or corrected part or all of it in various drafts. Among these are Tom Manning, Peter Bennett, Dick Keeling, Jackie Manning, Handa Bray, J. Tuzo Wilson, Omond Solandt, John Macdonald, George and Jessie Falconer, Curtis Merrill, Harald Finkler, Gerard Kenney, Arch Mackenzie, Rhoda Innuksuk, Margaret Stevens, Don Akenson, Philip Goldring, Mary McDougall Maude, and, of course, my family, especially my wife.

I am particularly grateful to Dalton Muir for the way he has produced clear illustrations from small, old, scratched negatives; to George Falconer for his assistance with the maps, and to Brenda Carter for most of the line drawings that enliven the text. The maps were drawn by Signy Fridriksson-Fick, using as base the Canada Base Map Series of Geomatics Canada, Natural Resources Canada.

I thank the Scott Polar Research Institute for giving me permission to reproduce the drawings "Building an igloo," which illustrated an article I wrote in the *Polar Record* 2, no. 16 (1938). I also thank the Cambridge University Museum of Archaeology and Anthropology and Dr Jørgen Meldgaard, of the Nationalmuseet of Denmark, for permission to reproduce their photographs of artifacts from my excavations.

The title of the book is taken from the final scene of Shakespeare's *King John*.

PART ONE

... this part of the world, so little known and so terribly represented by people who, in order to raise their own merit, make dangers and difficulties of common occurrences; merely because the places are unknown, and there is little or no probability of their ever being contradicted.

– Lieutenant Richard Pickersgill, Commander of His Majesty's Armed Brig *Lion*, describing a voyage to Davis Strait and Labrador in 1776

Preparing for an expedition

One morning in June 1935 Tom Manning came to see me in Cambridge. I did not know him, but he gave me a letter from Louis Clarke, the eccentric and respected curator of the Cambridge University Museum of Archaeology and of Ethnology, who added style and unpredictability to the museum's activities. His letter was short:

June 12, 1935.

My dear Rowley,
This is to introduce Mr. Manning with whom, I hope, you will go to the Arctic. He will explain things to you.

Yours sincerely,
Louis Clarke.

Tom Manning was of average height, as I am, but in no other way was he average or did he resemble me. He had just spent nearly two years on his own on Southampton Island, in the northwest corner of Hudson Bay, where he had been mapping the island, making zoological collections, and learning how to live and travel in the Arctic. In April he had driven his dog team across Roes Welcome Sound to the mainland and south to Churchill, continuing by train to Montreal and ship to England. He was still deeply tanned from driving south into the sun.

I was just finishing my fourth year at Cambridge University. I had graduated in natural sciences and then studied archaeology, and I had no idea what to do next. My father, who had died several years earlier, had been an engineer and my older brother had taken over the business he had built up. My other brother was a doctor. I had wanted to be a farmer but everyone considered this a silly idea, pointing out how little I knew about farming.

Tom told me he was planning a small scientific expedition to the Eastern Canadian Arctic, for which he was recruiting four men to join him. The expedition would leave England the next spring and spend up to three or four years in the north. He asked me to be the archaeologist, and said little else. I had not thought about the Arctic until reading Louis Clarke's letter, so I did not know what sort of questions to ask him. However, nobody else had said they wanted an archaeologist, and going to the Arctic would give me an excuse for postponing any decision on my future career. I took the easy course and agreed to become a member of the British Canadian Arctic Expedition, though I knew even less about exploring than I did about farming. I gave little thought to how many thousand miles of travel this would entail, by small boat or by dog team or on foot. Still less did I realize that, in trying to evade the issue, I had in fact determined how I would spend most of the rest of my life.

Tom persuaded Reynold Bray, an old school friend of his, to be the ornithologist. Reynold had been on an Oxford University expedition in the summer of 1931 to Akpatok Island in Ungava Bay, south of Hudson Strait. He was slight in build and had a quick mind that often reacted swiftly to the unexpected. His opinions on any subject were free of conventional limitations and always disarmingly frank.

Tom and Reynold had not only been at Harrow together. At the end of his second year at Cambridge, Tom had walked about one thousand miles along the coast of Norway to Bödo, where Reynold had joined him, and, rather than return to university, they had continued east across the mountains. When fall turned to winter they bought a reindeer and sledge, passed through northern Sweden and Finland, and crossed the border into Russia. Soldiers soon arrested them and, after an interlude in Leningrad jail, they were allowed to return to England. Tom had then gone to Southampton Island.

Pat Baird was our geologist and had also some interest in botany. He was a tall and rather reserved Scot and in 1934 had been a surveyor on a summer expedition to the east coast of Baffin

Island. He liked climbing mountains and walking long distances carrying a heavy pack. He tended to be uncommunicative, keeping most of his observations for the detailed diary he always wrote. It was never easy to know what he was thinking.

Dick Keeling, who was soon to qualify in medicine, offered to spend the first summer with us. His arctic experience was limited to a visit to Svalbard with a Cambridge party in the summer of 1933. His helpfulness and quiet competence were sure to make him an excellent doctor, but as he was intending to specialize in gynaecology, he was unlikely to gain professionally from his summer with us, which would really be a long and enterprising vacation for him before taking up a hospital appointment. We would certainly gain from his help and friendship.

The final member was Peter Bennett, a lieutenant in the Royal Engineers, who was at Clare College with me. I met him by chance in October, and he asked what I was doing. When I said I was going to the Arctic he said that he would like to come too. Tom agreed and the War Office gave him permission to join us as a surveyor at the end of the first summer, when he would have completed his degree. He would then replace Dick. Neither Peter nor I had ever been in the Arctic, nor had we more than a passing interest in the polar regions.

Other than Tom and Reynold we were essentially a group of strangers. We had had rather similar lives but we had few common interests and held very different views on many subjects. We were all in our early twenties, single, and had been up at Cambridge, except Reynold, who was married and had been sent down from Oxford.

In 1935 maps of Canada showed some of the northern coasts by dotted lines because they were still unknown. No ship had sailed there and no aircraft had yet flown through the sky above. The least explored part of Canada, and indeed of the entire circumpolar north, was the east coast of Foxe Basin, the sea that lies between Baffin Island and the mainland of Canada. This was where Tom was planning to take us. Part of this coast and much of the interior of Baffin Island had remained beyond the reach of expeditions and were rarely visited by the Inuit because the hunting was unpredictable. The reasons that an area comparatively far south had been so little explored, long after the more northern islands had been mapped, were both historical and geographical.

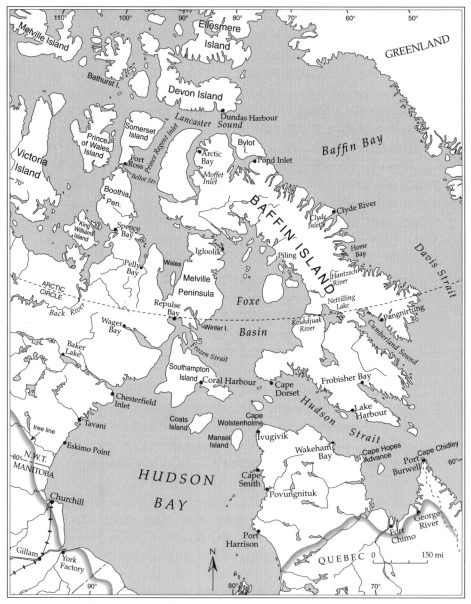

Map 1   General map of area. Place-names are those used at the time of the expedition; some have since been replaced by official names.

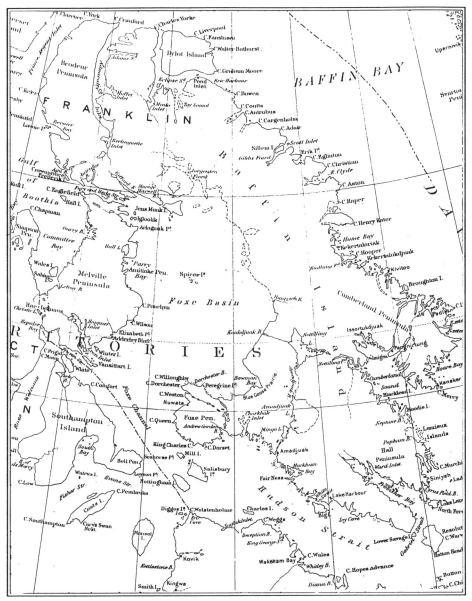

Map 2   Baffin Island showing coastline as known in 1935.
From Dominion of Canada Map, 100 miles to 1 inch, 1937

Historically, most of the Canadian Arctic had been discovered by the many parties searching for the expedition led by Sir John Franklin that had disappeared in the middle of the nineteenth century. His two ships had been seen entering Lancaster Sound so there was little point in looking for them through Hudson Strait. Once the fate of the Franklin Expedition was known, explorers became more interested in reaching the north pole than in completing the map of Canada, and Foxe Basin was again bypassed.

Geography had also particularly isolated Foxe Basin. North of Cumberland Sound, the east coast of Baffin Island is precipitous and in only two or three places is it possible to cross the island to Foxe Basin without first climbing a wall of cliffs three or four thousand feet high and often vertical. Foxe Basin itself usually remained choked with ice until early September, by which time ships in Hudson Bay or Hudson Strait were thinking of returning to the south rather than sailing through Foxe Channel into the unknown.

Tom's plan was for the five of us to sail in a small boat from Churchill to Southampton Island as early in the spring of 1936 as we could. He had already mapped most of the island but his radio had broken down and he wanted to fix some key points accurately by astronomical methods; to do this radio time signals were essential. At the end of the summer we would move north to Repulse Bay, a trading post in the extreme northwest corner of Hudson Bay. That winter we would travel by dog team and map to the west as far as Pelly Bay and to the south to Chesterfield Inlet. The next summer we would sail to Cape Dorset on the southwest corner of Baffin Island and then into Foxe Basin as soon as the ice allowed us, making our way north along the west coast of Baffin Island. We would map, excavate, collect, and record along our route. There would be plenty to do because the country was so little known.

We lived in different parts of Britain and never all met together though preparing for the expedition took much of our time. Letters had to be written to firms who might be helpful, books had to be read, instruments and equipment to be bought, and arrangements made for collecting and storing our supplies and shipping them to Canada.

A major constraint was money. The Royal Geographical Society awarded us £200 and lent us surveying instruments: theodolites to measure angles and make astronomical observations, radio sets to receive time signals for determining longitude, and chronometer watches to keep accurate time between radio time signals. Louis Clarke gave the expedition £100, and we received two or three smaller grants, one of which was from a scientist to encourage us to collect lice from the skins of any birds we shot. Generous manufacturers produced some Barneys tobacco, Haig whiskey, Chivers jam, Coleman's mustard, Cadbury chocolate, Lyons tea, Li-lo inflatable mattresses, and Crosse and Blackwell tinned meat. Bovril sold us man and dog pemmican at cost price. I asked several manufacturers for a motorcycle to test over the arctic beaches and sea ice, but they were not interested. The Canadian government agreed to allow us to import our equipment duty-free. Our grants and the value of what we were given totalled about £600, which in 1935 was probably equivalent to less than $40,000 today.

The expedition was expected to take three or four years and would of course cost very much more than our grants. We would have to make up the difference ourselves. As we were not rich, we had to do everything as cheaply as we could to keep the cost within the £200 or £300 a year that each of us hoped to be able to contribute to the expedition. With more money we might have been more comfortable but at that time a little money could go a long way in the north.

Early in September Tom invited me to go climbing in Wales with him and Vivian Fuchs, who twenty-two years later crossed the Antarctic by tractor. After a few days an unexpected telegram arrived offering me a job teaching science for a term at Oundle School. I had found rock climbing rather alarming, and was not altogether sorry when I had to leave them as they attempted progressively more difficult ways of reaching the summit of Snowdon. The teaching job provided part of the money towards my share of the cost of the expedition.

2

The Eastern Canadian Arctic in 1935

While teaching at Oundle I read all I could find about northern Canada and the history and prehistory of Foxe Basin. The history was easy as it was so short, beginning in 1821 when a British naval expedition entered Foxe Basin in search of a Northwest Passage.

The expedition's two ships, HMS *Fury* and *Hecla*, commanded by Captains W.E. Parry and G.F. Lyon, were following the coast of the mainland of Canada north from Repulse Bay. They examined the inlets of Melville Peninsula, wintering first on Winter Island off its southeast coast, and then at Igloolik, near the entrance to Fury and Hecla Strait. Here they were stopped by ice and had to return to England in 1823. During both winters Inuit frequently visited the ships where they were welcome guests. Parry and Lyon wrote, often with admiration, of how the people managed to live under such severe conditions. Their sensitive accounts were eagerly read in Britain and were largely responsible for the southern concept of Inuit.

Whaling ships had begun to fish along the eastern coast of Baffin Island at about the time the *Fury* and *Hecla* were at Igloolik, but they did not enter Hudson Bay until the second half of the nineteenth century and never penetrated far into Foxe Basin. Over a hundred years passed before R.A. Bartlett with the U.S. schooner *Morrissey* repeated Parry's voyage along the coast of Melville Peninsula in 1927 and again in 1933. The *Morrissey* party had mapped Foxe Peninsula in the south of Foxe Basin, but in northern Foxe Basin they added nothing to Parry's chart.

The man who had done most to try to complete the map of Baffin Island was Bernhard Hantzsch, a German zoologist and explorer. Starting from Cumberland Sound in April 1910, and travelling with a party of Inuit, he crossed Baffin Island south of the mountains by way of Nettilling Lake and the Koukdjuak River to Foxe Basin. They then turned north along the low flat west coast of Baffin Island, and spent a hard and hungry winter at the mouth of what is now named Hantzsch River. Hantzsch continued his journey with an Inuit couple on 16 April, and had nearly reached an area known to the Inuit as Piling, when he became ill from what must have been trichinosis after eating raw polar bear meat. He had to turn back but his condition deteriorated, and he died at the site of the camp where he had spent the winter. The Inuit who had been with him and had cared for him during his sickness brought his record of this journey to the missionary in Cumberland Sound.

Shortly after the First World War, Knud Rasmussen, the famous Danish explorer, led his Fifth Thule Expedition in a comprehensive investigation of the ethnology, folklore, and prehistory of the area north and west of Hudson Bay in an attempt to determine the origin of the Eskimo culture. His expedition established a base at Danish Island, not far from Winter Island where Parry had spent his first winter. Their plans included sledging from Igloolik to Piling to complete the map of Baffin Island, but they had to abandon the two attempts they made.

The Fifth Thule Expedition carried out the first professional archaeological excavations in the Eastern Canadian Arctic. Most Inuit were then spending their winters in snow houses, but old abandoned houses made of stone, whalebone, and turf were known throughout the area. Therkel Mathiassen, the expedition's archaeologist, excavated several of these, finding harpoon heads and other artifacts that were different from those being used by the Inuit he met. He concluded they had been made by a different people, whom he called the Thule people, because very similar artifacts had been found at Thule in northern Greenland. The Inuit told him that their ancestors had arrived in the Eastern Arctic to find it already inhabited by a race they called the Tunit, a strong but timid people, who had moved away to avoid trouble. Mathiassen thought the Thule people must have been the Tunit of

Eskimo tradition, and that they had been displaced by the Inuit. The work of the Fifth Thule Expedition was of such importance to me that I went to Copenhagen in February to see the material Mathiassen had excavated and to meet him and the expedition ethnologist, Kaj Birket-Smith.

The Inuit described in the reports of the Fifth Thule Expedition were living rather different lives from those of their forefathers who had greeted Parry. The whalers had introduced guns, whale-boats, and other southern influences, first along the east coast of Baffin Island and then in Hudson Bay. After the whaling industry collapsed early in this century, fur trading spread from the whaling centres to numerous small posts. The Hudson's Bay Company (HBC) gradually took over those it had not built itself and by 1936 held a monopoly, with a number of posts along the coasts of the eastern half of the Northwest Territories, each with a manager and usually a clerk: at Eskimo Point, Tavani, Chesterfield Inlet, Wager Bay, Baker Lake, and Repulse Bay on the mainland; Coral Harbour on Southampton Island; and Cape Dorset, Lake Harbour, Pangnirtung, Clyde River, Pond Inlet, and Arctic Bay on Baffin Island.

About half these places had a two-man Royal Canadian Mounted Police (RCMP) detachment. Some had either an Anglican or a Roman Catholic mission; one or two had both. There were two small mission hospitals; that at Chesterfield Inlet was operated by the Catholic church, the other at Pangnirtung by the Anglicans, each with a government doctor. Chesterfield had in addition a government radio station, established as an aid to navigation for the grain ships on the Hudson Bay route to Churchill. The total white population in the Eastern Arctic was not much more than fifty, and for most of them the north had become a lifetime commitment.

Few of the four or five thousand Inuit in this vast area lived near the trading posts; most hunted and trapped from small camps along the coasts, making their homes in igloos in winter and tents in summer. Trapping was an important activity, providing them with the imports they wanted from the south, and for many the missions had brought a faith with a message of hope, replacing one they had told Rasmussen was based on fear. Change had been gradual. Hunting patterns had been adjusted to meet the needs of trapping, with the Inuit following much the same way of life they had known for generations.

Once a year a small HBC ship called at every post bringing supplies, of which guns, ammunition, tea, tobacco, coal oil, sugar, flour, canvas, and the blanket material called duffle were the most important, and taking out the fur, almost exclusively white fox. Each post had a radio receiver, but no way of transmitting messages. The HBC manager, on whom everybody depended to some extent, was usually the most influential man in a settlement.

The RCMP represented the government in the north, carrying out such administrative duties as recording births and deaths, issuing relief, and taking the census. They had plenty of time for administration as there was little crime. In the spring they made long patrols by dog team with Inuit special constables, visiting the larger camps to make sure they were facing no unusual hardship.

The missionaries also travelled by dog team to hold services with their converts and to recruit new ones. Inuit would often visit the trading posts and the missions, particularly at Christmas and Easter. In the absence of any formal education, some missionaries taught the small number of children living in their settlements for a few hours each week.

Except at Chesterfield and Pangnirtung there were no health services. The RCMP, the HBC, and the missions all had some medicines and varying degrees of skill in administering them. For professional treatment the only course was to wait for the doctor on the steamer that called once a year. He could arrange for serious cases to be taken to hospitals in the south.

This was the setting for our expedition. It was a north very different from that of today. The people were close to the land and the sea, dependent on the resources they found, which sometimes failed. Starvation was the control that limited the population. The influence of the south had not grown powerful enough for its attractions to seduce or subordinate those who lived in the north.

3

Ottawa, Winnipeg, and Churchill

28 March – 9 June 1936

Reynold Bray, Pat Baird, and I sailed from Southampton late in March 1936 in the *Alaunia*, one of the Cunard "A" ships that took eight leisurely days from Southampton to Halifax. We arrived on a perfect spring afternoon and were soon westbound by train through the beautiful countryside of the maritimes.

Our first night in Canada was unusual. Johnny Buchan, the son of Lord Tweedsmuir, then governor general of Canada, had been with us in the *Alaunia* and was an old friend of Reynold. His mother had come to meet him in Halifax and she invited us all to a delightful dinner in the vice-regal coaches. The evening sky was cloudless and, in a rising full moon, the snow-covered lakes shone like silver against the dark woods. After this memorable start I slept in my clothes in the day coach. We had bought "colonist class" tickets, which cost only $35 to travel from Halifax to Ottawa and on to Winnipeg and Churchill, a journey of nearly seven days' travelling time, and included a very generous baggage allowance.

Tom Manning, who had preceded us, met us in Montreal and the next day we went to Ottawa, Tom continuing on to Winnipeg and Churchill. I spent two or three weeks in Ottawa where there were many things to do. They included buying additional equipment, arranging not to pay duty on the whisky we had been given, and seeing various officials to tell them our plans and to receive permits to kill wildlife and migratory birds. We were also each given a "License to Scientists and Explorers to enter the North West Territories of Canada." These were nicely engraved documents, each with a large red seal. Framed and hung in an office, they would impress anybody.

One visit I remember well was to the Dominion Observatory. We had been asked to measure the magnetic variation and declination wherever we could, and we had to be shown how to use the dip circle we were being lent. A scientist set the circle on its tripod and noted the angle the magnet dipped with the circle and the needle in different positions, but the readings showed no consistency. It was a long time before he discovered his steel-rimmed glasses were magnetic.

By far my most important visits were to Dr Diamond Jenness, the renowned archaeologist at the National Museum. He showed me the museum collections, arranged for me to meet some of those who had been with him on Vilhjalmur Stefansson's 1913-18 Canadian Arctic Expedition, and helped me in every possible way. He described how he had compared the Thule culture specimens excavated by Mathiassen on the Fifth Thule Expedition with collections the museum had received from other places in the Arctic. After he had removed all specimens that resembled those found by Mathiassen, the remainder looked older, most of them were smaller, and none of them had any drilled holes, which were very common in Thule artifacts. He thought they must have belonged to people of a different and older culture, which he had called "Cape Dorset" because many of these strange pieces had come from there. Mathiassen and some other archaeologists did not agree with Jenness, suggesting his Dorset specimens were from Thule sites where they had been used for some special purpose. When I asked him how an archaeologist could be most useful in the Arctic, he said the Dorset culture would not be accepted fully until a site was found that had artifacts from only that culture, unmixed with Thule material. He suggested that finding such a site would be a very worthwhile task.

From Ottawa I took the night train to Toronto and, after a diversion to see Niagara Falls, continued on to Winnipeg, where Pat Baird joined me. He had been to the factory in Oshkosh to learn how to look after the make of engine we would have in our boat, and what to do if it gave any trouble. I had intended to resume my journey to Churchill with him next day, but a scratch on my head had become infected. A doctor advised me not to travel until it had cleared up, so I decided to wait in Winnipeg for the next train. Fortunately the train to Churchill had just changed from its winter schedule of once every three weeks to a weekly summer service.

I did not regret the week I spent in Winnipeg, then the gateway to the Arctic. The HBC fur trade was centred there and the city had a northern atmosphere, especially in the Empire Hotel where I was staying and where people from the north congregated. There were several things I could usefully do, and it was a friendly town. I particularly remember being taken to see the great flocks of migrating geese. During the week I was joined by Reynold, who had stayed longer in Ottawa to study the collections in the National Museum and discuss his work with the Dominion Wildlife Service. A day later Dick Keeling arrived. He had left England as soon as he had completed his final medical examinations, and I now met him for the first time. After a reference to our expedition appeared in the newspapers, we received more social invitations than we could possibly accept.

From Winnipeg a day and a night on the train took us to The Pas, the southern terminus of the Hudson Bay Railway, which had been built to carry grain from the prairies to Churchill for export. As the Churchill train did not leave until the next morning we had a day to spend at The Pas. To our surprise the mayor of the town had heard about us, and he made sure we enjoyed our stay. It was break-up time and he drove us to see the Saskatchewan River. Great blocks of ice were churning and rafting in the powerful eddies of the dark waters of the river in flood. Sometimes the ice formed a dam, and water and ice paused, but the pressure of the river soon broke through and the ice resumed its rush to the sea, leaving spring in place of winter. It was a spectacle that could not fail to impress visitors fresh from England, where everything is on a much smaller scale and seasons change more slowly and more gently.

The hospitable mayor then asked us to dinner at his house with a group of Hudson's Bay Company men, also on their way north. Among them was W.E. Brown, who was always called "Buster" and was the company's manager for the Nelson River district, which included several posts we hoped to visit. He had been in France in the First World War at the age of fifteen or sixteen, had then enlisted in the RCMP, and been stationed for some years at Chesterfield. His interest in the north led to his joining the HBC where he had soon been promoted district manager. He was always generous with his help and a source of sound advice.

Next morning, 1 May, we boarded the "Muskeg Express," a mixed train, mostly freight but with two or three passenger coaches. Three days were needed to cover the 510 miles to Churchill because there was only one train crew. Nobody who travelled on the train in those days could forget "Newsy," a silent and rather austere man, who sold magazines and chocolate bars but also cooked delicious inexpensive meals, usually of caribou or other country food. In contrast, the brakeman, Tommy Jack, was an extrovert with an unfailing stock of northern stories he told so well that he made the long journey seem too short.

The first day's run was only 137 miles, yet we were three hours late when we reached Wabowden. Here there was an inn where drinks could be bought and most of the passengers had arranged beds for the night. We considered beds an unjustifiable expense and spent much of the night in the beverage room before we slept on the hard wooden seats of the colonist coach.

As the train continued its unhurried journey for the second day by lakes and through woods with increasing depths of snow, trappers would jump on to sell their fur – beaver, mink, fox, muskrat, and lynx – to three or four fur buyers on the train. It was a buyers' market. The longer the trapper bargained, the farther he would have to walk home. The night was spent at Gillam where arrangements for refreshments and sleeping were similar to those at Wabowden. Here a toast was always drunk to the Gillam cow, the most northerly and loneliest cow in Manitoba. According to Tommy Jack, one year some cattle had passed through, having been shipped by rail for export from Churchill. The following day the Gillam cow was found thirty miles along the track headed doggedly for Churchill.

Early next morning we crossed the Nelson River at the Kettle Rapids on a steel bridge, which had replaced a wooden trestle bridge that nobody trusted. Tommy Jack's story was that the train used to stop before it reached the wooden bridge so the brakeman and any passengers could alight and walk across. The engineer would then start the train slowly and jump off. At the other side of the bridge the brakeman would jump on to stop the train while the engineer walked over to restart it.

Past Gillam the line, originally planned to end at Port Nelson, turned due north to Churchill, which had been shown to have a much better harbour after the roadbed had been completed to Nelson. The forest thinned as we neared the tree line and around midday we left what was then known throughout the Arctic as the "Banana Belt" and entered the Barrens. We had been told that herds of caribou could sometimes be seen along this section of the line and had been known to stop the train, but we saw no sign of life in what seemed a white desert. In places the snow had drifted across the track. We got through one deep drift with a terrific jolt, but stuck in the next. The engine was then uncoupled and charged the drift with the plough, disappearing in a cloud of snow before returning to continue with the train.

We were an hour or two late when Tom and Pat met us at Churchill. The expedition now had four dogs, so we put our bags on a sledge which Tom drove to our tent, which was large and dome-shaped, and was pitched on what was to become, according to the town plan, Hudson Square. Tom and Pat had shot several ptarmigan – a form of grouse that has adapted to the north by

" WILLOW PTARMIGAN "   BCarter

turning white in winter and growing feathers on its feet – for the first meal we all had together. They were good to eat, but would have been better if any of us had known the first thing about cooking.

The author at Pond Inlet

The port of Churchill, April 1936

Preparing to leave Churchill

Polecat near Cape Fullerton

Expedition members at Nuqsarnaq: left to right, Graham Rowley, Reynold Bray, Tom Manning, Pat Baird, Dick Keeling

Walrus on Walrus Island

Polecat caught on lee shore of Walrus Island

John Ell enjoying the expedition's pneumatic mattress at Coral Harbour

Tom drying out equipment on Walrus Island

Sadlermiut house at Nuqsarnaq

Graham excavating a Sadlermiut house at Nuqsarnaq

Loading dogs on *Polecat* in Duke of York Bay

Lashing a komatik

Hudson's Bay Company house at Repulse Bay

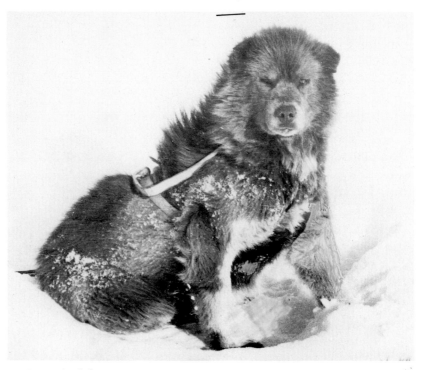

Kutuk, our lead dog

The railway had reached Churchill seven years earlier and the first grain ships had sailed in 1931. The town was still small though expected to grow rapidly. Its year-round population consisted of some Cree and Chipewyans, a few white trappers, a handful of traders to buy their fur and supply their needs, Anglican and Roman Catholic missionaries, railway workers, and the maintenance staff of the port. The Port of Churchill was the dominant influence in the town: it was under the jurisdiction of the federal Department of Railways and Canals, and it included both the port installations and the massive grain elevator which could be seen from afar. The town was much busier in the summer with port workers and the crews of the grain ships, which began arriving in the last week of July and had all left by mid-October. An average of eight ocean-going vessels a year were then loading grain there for Europe.

Tom told us we might be delayed at Churchill for up to a month. The previous year he had arranged for a boat to be built by a Norwegian trapper named Borge, who lived at Scandinavian Creek on the north side of the Churchill River where the HBC still kept a post. Some of the material he needed had arrived very late so the boat was not ready. This must have been particularly disappointing for Dick who would be with us for little more than three months, but nothing ever disturbed his good humour.

After much discussion we decided to name our boat the *Polecat*. She was a thirty-foot wooden whaleboat, open except for the first eight feet which were decked to provide a small fo'c'sle. Here a few things could be kept dry and two men could just stretch out, but it was too low for anyone to sit in comfort. Her 30 horsepower gasoline inboard engine required more patience than Pat could supply, and gave us constant trouble, which was probably largely our fault.

There was always plenty to do at Churchill – hunting, shopping at the local stores, cooking, buying two or three more dogs, and learning how to drive them. Sometimes we crossed the river to help in completing and painting our boat, and to try out a pair of skis I had brought with me.

Most of the expedition's supplies had been sent by rail to Churchill. They had to be repacked in separate consignments for shipping either in the HBC steamship *Nascopie* to posts we were planning

to visit on Southampton and Baffin Islands, or in the company's
schooner *Fort Severn* to Repulse Bay.

We also had to buy suitable clothing for the summer: lumber
jackets, heavy trousers, and parkas of duffle, the well-known HBC
blanket material. On our feet we wore *mukluks*, the name used
in Churchill for the Eskimo *kamik*. These knee-high boots were
made of the skin of the common ringed seal, with feet of the
much tougher square flipper seal sewn on very carefully to ensure
a waterproof seam. The best way to soften the square flipper sealskin for sewing or after it had got wet and been dried was to
chew it, a task that fell to the women for those lucky enough
to have wives. A measure of the diligence of a woman was said
to be the extent to which her teeth had been worn down through
caring for her family. Unfortunately we were all male and rarely
enjoyed the comfort of soft boots.

A number of other minor but necessary skills had to be acquired. One was how to make bannock by mixing flour and baking
powder, one cup to one tablespoonful, with a little salt, into a
stiff paste with water and heating it very gently for a long time
in a slightly greased frying pan over a primus stove. A tin lid
was always put over the primus flame to prevent the bannock
from burning. Another was sewing dog harnesses. I remember
learning how to join two ropes in a long splice, something I had
never heard of, for a block and tackle.

The birds also appeared to have been delayed at Churchill.
Flocks of oldsquaw duck filled the air with their penetrating but
tuneful call as they flew low, circling over the sea ice. Like the
migrating geese at Winnipeg and the break-up of the Saskatchewan River, they seemed to emphasize the urgency and vitality
of the northern spring. Reynold and Tom were kept busy skinning
the twenty-five species of birds we were able to shoot, search
for lice, and send to the National Museum in Ottawa before we
left Churchill.

Tom had made a very large and very strong *komatik*, the Eskimo
name for the type of sledge they use. A komatik has two runners,
curved upward at the front end and slightly canted, with the top
an inch or two closer than the bottom, lashed onto cross-bars.
Towards the end of May the *Polecat* was ready for us to load on
Tom's komatik to be dragged by tractor to the ice of the Churchill
River. We could then launch her, still on the komatik, from the

ice edge. This went without a hitch except that we had neglected to tie the komatik to either the *Polecat* or the tractor. It floated quickly away and we had to search for it in a freight canoe that Tom had bought. We found it washed ashore a mile or so downstream.

It was not long before our problems with the engine began. During an unexpectedly cold night, the water pump froze and stripped one of its gears when Pat started the engine. We were embarrassed, but the ever-helpful Department of Railways and Canals repaired it for us overnight in their machine shop.

The following night we had our first memorable arctic experience, which could easily have become our last. The *Polecat* was anchored to the ice edge and Tom, Pat, and I were loading supplies when a strong northerly wind forced us to move her to seek shelter on the north side of the river. Just after Tom and I turned in, leaving Pat on watch on deck, the river ice began to break up, without warning and weeks earlier than usual. Pat roused us because great pieces of ice were sweeping downstream in the powerful current while the wind, now nearly of gale force, was blowing us in the opposite direction among them. The engine kept stopping, and the rudder proved far too small to have much effect, and in any event was soon smashed by the ice. A large crate on the fo'c'sle deck, with supplies we had not yet stowed away, caught the wind, acting like an immovable sail and compounding our difficulties.

Throughout the night we kept dodging or failing to dodge the ice, sometimes having to jump onto the larger pieces to push them away or to pull the *Polecat* into a better position, while trying to avoid losing contact with her and floating out to sea on a pan of ice. It was well into Sunday morning before the wind slackened a little and, wet and cold, we could inch our way across the river into a small sheltered cove near the town and close to where we had moved our camp for our final preparations. The night had been light enough to provide the population of Churchill with the best Saturday night's entertainment they had had for years.

We had to repair the propeller which had been damaged, and were further delayed by deciding to reduce our load and then by ice packing into our cove. Finally, after one or two false starts, and with a new, much larger and sturdier rudder, we loaded the *Polecat* and the canoe which we were going to tow to carry part of our belongings. As a parting gesture, the cook of the Department of Railways and Canals brought us a rhubarb pie and some cakes. With the five of us, gasoline for the journey, food and fuel for the summer, tents, equipment, instruments, baggage, and the dogs on top, we were low in the water. The weather was beautiful and most of Churchill was present to see us off and to hear an old trapper's parting sally, "If one of them dogs pisses, she'll sink."

4

Churchill to Bay of Gods Mercy
9 June – 18 July 1936

The Churchill elevator, standing out against the clear blue sky, sank slowly below the horizon as we sailed north keeping close to the floe-edge, the limit of the land-fast ice. We were now on our own. It was 9 June, later than we had hoped, but several weeks before the Port of Churchill would open, and much earlier than small boats normally travelled along this coast. Our intention was to head about three hundred and fifty miles north to Chesterfield and from there another one hundred and fifty miles east to Southampton Island.

The band of land-fast ice between the floe-edge and the shore was several miles wide in the bays, though much less or absent near the points. In those days Hudson Bay was believed to remain open throughout the year. During the winter one could rarely see far across the water from the floe-edge because of mist rising from the sea, which was much warmer than the air. Everyone assumed this open water continued across the bay. Not until the Second World War, when aircraft first flew over Hudson Bay in winter, was it realized that the whole bay froze over late in the fall. What appeared from the floe-edge to be open sea was really a narrow lead of water, rarely more than a few miles wide, which was kept open by the prevailing northwest winds. Winds from the east soon closed the lead.

We had a good run with a following wind and found we could make seven miles in an hour. In twenty-four hours we were near to Eskimo Point where we anchored in shallow water. Tom and Dick took the canoe to the land-fast ice and then walked the two or three miles to the settlement to deliver mail we had brought

Map 3   Boat and sledge routes, 1936-37
For enlarged detail of area indicated, see page 92.

from Churchill, and to pick up gasoline to replace some of what we had used. The *Polecat* made rather less than four miles per very expensive gallon.

While Tom and Dick were away the ice nearby broke up, forcing us to raise anchor. We drifted out to sea, while Pat tried but failed to start the engine. Though Pat appeared in every way to be a phlegmatic and imperturbable Scot, he quickly became frustrated with anything he could not control. We had to row the *Polecat* about a mile back to tie up at the floe-edge.

Next morning Donald Marsh, an Anglican missionary who many years later became bishop of the Arctic, and three Inuit, brought Tom and Dick by dog team with twenty gallons of gasoline. These were the first Inuit I had ever met. Dick had been able to treat two sick people at Eskimo Point, his first patients as a fully qualified doctor. At that time the term Inuit was rarely heard, except to mean people in general. Everyone in the Eastern Arctic, including those Inuit who could speak some English, used "Husky," a contraction of Eskimo. A sledge dog was called a husky dog, and never a husky.

Before he left, Donald Marsh gave us two geese and a snowy owl for Reynold to skin and all of us to eat. We drew lots and Reynold and I won the owl for lunch. It proved to be literally tough luck.

Eventually we started the engine and set off late that afternoon. The wind had risen a little and our canoe soon swamped, but we recovered it with most of its cargo. During the night poor visibility, owing to mist and snow, halted us and by morning the ice had closed around the *Polecat*. We carried a block and tackle and began to prepare to haul her out of the water, but had made little progress when the ice appeared to be packing less tightly. We stopped and waited, realizing that in an emergency we were unlikely to have time to unload the *Polecat*, fix up the block and tackle, and haul her onto the ice.

Towards evening the ice loosened enough for us to make our way as far as Marble Island, its steep white cliffs shining in the low sun. The island was the most historic as well as the most prominent feature along this coast. Here James Knight, exploring to the north for the HBC, perished with the crews of his two ships between 1719 and 1721. Last century several whaling ships used to winter in the small harbour on its southwest coast, and two were wrecked there. To the Inuit it was a sacred place where powerful spirits dwelt and men should crawl on their hands and knees at least as far as the high-water mark.

We were again held up here but after a few hours were able to continue under calm and dove-grey skies, at first picking our way through pack ice. Shortly before midnight we saw in the dusk the radio masts that marked the settlement of Chesterfield Inlet and, five days after we had left Churchill, we anchored to the floe-edge.

Reynold and Dick stayed with the *Polecat* while Tom, Pat, and I walked to the settlement, a long wet walk through pools of water, sometimes over a foot deep, covering much of the blue sea ice. Though only seven or eight miles, it seemed much more.

At Chesterfield, Lofty Stewart, the post manager, Leslie Livingstone, the doctor, Corporal Bill Kerr of the RCMP, and Freddie Woodrow, the radio operator, were all well-known characters who had spent years in the north. They were particularly pleased to see us because they knew the doctor's whisky, which had missed the supply schooner at Churchill the previous summer, was on board the *Polecat*. A man was then allowed to import two gallons each year into the Northwest Territories.

Chesterfield Inlet was the most important settlement in Hudson Bay north of Churchill. The largest in the cluster of buildings around the harbour was the small hospital operated by the Grey Nuns. The inlet penetrated nearly two hundred miles into the interior and, as all supplies then moved by water, Chesterfield could have been described as the gateway to Keewatin. It was a gateway that was little used.

My most vivid memory is of visiting Dr Livingstone. I had lost a filling in a tooth during the journey from Churchill and he offered to replace it. The first problem was what to use for the filling. This was solved by making an amalgam by filing down a dime, then a silver coin, and mixing the filings with mercury from a broken thermometer. Dr Livingstone had a foot-drill but found he could not work the treadle and drill at the same time, so he asked a nun from the hospital to pedal while he drilled. As she did this with averted eyes, synchronization was poor. He would stop and she didn't, or she would stop and he didn't. I was glad when it was over. I would like to say I still have the filling but it fell out three days later.

I also went to see Lofty Stewart, who had been on Coats Island when the HBC had had a post there. Some of the Dorset culture specimens in the National Museum in Ottawa were said to have come from the island, which we were planning to visit. Unfortunately he could only say they were from the northern end of the island.

The return to the boat was easier and quicker than the walk to the settlement had been. Chesterfield, like other HBC posts, had some Inuit helpers. Two men and a young high-spirited boy loaded a dozen ten-gallon kegs of gasoline on a komatik for the *Polecat*. Enough room was left for us all to ride back in comfort over the wet sea ice. On their return journey the Inuit carried the doctor's case of whisky to the thirsty settlement.

Our objective was now the estuary of the Boas River, which runs into the head of the Bay of Gods Mercy on Southampton Island, where large numbers of blue and lesser snow geese were known to nest. Reynold wanted to spend the summer at the goose colony to determine if the blue and lesser snow geese interbred, and hence whether they were colour phases of the same species, as Tom suspected, or should continue to be considered separate species. To reach Southampton Island we had to cross Roes Welcome Sound.

We continued along the coast to Cape Fullerton, hampered at times by ice brought in by a southerly wind. Two groups of Inuit hunting on the ice came out to see who we were and gave us some seal meat, fish, and a pair of boots in exchange for tea and tobacco. At the end of the second day the wind changed to the north, and by morning we could head for Southampton Island. We were able to pick a route through loose pack ice, and early in the afternoon could distinguish the low, grey, featureless coast of the island.

Bay of Gods Mercy, so named by Captain Lyon in 1824 when HMS *Griper* was mercifully saved from shipwreck there, proved very shallow, and we began to graze the bottom about five miles offshore. We had been lucky in crossing Roes Welcome Sound so easily and decided to tie up to the floe-edge and sleep. Next day we sailed carefully along the Southampton coast to find a convenient place to land Reynold and his supplies near where Tom thought the Boas River reached the sea. We had to carry everything for several miles through pools on the ice before reaching

"SNOW GOOSE and JUVENILE" BCarter

the shore and then across flat frozen marshland covered with melting snow, as featureless as the sea ice, until we came to a solitary patch of snow-free ground. The abundance of geese, ducks, swans, waders, and other birds showed that Tom had found the right place, and Reynold decided to set up his summer camp here. It took us nearly two miserable days to carry in all he needed for the summer. Everybody broke through the ice into shallow water to be soaked to the skin at least once. In his diary Dick describes the first day as "the bloodiest day of the expedition so far" and the second as "even bloodier than yesterday."

Reynold and I returned after midnight the second day to find the *Polecat* had had to anchor out from the floe-edge because of a swell. Pat fetched us in the canoe with its outboard Johnson engine. During the night the *Polecat* drifted farther out. In the morning her engine would not start so we tied up to a flat piece of ice, on which we landed to sort out the sails. This proved rather complicated as they did not fit properly, and the wind had dropped by the time we had agreed on how to rig them. Pat took Reynold in the canoe to the shore, now about ten miles away. Meanwhile a mist formed and we had to fire several shots to guide him back to the *Polecat*.

Next day we tried a new but not very efficient way of making progress in the continuing dead calm. We lashed the canoe with its outboard engine to the side of the *Polecat* and in this way crossed the bay to Nuqsarnaq, an abandoned Inuit camp site near the-mouth of a small river. This was one of the places whose position Tom wanted to fix accurately for his map, and there were also some old houses made of stone, whalebone, and sod, which I could excavate. We unloaded, pitched our tents, and were able to sleep in reasonable comfort for the first time since Churchill.

The *Polecat* could not be left at anchor in so much ice, but we found we could beach her in the mouth of a river less than a mile away. As neither engine would start we rowed, poled, and paddled her there. Pat and Dick returned in the canoe to our camp, while Tom and I remained with the *Polecat* until after high tide and then walked back. We had to cross the river and I thought I had found a shallow place, but was soon swept off my feet and had to swim the rest of the way. My duffle parka acted like a life jacket and kept me quite warm.

Next day Pat helped me map and photograph the old houses. I chose two to excavate, and began to remove the stones and turf from the surface. The ground was still frozen below the turf and I could dig only what thawed. Tom set up the radio so he could receive time signals to determine the longitude and latitude of Nuqsarnaq with the theodolite. He and Dick then worked on the engines with some success, while Pat looked for fossils. We were also able to measure the magnetic declination with the dip circle.

The coast was so flat that nothing could be seen inland from our camp except a series of low ridges of broken limestone, marking old shore-lines, with long narrow pools between them. We could however turn our backs on this dreary scenery to be rewarded almost every evening with magnificent vivid skies. The sun, sinking slowly to just below the horizon, painted the northern sky with pink and turquoise, while the blue and green of the sea and ice reflected its low rays in gold.

We had left Reynold enough food for several weeks and realized that we could ourselves run out well before we reached the HBC post at Coral Harbour. Some flour and baking powder remained, but little else. We calculated we could use the flour at the rate of two large cupfuls a day. This would make two bannocks. Half a bannock each left us hungry, and hunting therefore had to take up any spare time we had. Fortunately there were numbers of birds around. I am a reasonable shot but, possibly owing to childhood impressions fostered by Beatrix Potter, I had never really wanted to kill things. However the fact that we needed the meat to eat, and the skins to search for lice and add to the National Museum collection, made hunting an enjoyable break from excavating. Geese, ducks, swans, loons, gulls – we skinned and ate them all and gathered their eggs.

Tom and Dick took the canoe to visit Reynold. A few days later they came back with him and seventeen geese, as well as a large number of rather incubated gull, duck, and goose eggs. While they were away the first mosquitoes had appeared, but there was usually a wind from the sea and we did not then realize how lucky we were. Tom ran Reynold back in the canoe for his solitary summer with the geese, and on the way was able to get another astronomical fix.

We had intended to continue our journey soon after Tom's return, but the ice packed into the bay and until it cleared there was no point in launching the *Polecat*. The next few days were warm and sunny, without a breath of wind. This was just what we did not want. We would remain prisoners until a wind from the east blew the ice away from the shore. For the mosquitoes the conditions were ideal. I can find no words to describe how they tormented us all except Tom, who seemed to enjoy discomfort of any kind.

While waiting for the sea to clear, I continued excavating, often with Dick's help. Southampton Island had been inhabited by the Sadlermiut, a people who by the end of last century numbered fewer than a hundred. For a long time they had had little contact with the Inuit on the mainland and Baffin Island, and had kept away from the whaling ships. In 1899 however a Scottish whaling captain had established a shore station just north of Cape Low, the southernmost point of the island, taking some Aivilingmiut from the west coast of Hudson Bay as helpers. Two years later the whalers brought a virulent infectious disease which was contracted by some of the Sadlermiut who visited the station and spread to their camps. All the Sadlermiut died except for a woman and four children who were then adopted by the Aivilingmiut.

The Sadlermiut were said to have been different from other Inuit in how they lived and spoke. This suggested they might not be Inuit, but instead the last remnant of the Dorset culture. All the artifacts I excavated were however in the Thule tradition, often of whalebone and with all holes drilled, apart from those on one harpoon head of a Dorset type, which had probably been collected by some Sadlermiut hunter with an archaeological mind. Tom, who had begun to dig a house of his own, also found only Thule-type material.

Those last days at Nuqsarnaq were not enjoyable. Wherever we walked in the open we were accompanied by a cloud of mosquitoes. Thickest close to the ground, they covered the old houses like a blanket. The only repellent in those days was oil of citronella, which they ignored. We smoked as much as we could, but most of what I was digging was soaked in old blubber; my hands were greasy with it, there was no way of keeping it from the cigarettes I had to roll, and old blubber tastes bad and smokes worse. Nor is it easy to smoke when wearing a head net. To the arctic archaeologist the development of effective fly repellents has meant more than any other technological advance of the Second World War.

The mosquitoes were marginally fewer during the short nights, so I used to dig early in the morning as soon as there was enough light, and to rest during the day. When the sun was high in the sky the tents became too hot for sleep. This was not what I had expected in the Arctic. Lying down I could see the tent canvas darkened by the layer of mosquitoes that had alighted on it. Since that time I have visited many places in the Arctic and other parts of the world, but nowhere have the flies compared with those on the coast of Southampton Island that summer.

What gave us most pleasure was the appearance of the arctic char. By setting a net at low tide, we would be rewarded a few hours later with one or more delicious fish. On one tide we caught twenty. Unfortunately two of our three nets were carried away by pieces of ice; the third had then to be moved at the first sign of danger.

July 17 seemed the hottest day we had had, and the air was dead calm. We were in the tent that night trying to get the BBC news on the radio. It was the day before the Spanish Civil War began. The chimes of Big Ben were followed by a rustling sound outside, caused by a sudden and unexpected breeze, which quickly cleared out the ice and the mosquitoes. We packed and at high tide dragged the *Polecat* into the water. I went back for a last look at the old houses, and we loaded the boat amid a cloud of mosquitoes which reappeared the minute the wind dropped. They made us all the happier to sail away early in the afternoon.

5

Walrus Island

18 July – 22 August 1936

Our next objective was to visit Coats Island. Its northwest coast had never been fully mapped, and we hoped to survey it and then sail to the HBC post at Coral Harbour which we had to reach before the HBC steamer *Nascopie* called. Tom thought this might be as early as 17 August. She would be bringing Peter Bennett to join us and would take Dick back to the south. To be reasonably confident of getting to Coral Harbour in time, we would have to reserve enough gasoline for the leg from Coats Island to Coral Harbour, and this meant using the engine as little as possible until then.

In the first twenty-four hours I do not think we made more than ten miles along the coast, but the second evening brought a fresh breeze. Sailing was not easy in such a crowded boat, and both Tom and Dick were dumped in the icy sea when gybing.

When the sun rose we found we had sailed a few miles past Ranger Brook, where Tom needed an astronomical fix and Pat had cached some rock specimens on a geological walk. We anchored and Tom and Pat went back in the canoe. Dick and I tidied the boat, moved to a more sheltered place to beach her, and set the fishnet. Two is usually an easier number than three or four, and Dick was good company. What one remembers best years later is sometimes surprising. Always reliable and careful in everything he did, Dick had one unusual idiosyncracy. The boot he put on his left foot was often one of a different pair from that on his right. He rarely seemed to notice this, and if he did he left them as they were.

We had two good days' hunting before Pat returned, having walked from Ranger Brook. The sea had become too rough for the canoe. He said Tom wanted us to take the *Polecat* there, so at high tide we sailed her back.

Two more days were spent at Ranger Brook. I took magnetic readings with the dip circle while we waited for a clear night sky for observing and good radio conditions for a time signal. We then rounded Cape Low, and had to use the engine to make our way to Walrus Island, a small granite island rising over 150 feet out of Fisher Strait, so isolated that no land could be seen from it.

As we approached Walrus Island the reason for its name became evident. We passed small herds of walrus cavorting in the sea, and its rocky coast was covered with many hundreds more, enjoying the evening sunshine. Most of them plunged into the water when they heard us, and it seemed as if a brown blanket had been stripped from the rocks. Our first priority was to secure one to feed ourselves and our dogs, and we anchored in a small bay. We drew lots to determine who would stay with the boat and I lost.

The others were back within two hours, having shot a walrus which had fallen into the sea and sunk, but which they hoped to retrieve nearer low tide. After supper we went out again, this time leaving Dick with the boat. The walrus, a young bull, was in about six feet of water but nearly floating, and we easily pulled it in with a boat-hook. Tom cut it up into big pieces while Pat and I were constantly keeping the knives sharp and dragging the heavy lumps of meat and blubber, dripping with blood, onto a rocky slab well above high-tide level. This took two or three hours, and I said I would stay to guard the meat while the others went back to make camp and rest.

It had been a very long day, it was a warm night, and after a few hours I became drowsy. I cannot recollect falling asleep, but I do remember waking up to find that some of the walrus had lumbered ashore again and were lying on the rocks, as I was, a few yards away to my right and left. This was closer to joining the herd than I wanted to get.

The sound of the outboard engine had woken me. The others had already unloaded and beached the *Polecat*, pitched two tents, and had come in the canoe to collect the meat. While we had been butchering the walrus, a polar bear had approached the anchored *Polecat*, and Dick had shot it. A few hours earlier we had been short of food; now we had several hundred pounds of meat.

Small uninhabited islands have a special appeal anywhere in the world. Walrus Island, a complete contrast to the flat, light grey, rather dreary limestone of the Bay of Gods Mercy, delighted us. It was an outcrop of the Canadian Shield with dark Precambrian rocks defining a steep coast, except where a narrow shingle beach formed an isthmus between the main body of the island and a barren knoll, which was its northern extremity. Small bays to the east and west of this beach could provide some shelter for the *Polecat*, in the one case from the prevailing northwest winds, and in the other from the southeasterlies which were common in summer. The beach was the obvious place to camp; nowhere else was level, and everywhere else was covered with boulders.

Exploring the island did not take long because it was not much more than a mile across in any direction. A few black guillemots, often called sea pigeons, were nesting on ledges in the rocks, and we came across three dead polar bears in different stages of decomposition. They may possibly have been wounded by the walrus and come on land to die. Of more interest to me were the remains of five small old houses which had been built in hollows.

I started to excavate two of the houses, with Dick and Pat coming to help when they were not busy in camp. Tom dug a house of his own. After two or three days we anchored the *Polecat* in the western bay rather than leaving her beached, because there was a heavy swell combined with high spring tides. Dick slept aboard.

It was still dark when I woke to find a rising wind blowing from the west and the boat dragging her anchor and being driven towards the beach. Dick was able to leap ashore and we all tried to push her out. Tom and Dick then decided to take her to the shelter of the other bay but the engine would not start. When they reanchored her she began to drag again, and they shouted to Pat and me to help row her round the point, but the wind and swell were much too strong for us to make any headway. We could not prevent her being blown ashore, and we unloaded everything through the waves and heavy spray onto the beach.

The *Polecat* filled to the gunwales and we watched, anxious but helpless, as the waves broke over her and she struck the rocky beach, regularly and heavily with every wave, while the tide rose and fell. Without her we would be marooned until some Inuit decided to hunt in the vicinity, which might be a long time. We would survive but would certainly become tired of eating walrus.

Four days were spent in repairing the damage. Fortunately the *Polecat* had been built to be very strong, and with a little caulking her hull still seemed watertight. We had to haul her farther up the beach with the block and tackle. Little had been lost, but the precious remnants of flour, sugar, and tea, and all our clothes and papers were soaked. Everything had to be unpacked and spread out to dry, almost covering the beach. The engine had to be taken apart, cleaned, reassembled, and with considerable difficulty restarted. I stitched the sail which had been ripped, and untangled the fishnet which at first seemed impossible.

Two weeks had passed since we had landed on Walrus Island and killed a walrus and a bear. We had plenty of food for the dogs but the bear meat was already getting rather high for us. We had finished the walrus liver which had provided us all with two meals a day for several days, and the flesh was tough, oily, and aging. The net we set every tide remained empty, and we did not want to shoot another walrus, most of which would be wasted because we already had all the dog-food we could carry in the boat. We had to rely on the guillemots on the island. Judging by their taste, we decided they were living exclusively on shrimp, which are better fresh than second-hand.

The planned visit to Coats Island was now very doubtful as there would be little time to work there. The decision was taken out of our hands when a sudden wind with an exceptionally high tide completely swamped the *Polecat* again. Our salvage operations were repeated with one exception. On the previous occasion I had, to my surprise and everyone else's astonishment, succeeded in restarting the engine when everybody else had failed. This time it resisted all efforts. The lack of both time and engine made a visit to Coats Island out of the question. All we could now do was to wait and hope for a southerly wind to take us to Coral Harbour before the *Nascopie* had come and gone. We thought she was due in a week and the wind was blowing strongly from the northwest.

I had been able to resume excavating now and again in the intervals between more pressing activities. Walrus Island had attracted walrus, and they in turn had attracted walrus hunters. Many of them had doubtless camped on the beach, as we had done, but I found no indication of those earlier camps. They would have been destroyed by the sea, which probably swept right over the beach in exceptional storms. The land here is rising at a rate of about one metre a century, and two or three hundred years ago there would have been sea where there was now beach. The few old houses in sheltered hollows on the higher parts of the island would have been built by hunters before the beach had been formed, or by later visitors who could not leave the island and had to find a place to camp that was sheltered from the winds and beyond the reach of the sea, as we might soon have to do.

Some of the objects I found were like those excavated at Nuqsarnaq, but many were quite different, being similar to those that Dr Jenness had ascribed to the Dorset culture. Unfortunately the few possible camping sites on the island were very small and had been occupied again and again, with the same stones constantly being reused. This had destroyed any stratigraphy that might have separated the two cultures.

It blew hard from the northwest for the next three days, and even the nicest small island loses its charm when it has become the limits of one's universe for an indefinite time. During the morning of 14 August, however, the wind seemed to be slackening. We started to get ready to leave and Dick, now more confident of catching the *Nascopie*, instructed me on what was in the medical kit, when to use it, and how to amputate a finger. By the time we had packed, launched the *Polecat*, and carried on board a few hundred pounds of maggoty walrus meat as well as our normal load, then caught the dogs, it was late afternoon and the wind, now light, had veered to the south. This was just what we wanted because the *Polecat* could not sail against the wind. The swell was still heavy but we could make quite good progress in the right direction. For me, the shorter the voyage the better. I have never been a good sailor, and the combination of swell and a cargo of rotting walrus meat made it difficult for me to enjoy what was certainly a dramatic change in our fortunes.

By morning we were nearing the shore of Southampton Island, and through binoculars we could make out some tents on the beach and a boat under sail heading towards us. When we met, Tom recognized Harry Gibbons with his young son and an old man. Harry, whose father had been the skipper of a whaler, spoke good English, better than any other Inuk in Hudson Bay. He looked at the magnetos of our engine but could get no life out of them.

A few hours later we met another whaleboat. It had an engine and Tom soon greeted Makik, who with about fourteen other Inuit of all ages, had been on his way to Harry's camp, called Nunariak. They gave us some flour, which we had run out of several days earlier, and a fish. We thought this was in exchange for a few gallons of our gasoline. However, Makik's knowledge of English was not as good as Harry's and we were surprised as well as pleased when they turned round and towed us the last ten miles into Coral Harbour, while we made bannock on the *Polecat*.

Sam Ford, the HBC post manager, met us and took us to his house for a drink. The *Nascopie* had not yet called, and he did not expect her for a few days. His radio had stopped working the previous November so he had had no news since then of "the outside," the term used throughout the north for anywhere else in the world. We were able to bring him partly up to date, telling him that King George V had died and been succeeded by Edward VIII, that the Italian invasion of Abyssinia had reached Addis Ababa, that there was civil war in Spain, that Jimmy Thomas, the chancellor of the exchequer, had resigned from the British cabinet owing to a budget leak, and anything else we could remember. Then, with the willing help of several Inuit, we unloaded the *Polecat* and pitched our tents.

The next two days we had to pack our specimens and artifacts into boxes to send out on the *Nascopie*, as well as write reports and letters. We also met Sam Ford's family and his clerk Peter Nichols. Sam Ford was from Labrador, a member of a family that had played an important part in the fortunes of the Hudson's Bay Company in the north. He was very well liked by the Inuit, who accepted him as one of them, and whose language he spoke as his own. To him the activities of the Inuit and the HBC in the north were complementary, and his role was to help both to prosper. No other white men lived on the island at the time.

Two groups of Inuit had replaced the Sadlermiut on Southampton Island. The Aivilingmiut had come from Repulse Bay and

Chesterfield Inlet on the mainland, had first moved to Southampton Island with the whalers at the turn of the century, and tended to be Catholic. The Baffin Islanders had arrived about twenty-five years later and were originally from the north side of Hudson Strait. They had been taken first to Coats Island where the HBC had established a post in 1918. It was closed in 1924, the company taking the Inuit with them to help establish the Coral Harbour post. The Coats Island post was reopened in 1927 but closed again the next year. The Baffin Islanders were all Anglicans and religion was one factor that tended to keep them rather apart from the Aivilingmiut.

One thing that brought everybody together was dancing. This was not the traditional Inuit drum dancing, but square dances introduced by the whalers. Mrs Ford and several Inuit women could play the accordion well, and a few notes would bring four couples forward to start the American Promenade, usually to the tune of the Arkansas Traveller. My only experience had been of formal dances in England. These square dances were much more fun, and the music was irresistible. It did not matter at all that you did not know what to do. Your partner, whoever she happened to be, would push or swing you in the right direction. The dancing could last all night and my only regret was that nights in the arctic summer were so short.

Tom had asked John Ell, the most renowned of the Inuit on the island, to look at our engines. He soon fixed the *Polecat* engine, and on the third morning he gave us back the outboard in good running order. John was about to become a grandfather and Dick was able to assist with the birth, which was not completely straightforward. He was surprised and delighted when the father gave him a pair of sealskin boots, his first professional earnings.

Tom, Pat, and I were now able to go in the canoe to Kuulluktuq, a few miles to the west. Here a small river ran into the sea and there were several stone houses. Tom left us there, taking back some material he had excavated two years earlier. I looked at the houses and pitched the tent while Pat went for a geological walk. He returned very wet, having been swept off his feet where he had first tried to cross the river.

Pat spent a day helping me excavate in intermittent rain before walking back to Coral Harbour. I continued digging another two days, but the site was recent and had no Dorset artifacts. The rain was heavy early next morning, so I wrote a letter and read *Tristram Shandy*. The Arctic is an excellent place for reading books one feels one should read but never does if there are any distractions.

After breakfast the rain on the tent sounded lighter and I crawled into the open. The first thing I saw was the *Nascopie* making her way through light ice towards Coral Harbour. I immediately struck the tent, cached everything, and set off to walk to the post. I arrived early in the afternoon to find the *Nascopie* at anchor, scows running to and from her, and the shore alive with people of all ages carrying supplies from the scows and stacking them on the beach.

6

Ship-time at Coral Harbour –
Coats Island and Duke of York Bay
22 August – 25 September 1936

Life in an arctic settlement reached its annual peak when the supply ship arrived, which in those days provided virtually the only contact between the north and the south. Supplies for the coming year had to be offloaded into scows, ferried to the beach, carried above high-water mark, checked, and stacked. The year's catch of fur had to be sent aboard. The HBC district manager would inspect the post and there might be unexpected personnel changes. A year's mail would be received, scanned, and in urgent cases answered in time for the outgoing mail.

The ship did not serve only the fur trade. The government was there too to demonstrate its authority. Some matters might have occurred that the RCMP had to investigate, and a magistrate's court might be held. It was the only time in the year when one could see a doctor. Two or three scientists would come ashore to collect plants, rocks, insects, or artifacts, and to ask questions. A handful of tourists would be taking photographs and asking different sorts of questions. There might be a wedding, baptisms, and, if a bishop were aboard, confirmations.

There could be newcomers to be welcomed to the settlement and farewells to be said to those leaving, with all their possessions. Old acquaintances would be on board, bound for some other post or on their way out of the north. All the Inuit came to ship-time if they possibly could, to see new and exciting things, and to be employed unloading the ship and, for a few days after, sorting and storing the supplies she had left. All this took place in an atmosphere charged by the captain's understandable anxiety to sail from the moment the ship dropped her anchor.

We were very sorry to lose Dick who had helped each of us in many ways and who always remained unperturbed in any situation. He joined the government party as the doctor for the remainder of the *Nascopie's* voyage. On the positive side Peter Bennett had arrived and soon proved a worthy replacement. He and Dick had similar strengths, and if they had any weaknesses they were well hidden.

One of the scientists on board the *Nascopie* was Nicholas Polunin who had been on Akpatok Island with Reynold five years earlier. He was collecting the flora at every port of call. Reynold was at his camp on the Boas River, and was probably the only person on the island not at Coral Harbour for ship-time. I must have received some mail, but I can remember nothing about it except a notice that a parcel had been sent to me containing many things I wanted. The parcel itself never reached me.

Ship-time did not last long at Coral Harbour that year. Though high winds made landing cargo difficult, the *Nascopie* sailed at 4:00 A.M., sixteen hours after she had anchored. Following the frenetic activity during her stay, the prevalent feeling was one of relief. One could well understand why the second-best day of the year at an arctic post was commonly considered to be the day the annual ship arrived, but the best was the day she left.

The expedition's next objective was to reach Repulse Bay to establish our winter quarters. En route, Reynold had to be picked up in Bay of Gods Mercy, and some positions on the west coast of the island had to be fixed by astronomical observations. The nights were getting much longer so it would be easier to observe the stars than it had been in midsummer. A group of Inuit, led by John Ell, were going to Coats Island to hunt caribou and were planning to sail around it. Tom decided we would split into two parties. Pat and I would go with John Ell to Coats Island and back to Coral Harbour and then cross Southampton Island by sledge north to Duke of York Bay, while he and Peter in the *Polecat* would collect Reynold and make the observations on the west coast before picking us up at the head of Duke of York Bay on 24 September.

Reading mail, getting ready, and loading the *Polecat* took two days. We had one disappointment. Peter had borrowed a radio transmitter with which he planned to carry out a number of tests, and which would have made it possible for us to communicate with the south. Unfortunately it was heavy and Tom thought the *Polecat* already had all she could carry, so it had to be left at Coral Harbour when Tom and Peter sailed early on the morning of 25 August.

Pat and I did not leave for another two days. In the meantime John Ell took me to Kuulluktuq to collect the cache I had left there. For the Coats Island expedition there were about twelve of us, all men, in two Peterheads, boats which were about forty feet long, decked, and with reliable inboard engines. Both were much tidier and more comfortable than the *Polecat* had ever been. Pat and I were in John Ell's boat along with his father, Angutimarik, and Joe Curley, an adopted brother. The skipper of the other boat was another Aivilingmiut, Tommy Bruce.

Once we got clear of the loose ice at the head of South Bay, the sea was rather rough with a southwest wind and we spent the night sheltering in the lee of limestone cliffs close to Harry's camp at Nunariak. We were near an old Sadlermiut village of more than twenty houses, which we went ashore to visit next afternoon in continuing bad weather. The following day was again very wet and windy, and we had to move to a small nearby harbour as ice seemed to be packing into South Bay. We woke to find we were firmly shut in, and we remained imprisoned by ice, and sometimes fog as well, for two more days.

We had not expected to be held up for so long and we soon read everything we had with us. Pat introduced me to the game of battleships which we played now and again from then on. Our greatest interest was however our companions. We had never before travelled with Inuit and did not know what to expect. I suppose there was a certain degree of apprehension. Our backgrounds were so completely different: we might find that they could not understand us and did not like us, just as we might not understand and might not like them. Any such fears were soon laid at rest. We were made to feel at home at once. Whatever they may have thought of us, they acted as if we were old and valued friends. I realized that mankind was a much nicer species than I had been led to believe.

With such companions the days of idleness were no hardship. We tried to learn a little of their language and how to write in syllabics. We practised throwing harpoons and using slings. We played hearts, a card game resembling whist with the important advantage in the north that it did not matter if a few cards were missing from the pack. We learned how to split a match with a needle first into halves and then into quarters to provide four lights. Angutimarik excelled in telling stories, parts of which we could understand. In one he described some incident from the whaling days repeating three or four times, "Plenty smoke, plenty fire, no cookum," accompanied with much laughter. We never discovered what had happened, but it had certainly made a lasting impression.

On our sixth morning near Nunariak the ice looked to us to be just as tight as before but a sudden decision was made to try our luck. For several hours we threaded our way through the pack, stopping now and again for someone to climb a pinnacle of ice from which to pick out a route. Eventually the pack became looser, and was gradually exchanged for mist and swell. At last the mist cleared and we could see Walrus Island to which we headed. We anchored in the bay where we had spent so many anxious days, putting up our tent for the night in the same place by the light of a clear full moon.

Next day we made for Coats Island, pitching and rolling in a heavy swell. Our course took us through a small herd of walrus near the land, resulting in some exciting hunting. Three were wounded before one was successfully harpooned and secured. Some of the meat and liver, the heart, and a few feet of intestine were cut out for us all to eat and the rest of the carcass abandoned. It seemed wasteful but I was not sorry to be spared sharing the bottom of the boat, where I often slept, with great lumps of slippery walrus meat.

We sailed southwest along the coast of Coats Island for an hour before anchoring by a gravel spit. Here we went ashore to hunt but we saw no caribou and returned with only a couple of swans. The country was like that around the Bay of Gods Mercy – low flat limestone, marshy, and with many lakes. After sleeping in the boat we sailed southwest along the coast for an hour or more and anchored again. Most of the Inuit went hunting while I tested a site where there had been a camp, but the only thing of interest was a young and very tame fox which came to watch me. The hunters soon returned with a caribou. We sailed again and then anchored where a second caribou was killed and we spent another night.

After continuing along the coast next morning for two hours, three caribou were seen. Both boats were run ashore and all the Inuit went after them. Pat and I were rather slower than the rest and realized that in the excitement the anchor of our boat had been forgotten and we were beginning to drift out. All I could do was jump off with the anchor into mud and water up to my waist and secure it to the beach.

By the evening a gale was blowing, and we had trouble pitching our tent. We did not expect it would stay up in the wind but it survived that night and the subsequent week as we stopped here much longer than planned because almost all of us came down with very bad feverish colds. Throughout the north the annual ship brought in not only the year's supplies but also that year's cold. Having been isolated from the south for a year, people in the north were very susceptible to infection, and the "ship's cold" quickly ran through the population. John Ell and Joe Curley were particularly ill, and there was no compelling reason to move until they had started to improve. The weather was wet and windy and a big tent was made of the sails. There were caribou in the area, so those who were still on their feet could hunt. For me there was a site about a mile away with some low circular walls which I could dig. In fact I found very little and what I did find was recent.

Joe Curley was beginning to feel better by the end of the week though John Ell was still weak. As I had a thermometer I took their temperatures. Joe's was 96.2° F and John's 101.0° F, but the weather was improving and John thought we should return to Coral Harbour and give up our plan to sail around the island.

One of the boats had been blown ashore and we had to refloat her. We then sailed northeast back along the coast to where we had first landed. Four of us went ashore, and I found a number of caches and old stone traps near the beach but no houses or tent rings. We returned to the boat and slept. In the morning we made an early start. As we were short-handed owing to illness a man from Tommy Bruce's boat joined us and he steered the whole way back to Coral Harbour in rough weather.

The expedition to Coats Island had taken longer than expected, and we had to get ready at once for our journey across South-ampton Island. Tom had arranged that Harry Gibbons would take us and try to find a few more dogs for the expedition. He had bought ten for us at six dollars each, a price suggested by Sam Ford.

The eastern half of Southampton Island is granite, with heights rising to nearly two thousand feet, and much rougher country than the low horizontal limestone in the west. To keep to the limestone we would have to start our journey from the mouth of Rocky Brook, some miles west of the post.

Within a day we were ready to leave but woke to find a violent east wind had blown sleet into our tent, soaking all our possessions, and one of the boats had been blown ashore. We dried everything in the warehouse while the wind changed to the south and blew Harry's boat ashore. Next morning the sea was too rough for us to sail and the jetty had been blown ashore. By the time the weather began to clear later in the day, we had missed the tide.

We got off next day in a choppy sea. It should have taken under two hours to reach Rocky Brook, but problems with the engine made it a six-hour journey and we were nearly too late for the tide to allow us to cross the shallow bar into the harbour. No time was lost during unloading so the boat could return to Coral Harbour. We made camp, fed the dogs, had supper, and turned in.

We were a party of four because Harry had brought Tautungi, his thirteen-year-old son. The dogs numbered twenty: six of Harry's, the ten he had bought for us, two that had been with us since Churchill, and two kindly lent to us by L.F. Hodgson, who had replaced Pete Nichols as clerk at the Coral Harbour post. It was of course very early in the year for sledging. There was only a dusting of snow and part of our route lay across bare limestone. Harry had shod his komatik with whalebone because it would pull more easily over rock than iron. Fortunately, we did not have a heavy load: tents, clothes, equipment, and food, fuel, and dog-food for two or three weeks.

Even with twenty dogs the start of the journey was hard work, particularly at first. The land rose gradually, there was little vegetation on the limestone, and we all helped to drag and push the komatik. We moved slowly, stopping often to rest, but our speed improved where there was any grass. We may have made ten miles and we could still see the sea when we camped that night. Next day was much easier because there were some patches of thin snow over which the komatik ran well and we must have covered over twenty miles in perfect weather. To lighten our load we had cached part of our coal oil, a heavy tent, and anything else we thought we could spare. They were left on the land in an obvious pile to be retrieved by Harry on his way home. There was no food so they would be safe from anything except an inquisitive polar bear.

Next day we set off in drifting snow which became worse, forcing us to stop after about ten miles. It was thawing as well as snowing and drifting. In these miserable conditions we pitched the tent. Pat started to cook, while Tautungi dried out and warmed up. Harry and I unloaded, and saw to the dogs. We then spent a happy night eating, smoking, talking, and sleeping while the tent flapped in the gale. It was still snowing and drifting next day and we could not travel. About midday the snow stopped and later the wind dropped. We went to sleep hoping for a frost overnight to give us good going.

It did freeze during the night and the first thing we had to do in the morning was to beat off the snow that had frozen on to everything. This delayed our start, but conditions were quite good for sledging and we soon came to a major river. We knew we would have to cross the Boas River, the biggest river on the island, which Harry called Goose River, and we expected it to be our greatest obstacle. Harry said he recognized this to be Goose River and we crossed it easily where it was frozen. Several hours later we really did come to Goose River, and it proved even easier to cross. We shot two ptarmigan which made a welcome addition to our dinner that night. For some reason ptarmigan were always called partridge in northern Canada, just as caribou were called deer, and hare were called rabbits.

The next day we came to many shallow lakes in the direction we were heading. They were a nuisance because they were not quite frozen enough for us to cross, though we made several exciting attempts. Sometimes we had to go a long way back to find a way around. The only birds we saw were snowy owls hunting for lemmings. The population of lemmings varies greatly from year to year, following a four-year cycle, and was now on the increase. Their other major predator, the fox, would also benefit, and the income of the Inuit, largely dependent on fox-trapping, would show a similar fluctuation.

"SNOWY OWL" BCarter

We had hoped to camp at one of three fish lakes known to Harry on the Cleveland River, so we could fish for our supper, but we had to stop before reaching there. We passed the lakes next morning; there was no time for fishing as it was September 24 and the *Polecat* should be waiting for us at the head of Duke of York Bay. Towards evening, light snow began to fall, and soon afterwards the dogs became very excited. They had picked up a scent, which we thought was most likely of a polar bear, but they lost it, and we could not find any tracks.

Though we had expected to reach the sea early the next day, it was not until the afternoon that Tautungi realized that what we thought was yet more snow-covered land ahead was really sea ice packed into the head of the bay. There was no sign of the *Polecat*. We wondered what had happened to the rest of our expedition as we continued to sledge towards the coast. Then Harry saw in the distance a man walking along the shore towards us. As we drew nearer we recognized Peter Bennett.

7

A long walk to Repulse Bay

25 September – 13 October 1936

Peter told us that he and Tom had picked up Reynold in Bay of Gods Mercy. Reynold had collected some hybrid snow and blue goose chicks, showing they were colour phases of the same species. They had also fixed the astronomical positions that Tom needed along the west coast of Southampton Island. In Roes Welcome Sound they had experienced the same stormy weather that we had. The *Polecat* had been blown ashore once and swamped, but they had been able to refloat her. Wind was packing ice into the head of Duke of York Bay and had stopped the *Polecat* about five miles away. Peter had been on his way to leave a message for us saying where they were, and that they were going to try to make their way back to Cape Munn, where they would wait for us until 1 October. There was plenty of dog-food in the *Polecat* because he had shot a polar bear two days ago.

It seemed a long five miles to the *Polecat*. Much of it was in the dark, and we could not see the lantern that was to have been put out to guide Peter back. At last, after firing several shots, we found where the boat was. The ice had packed around the *Polecat* and prevented Tom and Reynold from coming ashore in the canoe. After a shouted conversation with them, we camped where we were. The five of us passed a comfortable night in the tent. It was our last comfortable night for some time.

Peter and I hunted ptarmigan in the morning while Pat, jumping from one piece of ice to another, made a hazardous visit to the *Polecat*. When we returned we found the ice had eased enough for us to get everything on board, including our twelve dogs. I had not seen Reynold since June, and he had grown a long thick beard. The *Polecat* also looked rather different because Tom had cut too close to a high piece of rough ice, and she had lost most of her mast. I took Harry and his son ashore in the canoe, with some bear meat for dog-food on their journey home, and said goodbye to them. I had thoroughly enjoyed the journey across Southampton Island, largely owing to their knowledge and good nature.

We had little difficulty poling our way through the ice into open water, and we then turned north along the coast before crossing to White Island, its steep black hills already covered with snow. Darkness fell, but Tom wanted to continue in these good conditions for another hour or so before we anchored for the night. We then discovered that the canoe, which we had been towing and which held all our tents, some fuel and dog-food, and much useful equipment, had broken away in the choppy sea. It was a serious loss but searching for it in that great bay would have been a waste of time, even in daylight.

Our journey next day took us through Comer Strait, which lies between Southampton Island and the west coast of White Island and is the western entrance to Duke of York Bay. We found it to be longer and much narrower than shown on our maps. We then headed for the mainland of Melville Peninsula. Once out in the open the sea proved too rough for the *Polecat*; she pitched so violently that we had to run to shelter in a cove on White Island. Later we crossed Comer Strait to spend the night on Southampton Island in a protected anchorage near Cape Munn.

The engine had been satisfactory since John Ell had overhauled it at Coral Harbour, but our problems with it now returned. All next day was spent in trying to coax it into life and late in the afternoon the water pump must have frozen, as at Churchill, stripping a gear. Peter set to work to try to repair this while Tom improvised a way to use the Johnson outboard engine, which had not been lost with the canoe, as a sideboard. A second day was being devoted to trying to persuade this engine to work, when Peter succeeded in repairing the stripped gears and started the *Polecat*'s engine. Both Tom and Reynold were feeling ill which Tom thought was probably owing to carelessness with the arsenical soap they used to preserve birdskins.

The weather was fine and all seemed well next morning when we began to get the dogs aboard. We had had to put them ashore at night because we had 200 pounds of polar bear meat in the bottom of the boat. We could find only ten dogs, so Pat and Reynold set out to look for the other two. They failed to find them and Tom said we should wait a day for them to return. It proved to be a wrong decision. We went to collect the dogs next morning, hoping to find twelve, expecting to find ten, but succeeding in finding only nine. There was obviously no future in waiting any longer, so we again headed north across Frozen Strait.

Our original plan had been to sail to the Repulse Bay post, but the ice was known to break up there late in the summer. Tom intended to make an early start next year and did not want to risk being imprisoned by the ice. He decided it would be better to winter the boat in Frozen Strait, which was likely to be free of ice earlier than Repulse Bay. I had assumed we would sail to Repulse, unload what we wanted for the winter, take on more fuel, a tent, and a sledge, return to find a good location in Frozen Strait to haul out the *Polecat*, and then sledge back to Repulse. It was already 1 October, which was getting late in the season. Going to Repulse and back would take at least two days of good weather, and Tom decided instead to winter the *Polecat* at the first suitable place we could find in Frozen Strait. This would give us a long walk to Repulse at a difficult time of year but he thought we could reach the post in three days. Other disadvantages were that we had neither a sledge nor a tent for our walk, we had no really warm clothing, and as we could take little with us, we would have to return to the *Polecat* later for things we needed during the winter.

We passed Cape Frigid, on a small high island at the northernmost point of White Island, and found no difficulty in crossing Frozen Strait. A nice little cove on the north side seemed a perfect place to winter the *Polecat* until we went ashore. We then discovered we were on an island separated from the mainland by a narrow strip of open sea. In the meantime the tide had fallen, grounding the *Polecat*, so we slept there before continuing our search. We soon found another suitable cove, this time on the mainland. While we unloaded the boat, Tom made a sleeping shelter with walls of two rows of snow blocks and a canvas roof. It was too early in the winter for the snow to be either deep or hard enough to build a snow house. I remained in the fo'c'sle on the boat in a not totally successful attempt to keep the dogs on the beach away from the meat in the boat.

Our two immediate tasks were accomplished on the following two days. One was to prepare the *Polecat* for the winter. With the block and tackle we hauled her far enough up the beach that she would be safe from high tides and any sea ice that might be pushed ashore. We then selected what we would need to take with us, and stored most of the rest in the fo'c'sle. Our other task was to make a sledge. Tom cut the broken mast and the spars into two twelve-foot runners, used the boat hook for eight narrow cross-bars, and lashed them, widely spaced, to the runners. This was as effective a use as could be made of what was available, but the resulting sledge was low, giving little clearance over rough ground, and not very strong. We wondered how long it would last because we had to take food for ourselves and the dogs, a primus and fuel, some spare clothing, a radio and batteries for time signals, a large metal box containing mainly instruments, a gun, canvas for a shelter, our sleeping bags, two polar bear skins to sleep on, an assortment of pots and pans, and a dozen ptarmigan we had just shot.

We set out on our walk to Repulse on 5 October, going west along the coast and gradually veering inland. Sledging over the granitic formations of the Canadian Shield was very different from our journey across the horizontal limestone of Southampton Island. The Pleistocene ice sheet, scarring and scouring the rocks as it moved, and leaving sand, gravel, and boulders as it melted, had given the land a grain, like the raised grain on a plank of weathered wood. We were cutting across the grain to a great extent and were constantly faced with short but steep inclines.

At noon we stopped for a "mug-up," a Newfoundland term used widely in the Arctic for making tea and eating anything handy while on the trail. Snow started to fall steadily during the afternoon and we camped early in a steep-sided valley. Tom and Peter built a snow shelter for the night while Reynold and Pat repaired and relashed the sledge – which became a daily task – and I fed the dogs. We had covered about ten miles though not all in the right direction. Camping at night and starting in the morning were always slow as there was room in the shelter for only one man at a time to dress or undress and get out of or into his sleeping bag.

We woke to find drifting snow which made travelling conditions poor. The sledge stuck in the soft snow every few yards. One man walked ahead to find a good route, break trail, and encourage the dogs; the other four helped to pull and push the sledge. Gradually we climbed out of the valley onto easier ground, but in such bad visibility it was then difficult to keep in the right direction. Our shelter that night was in the lee of a large boulder. We were not much closer to Repulse than we had been in the morning.

Drifting continued throughout the night but stopped soon after we set out, and we were able to see where we were going. Although the snow was soft, progress was quite good until the afternoon when we came to a fiord, not then shown on any map, cutting across the direction we were following. It was unfrozen and bounded by steep rocky cliffs, so we had to turn back on our tracks and strike north to get around it. When we camped we fed the dogs and ourselves the last of the bear meat. From now on it would be bannock, and not much of that, unless we killed something on our way. From time to time on our journey we had caught sight of what appeared to be a stray dog in the distance. That evening the stray, which was a bitch, joined us, giving us one more mouth not to feed.

The next day dawned clear and sunny but much colder than it seemed. The temperature was probably below 0° F. We were travelling into the wind and found how easily exposed flesh froze when Peter froze a wrist. The stray bitch had been added to the team and pulled better than any of our dogs. We had attached hand-lines to the sledge and used them all day to make about eight miles in the right direction. While we were building the shelter, repairing the sledge, and carrying out the other daily chores of camping, Pat walked some distance ahead. He cheered us by reporting the sea was only two miles to the west and that he had seen the head of Haviland Bay, which forms the northeast corner of Repulse Bay, about eight miles away.

It took even longer than usual to get up and going next morning because our stockings and sealskin boots had frozen overnight. Sledging was rather better as the ground was less rough and we could follow a chain of lakes leading more or less in the direction we wanted. At noon we made a cache of any equipment we would not need immediately, including the radio, an axe, and the large metal box, in order to lighten the load. We would be able to retrieve them from Repulse when we were better equipped. The ice on the lakes appeared to have become thick enough to bear the weight of the sledge and this made our journey easier. Just before we camped Peter broke through the ice, luckily above a large rock surrounded by deep water. His footwear and gloves froze at once.

We were late getting up next morning because the alarm clock on which we relied to wake us at 4:00 A.M. had frozen, but we were away by 8:00. It took another seven hours before we got around the head of Haviland Bay. We knew that Inuit often hunted in this area and we hoped to find a camp, but were disappointed. We had to continue late that night because we could not find snow firm enough for cutting blocks to build a shelter. Eventually we dug a large square hole in a deep drift, covered it with the canvas, and crept in. This took less time than building a shelter and was not much more uncomfortable. Our estimates for the remaining distance to the post at Repulse Bay ranged from a low of twenty miles to a pessimistic forty.

The country appeared to be more level and we expected better conditions next day, but there was no improvement. The rough and rocky ground had only a light cover of snow. We made our way to the coast to try the young sea ice, but found it too thin for safety. It had broken off wherever there was a spit and we had to return to the land. The attempt cost us a couple of hours, and we had made only ten miles before we dug another hole in another drift where we slept.

A strong wind next day and more rough rocky ground made conditions pretty miserable, and again we covered ten difficult miles. In our hole in a snowdrift that night we agreed that the post could not be more than ten miles away. All the cross-bars on the sledge had broken except two, and the dogs could not be expected to pull any more until they had been fed. We decided that, if we left the remains of the sledge with most of our gear, we would have a reasonable chance of reaching the post before dark.

Snow fell during the night, and we had to dig our way out of the drift to find a beautiful morning. We set off with two small bannocks made from the last of the flour, a primus, a kettle, two cups, one camera, and a saw with which to build some sort of shelter if we failed to reach the post during the day. In the sunshine and without the sledge to haul, it felt like a holiday. We soon came to a small fiord and had to walk some distance up it before we could cross to the other side. We then reached a valley where we found the tracks of a man and a dog. Shortly afterwards Pat noticed a flagpole near the coast behind us.

We fed our bannock to the dogs, turned round, walked down a small hill, and saw the characteristic white and red HBC buildings. Here we found a very surprised Joe Ford, the post manager, and his clerk, Henry Voisey. They knew we had intended to winter at Repulse, but when the sea began to freeze and there was no sign of a boat, they thought we must have changed our plans and remained on Southampton Island. They had never expected to see us walking down the hill behind their post in mid-October.

8

Preparing for winter travel
13 October – 21 December 1936

Within a couple of hours we were washed, clad in dry clothes, and eating bacon and eggs prepared by Joe Ford and Henry Voisey. Joe came from Northern Ireland and was not related to Sam Ford of Coral Harbour. Among his many admirable qualities he was an excellent cook. Henry, a member of a Labrador family well known in the north, was an outdoors' man, never happier than when hunting with the Inuit, whose language he spoke fluently. We were very lucky in finding them at Repulse, and seeing so much of them while we were there.

There had been two fur-trading posts at Repulse – the Hudson's Bay Company and Revillon Frères – but the HBC had bought control of Revillon, and during the last summer had closed any posts that duplicated its own. Joe told us that Buster Brown, his district manager, had said we could use the Revillon house. This was really good news because it would give us space to live and work, as well as sort and store our equipment. The annual schooner had delivered our supplies, and there was even a letter for me from a friend in Malta. I did not receive another letter from "outside" until the following September.

We spent the afternoon talking and taking borrowed sleeping bags to the six-room Revillon house, which far exceeded our expectations. Then we returned to Joe's house for a second splendid meal, I think of caribou. Overfed, comfortable, and relaxed in my sleeping bag in our new house that night, I realized how much our situation had improved in the past twenty-four hours. It was 13 October but it had been a lucky day.

Repulse had a Roman Catholic mission, a few hundred yards from the HBC and rather nearer to our new house. There were three fathers, Armand Clabaut, Marc Lacroix, and Joseph Massé, the first two of whom became bishops within the next few years. We saw them frequently, sometimes having meals together and more often for a game of bridge. Only three Inuit families lived in the settlement. Though they often visited us, I never learned the correct Inuit names of the couple who worked for the HBC, Big Boy, who was taller than most of his people, and his small energetic wife, The Bouncer. Louis Tapatai and his wife Hannah, both Aivilingmiut, had been employed by Revillon. They had a son, about ten years old, called Felix, who was a frequent and very welcome visitor. He watched every movement we made and sometimes drew pictures of us. Years later he was the first Inuk in the Eastern Arctic to be ordained in the Anglican church and, as the Reverend Armand Tagoona, became responsible for the mission at Rankin Inlet. He also wrote and illustrated a sensitive book, *Shadows*, about his experiences and thoughts. We saw less of the third family, who were involved with the mission.

With the Revillon post closed, Louis had time to spare to help us, which he did in many unobtrusive ways, sometimes without our knowing. Late that spring he had only just escaped drowning. He had been hunting walrus with the Revillon manager when their canoe was attacked and destroyed by a wounded animal. Realizing their sinking craft was drifting out to sea, they had to try to reach the ice edge. The Revillon manager could swim, reached the edge, but could not climb up onto the ice. Louis, though unable to swim, was wearing caribou-skin clothing which acted as a life jacket, and he had a paddle. He too eventually managed to struggle to the edge, where he was able to pull himself up onto the ice. He could find no trace of his companion. He then returned to their camp, harnessed the dogs, drove about thirty miles back to Repulse, and returned with a search party, but they could find nothing. Only then did he sleep.

From freeze-up to the end of the year is a comparatively static time in the Eastern Arctic. The days are short, storms are frequent, the ice on the lakes, rivers, and sea is often unsafe, and the snow is rarely deep enough for long overland journeys or hard enough for building snow houses. We had however plenty to do over the next two months.

First we had to collect the caches we had left on our walk to Repulse and to move to our house the supplies we had shipped by the HBC schooner. They included a nine-gallon cask of a special Scotch whisky, generously given to us by Haig and Haig. By some mistake it had been sent, plainly marked "Produce of Scotland," as deck cargo on the schooner. The previous year the schooner had been delayed for a day at Churchill. After a night on the town with some friends, the mate, pacing the deck with a long knife, had kept the crew in the fo'c'sle and the captain and passengers on the dock until he fell asleep in the afternoon. It was hard to believe that with such a thirsty shipmate our cask could have arrived, safe and sound, at the last point on the schooner's itinerary. With it we could repay some of the hospitality showered on us by the HBC and the mission.

Most of our time was spent in making preparations for winter travel. Four of us had had no experience and we had a lot to learn. Tom, however, had already earned a reputation in the north as an exceptional traveller. He set a standard we had little prospect of approaching.

"KOMATIK" BCarter

We started by making two komatiks, one eighteen feet long and the other sixteen. The only materials needed for a komatik are two long wooden deals about ten inches wide and two inches thick for the runners, a number of planks around four inches wide and an inch thick to be cut into cross-bars about three feet long, and line made preferably from the skin of the bearded seal. A komatik has to be flexible: if it were rigid it would soon break up in rough ice. Skin-line lashed each cross-bar to the runners using holes drilled through their sides and then passing over the cross-bar. The cross-bars formed an almost complete platform. Before a journey, boxes, skins, sleeping bags, dog-food, and anything else were stacked on the platform and secured by a long piece of skin-line lashed over the load and around notches cut in the protruding ends of the cross-bars. The front end of the runners was curved up so the komatik would ride over the snow.

The most important part of a komatik is the surface in contact with the snow. Wood wears down quickly and does not slide well over either snow or bare ground. The runners were therefore usually shod with iron, but it is good only in comparatively warm weather. When the temperature falls below about 0° F, the friction between snow and iron increases rapidly. Bone from the ribs of the bowhead whale slides better on land and snow. We had used this for shoeing on our trip across Southampton Island, but it wears out and is not easy to replace. The Inuit had invented the most satisfactory shoeing for carrying heavy loads at low temperatures. They dug up peaty soil, warmed it with water, working it into a thick mud, and then pressed and moulded it into a layer an inch or more thick on the wooden bottom of the runners. It quickly froze and was then smoothed down with a plane. This mud surface would hold an ice coating better than any other. The final stage in preparing the runners was "icing up." A mouthful of water was squirted onto a small pad of bear skin, which was used to apply the water evenly on the mud shoeing. This operation was repeated until a smooth layer of ice covered both runners. The ice wore off quite quickly and the komatik might have to be unloaded, turned over, "iced up," and reloaded two or three times in a day's journey but it was well worth it, and often provided a welcome opportunity for a hot drink.

When sledging our main concern was steering the komatik to preserve both the ice on the mud, and the mud on the runners. Ice does not stick on iron or bone shoeing, and even on mud it quickly flakes off if the komatik runs over snow-free glare ice or stones. Much more serious was losing bits of the mud itself because it had to be replaced. Here again glare ice was the most common danger. Pieces of mud that broke off were carefully gathered up, thawed, and used to fill the gaps. This was much easier than finding suitable soil in land covered with snow and frozen as hard as concrete. Temporary patches could be made with porridge if any oats were in the food-box, but porridge patches were liable to be eaten by the dogs during the night.

Dogs became an increasing concern. We had arrived at Repulse with ten, and we were gradually buying more from visiting Inuit because we needed two teams. New dogs meant new harnesses and traces and more dog-food. We also had to learn how to drive them. In the Eastern Arctic, all dogs had separate traces of different lengths made of narrow sealskin line, with the leader having the longest, probably about twenty-five feet in length. Driving them was more a matter of controlling several individuals than a team.

With patience one could usually get somewhere, but it was easy to become frustrated and to confuse the dogs. Pat found driving dogs as difficult as starting engines – and for the same reason. There are basically two problems: to keep the dogs moving in the direction you want, and to encourage them to pull. A tug on the bridle and a shout will usually get them to start, and a low-pitched call to stop. Gradual turns are made by command, shouting the difficult-to-pronounce and impossible-to-write calls for right and left that the Inuit use. Abrupt turns involve cracking the whip on the opposite side of the team.

Dogs become bored pulling a komatik for hour after hour. A good driver often talks to them, and takes every opportunity to break the monotony. If there is something dark on the ice ahead he will tell them it might be a seal, and they usually dash forward; sometimes the calls are meaningless but encouraging. Turns on the sea ice are normally made very gradually with the commands for left and right repeated often.

The dogs form an irregular fan when they are pulling. They can jump over leads in the ice or scramble up snow banks without interference from their neighbours, and where the route narrows they can bunch together. It is of course aggravating when they choose different paths in rough ice, bringing the komatik to a sudden stop against a large lump, and in wooded country a fan hitch would not be practicable. One end of each trace is attached to the harness of the dog and the other has a perforated walrus ivory toggle. The bridle, a short piece of strong, bearded sealskin line, is attached near the front of both komatik runners and is passed through the toggles. As the dogs change their positions, which happens constantly, the traces become plaited. After an hour or two the plaited part of the traces will have extended to the point that the dogs are bunched together and pulling largely to each side rather than forward. It is then time to stop, release the toggles from the bridle, and unplait or "shake out" the traces while the dogs lie down to rest.

When pulling a loaded komatik on a journey, dogs either walk or trot. Only for short periods and when excited do they run. With a load that is heavy to pull, or when they are tired, cold, or hungry, they walk slowly with their tails dragging in the snow. With an easy load, well fed, and fresh, they move at a smart trot with their tails curled up and waving in the air, and the driver and any passengers have to sit on the komatik or they will soon be left behind. Guiding the komatik is from the front, the driver jumping off to pull or push it to one side or the other.

The driver has a whip which has to be longer than the traces. The lash, of tapered sealskin, is about thirty feet long and is attached to a short wooden handle. Hours of practice are needed before one can direct and crack it accurately, especially in a wind. At first we found it to be more dangerous to the driver than to the dogs. The whip is used mainly to stop dog fights, or when some dog is obviously not trying to pull its weight. The laziest dogs have the shortest traces and are therefore closest to the driver and the whip. Lazy dogs face another hazard. A slack trace is more likely to snag a piece of ice and drag its dog howling under the komatik.

We had of course to learn how to build igloos, the Inuit word for their snow houses. Using a saw or snowknife, the builder first excavates a trench about three feet wide and two feet deep in a snowdrift. He then cuts a dozen or so snow blocks, each a few inches thick, from the end, which extends the trench to about ten feet in length. Some of the blocks are arranged in a circle about eight feet in diameter, cutting across the trench near its mid point, where a block is put back to support the bridging blocks. The blocks in the circle lean in slightly to provide stability and to begin the slope of the roof. The builder from now on remains within the circle. If he is right-handed he makes a sloping cut from the right-hand bottom corner of one block to its top left-hand corner, discarding the top part, and fitting a complete block in its place, to begin an anticlockwise spiral. He continues

a   Stages in building an igloo

b   Grip of snowknife for chopping blocks. Gloves are always worn but would mask the position of the hands.

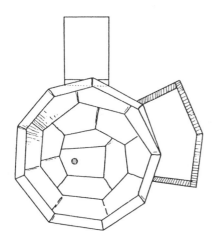

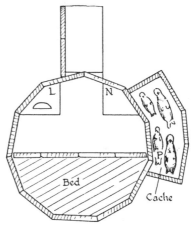

c   Completed igloo from above. The hole in the key block is for ventilation.

d   Plan of igloo interior: L indicates kudliq stand and N snow table for meat.

the spiral by cutting more blocks within the circle and fitting them to lean in at what appear to be increasingly improbable angles, until only a small hole is left. He then raises a block through this hole and lowers it into place, shaping it to fit well. This key block completes the house and gives it strength. As the blocks have been taken from inside, the house is partly below the original surface of the snow and much bigger than it appears from outside. The builder makes a raised bed of soft snow before cutting through the block in the trench, which becomes the entrance passageway. Any small gaps between the blocks are then filled in with soft snow.

I found that I was fairly good at building snow houses and quite soon reached the point that I was reasonably confident of completing an overnight igloo for two in under two hours. This is twice as long as an Inuk would take but it could be done by the light of a lantern without sacrificing any of the few daylight hours, so precious when sledging in mid-winter.

"DOG WITH HARNESS" Blaster

Winter clothing was not a problem because Tom had arranged for the HBC to send sufficient caribou skins to Repulse for us. We wore the same clothing as the Inuit and it was virtually all of caribou skin. While still sitting in one's sleeping bag, one could pull the *atigi* over one's head. This was a tunic reaching to mid-thigh, with a hood to pull up when one went outside the igloo. The hair was inside and it felt warm at once. Then came the *qarlik*, trousers to just below the knee, with two layers. The inner had the hair inside and the outer had the hair outside and was sometimes made of sealskin, which is not as warm but wears better than caribou. Stockings to just above the knee with the hair inside followed, and then outer stockings, made of the more durable skin from caribou legs with the hair outside, were tied below the knee. Mocassin-type slippers, hair inside with a pad of polar bear skin under the sole and tied round the ankle, completed the footwear. Mittens were usually made of skin from caribou legs, hair outside, and we often used a duffle liner. The final garment was the *kulitak*, an outer tunic with the hair outside, which one put on if it were very cold or windy but was often not needed. Two layers of caribou skin protected one from even the severest cold. The clothes were light, comfortable, and made to fit loosely in order to allow perspiration to escape and hence to remain dry. August and September skins, which had shorter hair, were preferred for the inner layer, and skins from animals killed later in the year for the kulitak. We all had double caribou-skin sleeping bags, while the Inuit usually slept under caribou-skin blankets. Pyjamas, like underclothes, would have been a nuisance and an unnecessary complication.

Our needs kept The Bouncer, Hannah, and any visiting women busy, but they were incredibly quick to produce well-stitched and well-fitting clothes. No measurements were made; a careful look was enough. Caribou sinew from the back muscles was used instead of thread, and plaited sinew for drawstrings. Sometimes a garment delivered at night had been made from skins provided early the same day.

Not much of our time was spent in cooking. We lived mainly on porridge, bannock, hard tack, caribou, arctic char, and seal. Peter showed most enterprise, sometimes making soups, pies, and, on one occasion, bread. He was no gourmet cook, but he had no need to be. We would have eaten anything. About once a week we spent an evening at the mission, and we visited the HBC rather more frequently. Sometimes they came to see us, often to give us something they thought we might need.

After the trapping season began in mid-November, Inuit from nearby camps started to come to the post to trade. Louis Tapatai usually brought them to see us. We had a dartboard and this became very popular. Darts were certainly less painful than many

of their own games which we also played. In one a string of plaited
sinew was looped around the left ears of two men who then had
a tug-of-war. This was repeated with the right ears, and then
with a left ear and a right ear. Any activity helped to warm the
house. As the Revillon post was to be closed, no coal had been
shipped to Repulse for the house, which daily grew colder. Our
only source of heat was a small space heater intended for a tent.
Banking the outer walls with snow made little difference, and
we gradually retreated to a single room with a bed we all shared.
Even there the temperature frequently fell below freezing.

Joe Ford had a trap-line a few miles long which he covered on
foot every four or five days, more for exercise than profit. Sometimes I went with him and learned where to place traps and how
to set and bait them. I also learned his views of the north, the
fur trade, and the people, which differed little from those of Sam
Ford at Coral Harbour. They were good servants of the company,
but would never contemplate anything against the interests of
their customers.

Our greatest problem was dog-food. The supplies Tom had had
sent to Repulse included a ton of Bovril pemmican but this was
nothing like enough for two teams of dogs. A working dog will
eat about two pounds of meat a day in the winter, so a team
of seventeen dogs requires nearly half a ton of meat a month.
The previous spring Tom had asked the HBC to buy several wal-
ruses for us locally. An Inuk hunter can usually kill more seal
or walrus in the summer than he needs for his own dogs. There
had been very few Inuit at Repulse that summer, however, and
they had none to sell. Fortunately a camp at Gore Bay, not far
from where we had left the *Polecat*, was said to have had an exceptional catch of arctic char in the fall. They could probably spare
some, but fish is poor dog-food for long journeys, as it has only
a fraction of the food value of the same weight of walrus. One
place that was sure to have plenty of dog-food was the Igloolik
area. It was renowned for its walrus herds and walrus hunters.
The Inuit there had several hundred dogs and a few more would
make little difference. Igloolik lay 225 miles to the north as the
crow flies, and very much farther by any possible sledge route.
Tom decided that Reynold and I would take one team to Igloolik,
starting our journey in December, and spend the rest of the winter
there.

This was a plan I liked, though Louis Tapatai warned us that it was much too early in the winter for us to attempt such a journey. He said it was the coldest time of the year and we would have very short days, poor snow conditions, and probably strong winds. A Roman Catholic missionary, Father Étienne Bazin, was at Igloolik, but no other white man had ever lived there. The nearest trading post required a journey of at least 300 miles, and Father Bazin's supplies had to be taken to Igloolik by dog team. We would therefore be living with the Inuit and I had liked all I had seen of them. Tom was a superb traveller, with great energy, determination, skill, and stamina. He also had a complete disregard of hardship. In fact he found contentment in discomfort. These qualities, so valuable to an arctic traveller, did not make him an easy man to live or travel with. I felt, as I am sure he too must have, that we would have a happier winter apart.

Only once was one of us really ill. On 20 October Peter and I had gone to recover our last cache. He was not well when we returned that night, and next day he felt worse and his muscles seemed very sore and painful. I took his temperature to find it 103° F, so he went to bed. It was just below 104° F by the evening. He continued to feel miserable with a high temperature and aching muscles, and it was not until 2 November that he was able to get up, though still far from well. In a few more days he had fully recovered. We had no idea what had been wrong with him.

Many years later Peter realized that he must have contracted trichinosis from the meat of the bear he had shot in Duke of York Bay which we had all eaten. It was not then generally known that many polar bears carry trichinella, the microscopic round-worms sometimes found in pork. Eating polar bear meat, unless it is well cooked or has been deeply frozen for some weeks, can lead to trichinosis, a very painful and frequently fatal disease. Trichinosis from eating polar bear meat had probably killed Hantzsch, the German explorer, on the west coast of Baffin Island twenty-five years earlier. Peter's symptoms were typical of the illness. If any of the rest of us had been affected, we had escaped very lightly. Tom and Reynold had not been well for a day or two soon after the bear had been killed, but they had recovered quickly. Pat's diary records that he felt sick some days later. Peter must have eaten a different part of the bear, or some that was not well cooked. We were very lucky that Peter had not felt really ill until twenty-seven days after his first meal of bear meat. Trich-inosis usually develops between two and twenty-eight days after ingesting trichinella. It might have struck him, or any of us, during our walk from the *Polecat* to Repulse, when we already had enough problems.

On 9 December Reynold and I set out on a trial run, sledging first along the coast to the northwest corner of Repulse Bay and then south to Beach Point before returning. We camped on the sea ice to avoid having to cross the tide-crack, the name for the margin between the fast-ice, which floats and moves up and down with the tide, and the ice-foot, which is fixed immovably to the shore. Where the tidal range is large and the coast fairly steep, the tide-crack is marked by broken and fissured ice which can be difficult to cross, especially at low tide, and pools of sea water may be encountered there at high spring tides.

The weather was good, the dogs seemed more responsive once we were well away from the post, and we had no difficulty finding suitable snow for our igloos. We returned after a week more con-fident about our journey to Igloolik than we had been when we started. The second night we had camped in a small unnamed bay. Reynold, following the tradition of Coronation Gulf, named by Franklin to mark the coronation of King George IV, suggested Abdication Bay as an appropriate name when we heard on the radio at Repulse that this had been the day that King Edward VIII gave up his throne.

Tom went to the *Polecat* twice during the fall, first with Reynold and later with Peter. On the second trip he and Peter had visited the Inuit camp at Gore Bay, confirmed the abundance of fish there, and carried out some preliminary mapping in the area. They re-turned to Repulse a day or two before Reynold and I.

9

Repulse to Igloolik – hard start
21 December 1936 – 22 January 1937

The coast between Repulse and Igloolik was quite well known. Every spring several Igloolik hunters, usually with their families, would come down to trade their year's catch of fox, and Mathiassen and Freuchen of the Fifth Thule Expedition had travelled with Inuit to Igloolik from their base near Gore Bay. Mathiassen had made a rough map of the route they had followed, which supplemented the chart published in Parry's report a hundred years earlier.

The most difficult part of the journey was sure to be between Cape Wilson and Cape Penrhyn. Here the ice breaks off close to the land and there would be open water, rough ice, or dangerous young ice that the strong sea currents in Foxe Basin could carry away with no warning. To avoid this we would have to leave the sea ice and make a land-crossing of eighty or more miles. Travelling over land, especially in rough broken country, is not as easy as on the sea ice. There are valleys, rivers, and watersheds to go up, down, and across. Rocks and glare ice have to be avoided to preserve the komatik's mud shoeing. The snow is less even, the komatik does not run as well, and the route is often hard to find.

We had to take everything we would need for the winter as well as dog-food for the journey. The only dog-food we could get was frozen whole fish, and several pounds of fish were needed to equal one pound of walrus as dog-food. This left little room for luxuries. We had of course a good stock of tobacco and tea, not so much for our own use as for giving to the Inuit and for paying them for anything they did for us. Tom said he would help us by taking much of our load along the coast to the beginning of the land-crossing.

Joe gave us all a farewell supper on 18 December, a splendid occasion that served as our Christmas. Final preparations took up the next day when a lot of soft snow was falling. We went to bed planning to leave in the morning, but by then it was drifting too badly for travel. We were not sorry because the wind would harden the snow and make conditions much easier.

Next morning, 21 December, the northwest wind was still strong with a temperature of -30°F, but visibility had greatly improved. It was the shortest day. Technically I suppose it was no day at all because the Arctic Circle passes right through Repulse, but even at that time of the year there was enough twilight to allow travel for six or seven hours a day and much longer on moonlit nights. Tom left just before nine o'clock and Reynold and I followed shortly after. Our komatiks were not heavily laden because we were going to add most of our dog-food at the Inuit camp in Gore Bay.

There is often an exhilaration about entering a new phase of an undertaking, and I think Reynold and I shared this feeling when we drove away from Repulse. The wind was behind us on the sea ice as we headed east along the coast towards Gore Bay. In a few miles we passed Harbour Islands. Here American whaling ships had started to winter in 1866 and had attracted many Inuit, but the last whaling ships had left Hudson Bay in the early years of the twentieth century and the Inuit had dispersed.

Reynold and I had ten dogs and were to get one or two more at Gore Bay. The best and by far the most important was Kutuk, a powerful red dog with a very broad chest, which had belonged to Louis Tapatai. A dog team has two positions. One is that of leader. He or she has the longest trace, responds to the commands, and is followed by the rest of the team. The other is that of boss. He is the strongest dog and the disciplinarian of the team; he appropriates the largest share of the food and has only to snarl and bare his teeth to make any other dog cower. He rarely needs to. In our team Kutuk held both positions, and filled them with distinction. Always pulling his hardest he set an example, as well as giving a lead to the other dogs. He was much the most efficient of us all.

The route we followed to Gore Bay was well marked by komatik tracks because several parties from there had already been to Repulse. We were slower than Tom but caught up to him while he was preparing to camp in an old snow house. The journey was uneventful and we reached the Inuit camp on the third day. We were welcomed by Qaunnaq, an older man, who was the one who made the major decisions in the camp and lived in the largest of the four big igloos there. In a society without books, the older people were the repository of knowledge, and knowledge is essential to survival. They had a vital role to fill, and were more important and held in higher respect than the old in our society, or indeed in their own society today.

An igloo in a camp is very different from an igloo built for a night on the trail, and the first time you enter one is like discovering a new world. First, there is an entrance tunnel, made of one or more small igloos where you have to stoop. Other small igloos, used as store rooms, lead from it. At the end of this entrance tunnel is a wooden door, or sometimes just an old skin as a curtain, with a lintel. You have to bend low to push open the door, and step up into the main igloo where people live and sleep. Qaunnaq's igloo was about twenty-four feet in diameter and nine feet high in the centre, with a pane of clear ice, cut from a lake when a few inches thick, inserted as a window. It was much lighter, more spacious, and warmer than I had expected.

'KUOLIQ" BCater

A married woman usually had her own *kudliq*, or soapstone lamp. She had possibly inherited it from her mother or grand-

mother. It rested on three wooden legs stuck in a table of hard
snow in front of where she sat and slept on the bed, so she could
easily tend it. In Qaunnaq's igloo kudliqs were burning and, since
they had plenty of seal-oil, each had a flame over two feet long
and one or two inches high for cooking and to give a bright light.

The floor of the igloo, originally of packed snow, had been
turned into ice by people walking on it. Most of the area inside
an igloo is occupied by the bed, faced with blocks of hard snow,
behind which soft snow has been shovelled and topped with a
layer of willow twigs. On this mattress polar bear and caribou
skins are laid, the bottom ones with the hair down and the others
with the hair uppermost. This forms a soft and comfortable bed
about two feet above the floor. During the day everyone sits on
the edge of the bed, sewing, repairing equipment, softening sealskin boots by chewing them, tending the lamps, drinking tea,
smoking, and talking. At night they take off all their clothes and
cover themselves in caribou skin blankets. In Qaunnaq's igloo,
where a son and his wife also lived, the bed was divided into
two by a narrow passage. Some of these igloos, which were lived
in for months and often throughout the winter, were lined with
canvas and skins and were much warmer. Qaunnaq's was one
of these.

Unusually low water levels in the nearby river at the end of
the summer had hampered the run of the arctic char upstream.
It had been easy to spear the fish through holes cut in the newly
formed sea ice, and many thousands had been caught and cached.
Qaunnaq could supply us with as many as we wanted. We spent
the next day feeding our dogs and arranging what we would take
with us. Some of the fish had been caught in the summer and
were now fit only for dog-food, but there were also large numbers
that had been taken late in the fall, when they had frozen quickly.
They were in perfect condition, as good as when they had just
been killed.

Tom wanted an astronomical fix in the vicinity of Winter Island,
where Parry and Lyon had spent the winter of 1821-22. Their
longitude for the Melville Peninsula coast was nearly a degree
different from that determined by the Fifth Thule Expedition. He
decided to leave Gore Bay on Christmas morning so we missed
the day's festivities there. On 28 December we camped on a small
island off Winter Island and waited a day for a clear sky for ob-

serving. Instead conditions became worse and on 30 December the snow was drifting too badly for travel. Together we had more than twenty-five dogs and our dog-food was diminishing rapidly. Tom decided he would go ahead and make a cache for us south of the land-crossing. In the meantime Reynold and I would return to Gore Bay for more dog-food.

With a light komatik we made a quicker journey back, but night overtook us on 1 January. We knew we could not be far from the camp though we were not sure of its direction. It was a dark night and we began to look for suitable snow for building an igloo. I think it was I who had a sudden idea. We both howled like wolves. Our dogs took up the cry and the wild chorus spread into the night. A minute's silence followed and then, faint in the distance, we heard an answering howl from the dogs at the camp. Our dogs also heard it and set off at a gallop over rocks and up and down small gullies. Within ten minutes we could see faint circles of light filtering through the ice windows of the igloos of the camp. We arrived, breathless and excited by the mad dash in the dark night, to be welcomed by the Inuit with cries of "Happynewyear," followed later by presents of mittens, dog harnesses, and skin-line. Two small girls shyly gave us two skins, one an ermine, the other a lemming.

To our surprise we found Pat here. He was accompanying Louis Tapatai who was checking his traps. We told Pat about our plans, and that Tom should soon be on his way back to Repulse. Qaunnaq again said we could certainly take what fish we wanted for dog-food. He consulted his Scripture Union card, distributed by the Anglican Church, which suggested a passage in the Bible to be read each day, and was widely used by Inuit as a calendar, and added that Ivalak, one of his sons, would be leaving on 4 January to trap in the same direction we were going, and could carry some of our load for us. This help was well worth the wait.

During the next two days we visited all the igloos in the camp. The only people who could speak a few words of English were some of the older men, who remembered visits of whaling ships at Repulse Bay. One of these men had lived in the Igloolik area and had visited Piling. He said it was possible to travel from there to Igloolik in five days. He also drew a rough sketch of the coast, showing two large islands, both called Sadleq, which did not appear on any map. This was exciting news to Reynold and me.

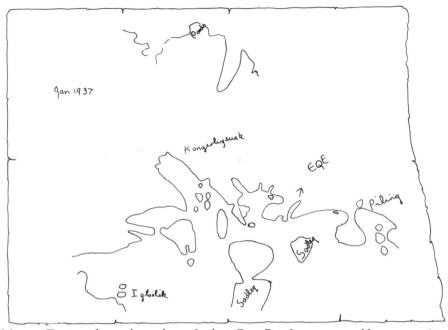

Map 4   Tracing of map drawn by an Inuk at Gore Bay, January 1937. Names as written
by author at the time.
Original width of paper, 6 inches

Clearly there would be other things to do at Igloolik during the
winter besides feeding our dogs.

The morning of 4 January was fine and most of the camp was
around to help us load the komatiks and harness our dogs. Ivalak
was bringing one of his young sons with him. Inuit often took
boys on journeys so that they would learn how to travel. Reynold
and I were touched when, just as we were ready to go, Qaunnaq
knelt and said a prayer. If we had not had so many other things
to think about, we might also have been rather alarmed. Ivalak
had a fine dog-team, and he took the heavier load and set a good
pace. We were a cheerful party as we headed north again.

We spent the first night at an abandoned snow house just before
a short land-crossing from Gore Bay to Lyon Inlet, and reached
our old snow house near Winter Island the next night. Ivalak
considered it rather small for four of us, so he built a new one

adjacent to it. He then converted our old house into a porch for our new one.

In the morning a thick mist brought very poor visibility so we started late and camped early. Ivalak built a snow house on the mainland facing an island some miles past Winter Island. We, like his young son, learned a lot watching how Ivalak did everything. Among our provisions for the winter was a small case of sweetened condensed milk. After stirring some into our tea, Reynold licked the spoon, remarked how good frozen condensed milk was, ate another spoonful, and passed the tin and spoon around. This continued for some time and, because Reynold had brought the case into the igloo, showed no sign of stopping. The rest of us could see no reason why he should eat it all. Next morning Ivalak and his son left us for his trap-line and I wondered what the boy had learned from watching us. Reynold and I set off, our load increased by the fish Ivalak had brought for us and decreased by our winter supply of condensed milk. It was no loss as I soon learned to prefer tea without milk or sugar.

During the morning we met Tom on his journey south. He described where he had cached our equipment on the sea ice near the beginning of the land-crossing. Reynold and I would now be on our own until we met Inuit who lived in northern Foxe Basin, those called Iglulingmiut. Strictly speaking, Iglulingmiut refers to the Inuit living on the island of Igloolik, who were first described by Parry and Lyon, but Rasmussen had extended the name to include all those in northern Foxe Basin, and he used the term Iglulik Eskimos to cover also the Aivilingmiut to the south and the Tununirmiut living on the northern coast of Baffin Island, because they shared much the same culture and frequently inter-married.

We continued along the coast towards Adderley Bluff, a prominent steep gneiss cliff, and it was still ahead when we reached the snow house Tom had left that morning. Next day we were delayed a little by having to make our way through rough ice but we rounded Adderley Bluff to find smooth sea ice before building a snow house for the night. The next two days were uneventful. We spent the first night in an old igloo of Tom's in Palmer Bay and the following night reached a small island where I had great difficulty in finding good snow for building the igloo.

Suitable snow for building igloos has been packed hard enough by the wind that walking across it leaves only shallow footprints. Snow that is softer than this will not cut into firm blocks. The top two feet or so of the drift must have been formed in the same storm or the snow will be layered. An area big enough for an igloo must be tested with a thin straight stick, or anything else that can be used as a probe. If it penetrates the drift smoothly, the snow is probably satisfactory; if it goes down jerkily, the snow is certainly layered. Blocks of layered snow are sure to break along the layers either in lifting them out or when used for building. The best snow I could find that night was very bad, but it is surprising what one can sometimes do when shelter, a meal, and a warm sleeping bag depend on it.

We had expected to be delayed by wind, drifting snow, darkness, and probably cold. In fact we lost most time because of mist. Possibly owing to a combination of low temperatures and open water off Cape Wilson, there were times when the mist was so thick we could barely see a foot ahead. The next morning was like that. We made some progress because we could follow komatik tracks, or it would be more accurate to say that Kutuk, our very efficient lead dog, could. Eventually we made our camp somewhere along the coast in Freuchen Bay. Another day, in much less mist, brought us to the cache that Tom had left. Here Reynold rearranged our supplies while I built an igloo as Tom had not spent a night there.

We reached the land next day and camped at the beginning of the crossing. The thick mist returned overnight. With no tracks to guide us, and little visibility, we could not travel. Within a few miles of here and fourteen years earlier to the day, Peter Freuchen had missed his way in a sudden blizzard. He became badly frozen when he fell asleep, and had lost a foot as a result.

When the mist cleared a little I climbed a small hill to try to determine the route we should take up the valley that lay ahead. Next day a strong wind brought drifting snow to replace the mist, and we were able to continue our journey. We travelled slowly as we had a heavy load and had to climb two or three hundred feet during the day.

We camped on a small lake. By now Reynold and I had evolved our camping procedure. When it was getting too dark to travel, I would look for suitable snow, and I always built the igloo. In the meantime Reynold unharnessed and fed the dogs, unloaded the komatik, buried the remaining bags of dog-food in the snow to keep them from the dogs, and then started to "chink" the igloo. Chinking meant filling with soft snow any gaps in the walls where the blocks had not fitted closely. I had much the nicer job. Building is reasonably hard work and makes one warm, while the rising wall of the igloo gives increasing protection from the wind.

When I had completed the igloo and made its bed of soft snow I would cut a door and crawl out, and Reynold would crawl in. I then passed him the caribou skins we carried to lay on the bed and our sleeping bags to put on top of them. The skins and bags had first to be beaten with a stick until they were free of snow to prevent their getting wet if the igloo became warm. Then came everything we would need for the night and anything the dogs might eat, like harnesses, traces, cameras, and clothing.

Reynold lighted a candle and soon had the primus lit, pumped, and roaring, a very comforting sound on a cold night. He melted snow or ice and began cooking. I checked the komatik and tried to make everything we left outside dog-proof. Finally I would crawl in, fit a block of snow to close the entrance, and beat the snow off my clothes. We could then sit on the edge of the bed and thoroughly enjoy a cup of tea as the temperature inside slowly rose.

Drinking quantities of tea after a hard day caused one physiological need that proved surprisingly simple to satisfy. The last thing one wanted to do was go outside again. Everyone in the north followed the Inuit practice of using a *quvik*, which was usually a small lard pail, that could be taken into the sleeping bag when required. Disposal was even easier; one had only to lift the skins on the bed and pour the contents into the soft snow beneath, where they disappeared immediately into the hole they melted. In a permanent camp they were poured into a bucket that was emptied every morning.

On our journey the snow house served one final useful purpose just before we harnessed the dogs in the morning. We would retreat to it for our other physiological need, and the dogs immediately cleared away all traces of its use. In a camp the operation was not so easy. Dogs were never tied up and roamed around the camp. One was sure to be followed when seeking a convenient rock to squat against. The dogs formed a semicircle and one gazed into fifty or more pairs of expectant eyes. If a single dog moved, the rest would dash forward and one had to swing a stick wildly before they would sit again to wait in a closer semicircle. In these circumstances one learned to be quick about one's business and to spring aside smartly as soon as one had finished.

Living in a new snow house is like living in a fairy tale. The candle light is reflected from the snow crystals in the wall in thousands of points of light, and the thick caribou furs on the bed provide an air of luxury and a promise of contentment. The contrast between its calm and the cold and wind outside increases its magic. On this journey we always had boiled char for dinner, sometimes with a handful of rice. The pleasure of not feeling hungry was soon added to the pleasure of not feeling cold. We would then crawl into our sleeping bags, drink tea, and smoke our pipes, while making bannock over a low primus flame, which also kept the igloo warm. Sometimes the oxygen level fell so low that the candle flickered. We took this as a sign that we should go to sleep, so we stopped cooking and turned off the primus and put a mitten in the ventilation hole. It was much too cold to let in more air. The snow walls must have been porous enough to restore the oxygen level once the primus was out, as we never had headaches or felt any ill effects when we woke in the morning.

Reynold was at his best in the mornings. We had an alarm clock to wake us up after a few hours' sleep in order to start getting ready hours before daylight. He would begin the slow job of melting snow or ice to boil water. Ice was better than snow which would absorb the water formed as it melted, with the danger of burning the bottom of the kettle. We still had some rolled oats so we made porridge. Reynold then cut a door in the snow block in the entrance trench and crawled out into the cold and dark to take on the nasty job of icing the komatik runners. Packing, loading, and lashing the komatik, catching and harnessing the dogs, and checking our route all took time and it was usually light before we started. We found that, despite good intentions, we camped too late at night and started too late in the morning to make the best use of the daylight hours.

One morning Reynold, after cutting open the door, turned round for his mitts. Three or four dogs suddenly dashed into the igloo. This could easily have become a disaster because the rest of the team would be sure to follow, and our food, clothes, boots, and sleeping-skins would be ripped or eaten in minutes. The usual ways of disciplining dogs are impossible in the confined space of an overnight igloo, and where there is nothing to hit them with. The only thing I could do was to grasp the first dog and bite his ear as hard as I could. He gave a piercing howl and dashed out of the door, followed by the other intruders. As a boy I had broken a front tooth which had been replaced by a crown. This was our only loss. Recalling the incident I wonder what else I could have done, but I can think of nothing as effective as my almost instinctive reaction.

Our route continued up the valley which rose gradually. Near its head were tracks of six or seven caribou and what might have been a man's footprint in the snow. We had reached about six hundred feet in altitude when we crossed an almost imperceptible watershed to follow a stream that in the summer would flow northward. We camped on a steep slope near the head of its valley.

Next morning we set off down what was marked on Mathi-assen's map as Moraine Valley. The number of boulders we had to avoid to preserve the mud on our runners demonstrated that the name was appropriate. Fortunately we came to a lake which provided us with four or five miles of easier going and took us almost to where our stream joined the much larger, eastward-flowing Barrow River. Here I saw a hare, the only wild animal we met on the land-crossing. We followed the Barrow River down-stream for a mile or two and came to a prominent cairn where a valley from the north joined ours. Here we camped. We agreed that the cairn had probably been built to mark the route of the land-crossing and decided to follow its valley next day.

We were becoming increasingly concerned at how fast our dog-food was diminishing and that our dogs were pulling no better though the load was getting lighter. The country ahead of us ap-peared to be rough, and we would need all the dog-food we had. Our load however included a number of things we would not want for some time, such as a theodolite, a radio and batteries for time signals, our reserve stocks of tea and tobacco, and some duffle in which we had carefully wrapped up two bottles of Haig's "Fine Old Scotch," one as a present for Father Bazin at Igloolik and the other to celebrate our arrival there. I think it was here that we made a cache, intending to recover it later when our dogs had had something other than frozen fish to eat and were in better shape.

When we had gone some way up this new, ill-defined, and moraine-filled valley, we came across tracks of two dog teams going south, indicating we had reached a recognized route. Komatik tracks in the north can last a long time. Where the snow is at all soft, the weight of the komatik depresses and hardens it under the runners. The frequent winds of the north soon blow away the soft snow and the komatik track, originally a depression, stands out in relief. These tracks appeared to be very recent.

The going became easier and we had little difficulty in finding a good route but it was reassuring to see the tracks now and again. Towards the end of the day they led us to an igloo that the unknown travellers had built. It seemed very large to us, but the light was beginning to fail and we decided to camp in it. Though there was no wind, it felt very cold, and while we were unharnessing the dogs we heard the ground crack, a sign of extremely low temperatures. When we were cooking, the primus did little to warm so large an igloo, which we were not sorry to leave after an icy night.

We were able to set off despite a thick mist because we had the komatik tracks to guide us. Later the calm and mist gave way to a strong northwest wind and drifting snow. We had reached a long lake, called Tasersuaruseq on Mathiassen's map, which we followed for the rest of the day, building our igloo near where it ended.

In the clear night sky the stars seemed much nearer than in England. Reynold thought he could detect shadows cast on the snow by Venus, then very close to the earth, and I imagined I could too. The moon had been new when we began the crossing and each night became a little lighter. We were too far north for the most spectacular aurora, which are at their brightest in a belt centred on the geomagnetic pole near Thule that passes through Chimo and Churchill. Every night, however, their flickering greenish rays darted across the sky, pausing, waxing, and waning to contrast with the stillness and silence of the moonlit land.

Drifting was less of a problem next morning. Our route followed a river course that ran north, and after a very long day we arrived within sight of the coast. We had been told we could expect to find Inuit here. There was an abandoned igloo but it had obviously been built by the party whose tracks we were following. As it was smaller than the one we had stayed in before we correctly thought it would be much warmer. Not having to build an igloo, I erected a shelter for the dogs because there was a strong and bitterly cold wind. They ignored it completely, preferring to remain in the open where the drifting snow soon converted them into as many little igloos.

We now followed the tracks along the coast. They did not move out onto the sea ice but ran along a raised beach of limestone. I was leading the dogs and after an hour or so I looked back and saw an animal silhouetted against the sky, following about a hundred yards behind us. It was the size of a wolf but when it came nearer we could see it was a black dog in miserable condition. It was very thin and the ice on its bedraggled tail rattled against the ice matted into its coat. The black dog continued with us all day and we fed it with the other dogs that night. They did not get much because we were down to our last bag of dogfood. It had been another long day by the time we found a suitable snow bank and built our igloo.

We slept rather late next morning because we had not got to bed until after midnight. We were drinking tea, while wondering how well and for how long our hungry dogs would be able to pull on little or no food. Reynold was about to go out to ice the komatik, and we were listening to the low whistle of the wind outside promising another cold day. Then we heard a rather different noise, a crunching in the snow, followed by a short cry of surprise. Reynold quickly took a knife to cut away the snow block in the entrance. A boy crawled into our igloo, and looked around it with a critical stare.

10

Repulse to Igloolik – easy finish

22 January – 6 March 1937

He looked no more than fourteen years old; he also looked rather surprised. He had gone out that morning hoping to find some ptarmigan: instead he had discovered a strange igloo and even stranger occupants. We were as happy as he was surprised. As we drank tea together we understood him to say that his name was Aipilik and that he lived nearby. Little did I then think that at various times during the next fifty years he, his wife, several sons, daughters, grandsons, and granddaughters, and even a great-grandson would come to visit me in Ottawa.

After we had loaded the komatik and harnessed the dogs, Aipilik led us to his camp on a point with the name Usuarjuk. There was only one igloo there. If we had gone another quarter of a mile the previous night we might have reached it. Yet it had been dark before we camped, the igloo was not on the raised beach we were following, and we might have passed it by. We would then have had another seventy miles or so before coming to the next camp, and they would have been hungry miles for our dogs at least.

Two men, Issigaituq and Piluarjuk, and their wives were sharing the igloo which had a single wide bed. There were two small children and Aipilik. Our knowledge of their language was very limited and they had no English. It was difficult to determine who was related to whom, as Inuit consider using a person's name to be disrespectful and usually refer to another Inuk by their relationship to him – my son, my father's older brother, and so on – or even to somebody who has the same name. This is no problem to the Inuit, who are thoroughly versed in family relationships, but is utterly confusing to strangers. Months later we were told that the two families had shared the same camp for some years. One summer Issigaituk went inland to hunt caribou, which meant walking long distances over rough country. As his wife was pregnant, Akitteq, who was then married to Piluarjuk, took her place. During the summer both couples found they were very compatible, and what had been intended as a temporary rearrangement had become permanent – to everybody's satisfaction. We also learned that Aipilik was Akitteq's much younger brother.

We spent several happy days in this igloo, one family on one side of the bed, the other on the other side, with Reynold and me in the middle. Aipilik never seemed to sleep and would stand for hours rather than sit on the bed because, so we were told, it would make him a good hunter. For our dogs as well it was a marked change for the better. They were brought one by one into the igloo and given thawed walrus to eat without having to fight to get their food and keep it, and they soon looked much fatter and fitter.

Our greatest surprise came when we told our hosts about the cache we had left on the land-crossing. We described where it was and asked how we could recover it. The reply was there was no problem as it was already here. There was obviously a misunderstanding so we repeated our story. Issigaituq said he understood, and then took us and showed us all the boxes we had cached, now neatly stacked in a side-igloo he used as a storeroom.

We gradually pieced together what we thought must have happened. Three men from farther north had passed through Usuarjuk on their way to Repulse to trade foxes for tea and tobacco as there was none left in the Igloolik area. Issigaituq had decided to go with them. It was their tracks we had been following, and they had built the two abandoned igloos we had used on the landcrossing. When they came to our cache they realized it had been left by somebody travelling north who would want it, and Issigaituq had turned back and brought it all along. We had probably missed them the morning we left the Barrow River. Issigaituq said he hoped we would not mind but, aware that the owner of the cache would be pleased and would want to give him something, he had taken a little tobacco for those continuing on to Repulse to smoke on the way. Of the fifteen or more pounds of tobacco we had had in the cache, we found he had taken less than an ounce to give them.

The wind blew strongly from the northwest almost all the time we were at Usuarjuk, and we were glad we were not fighting our way against it. Issigaituq offered to go with us to the next camp as soon as the weather improved. I think it was on 28 January that we resumed our journey. The wind had hardened the snow and the route was easy, either along raised beaches or across sea ice. He had a good team, and our own dogs had greatly improved. We made an early start, stopped only to make tea, ice the runners, and shake out the traces, and at midnight we arrived at the island of Ugliarjuk, where there were several igloos. We must have covered about seventy miles that day. From Winter Island to Usuarjuk, Reynold and I had walked all the way and sometimes pushed or pulled. This was a complete contrast. We all sat on the komatik, and anyone who got off had to run to keep up.

Issigaituq took us to the largest igloo, where Qidlaq lived. He was also known as Cleveland's Johnny, because he had worked for Captain Cleveland, a holdover from the whaling days who had become the first HBC post manager at Repulse. Johnny welcomed us warmly, and after we had shaken hands with everyone around we entered his house and soon there was a kettle of strong tea boiling for all in the camp to share. As he filled his pipe, Johnny, who remembered a little English, said, "So glad you come. You got tobacco. All winter my wife she smoke deer hair, me coal sacks." Sometimes he used pidgin-English expressions. When I asked him the distance between two places, he thought carefully about the route and where he would camp each night before replying, "Husky go catchum igloo, go catchum igloo, go catchum igloo, go catchum igloo – four sleep."

We were objects of great interest during the two or three delightful days we spent at Ugliarjuk. Everybody in the camp came to see us and we were surrounded by friendly faces. Only rarely did any white man come to the Igloolik area. Such visits were in the spring rather than mid-winter, and they were always with Inuit, while we had arrived in the area on our own. We were treated like members of the family, but rather spoilt members in the way that Inuit parents always indulge their youngest children. Reynold, as ever, was the perfect companion as we compared notes and drew one another's attention to the many unobtrusive ways

Martha, Nasook's wife with Kadlutsiaq in the hood

Kutjek

Ituksarjuat, the "King" of Igloolik

Ataguttaaluk, the "Queen" of Igloolik

Prominent bluff at Piling

Reynold and Mino leaving Angmaarjuaq for Igloolik

Graham building and Reynold chinking an igloo on the way to Piling

Jack Turner by his sledge on the way to Pond Inlet

Leaving Pond Inlet for Arctic Bay

Kutjek's wife scraping a sealskin with an ulu

Hunting narwhal in Strathcona Sound

Excavation camp in Strathcona Sound

The *Aklavik* at Fort Ross

Ship-time at Pond Inlet

in which our hosts were being kind and thoughtful. We felt we did not have a worry in the world, and I fully understood Reynold when he said he had found peace of mind, because I too felt completely at ease.

Something of interest was always happening in the igloos. Water was obtained from melting ice over the kudliq, and there was little to spare. We would sometimes see mothers lick their babies to clean them, as a cat licks her kittens. This must strengthen the bond between them. Though Reynold and I were not as helpless as babies, I am sure we felt the thoughtful attention we were always receiving was establishing a rather similar bond between the Inuit and us.

At night the women tamped the kudliq wicks until each had a very short flame, giving a glimmer of light. The Inuit pulled off their clothes and gathered their caribou-skin blankets around their families. Soft snores and the sounds of restless children filled the igloo. This comparative quiet would be broken occasionally by a loud shout when some hunter called to his dogs in an exciting dream.

We were now in a region where caribou were very scarce and walrus were by far the most important food for both the people and the many dogs of the large teams needed for walrus hunting. There was always a hunk of fresh walrus lying on a snow table with a knife as an invitation to help oneself. In Johnny's igloo there was also a walrus stomach with its contents, and Lewis Carroll came alive to Reynold and me. It was full of clams, neatly shelled by the walrus and ready for cleaning and eating a second time. Along this coast of Foxe Basin walrus were hunted throughout the year, but most were killed late in the summer. Large pieces of meat, weighing up to two hundred pounds, were cut off, made into rolls, and laced together with strips of the skin to form what looked like enormous sausages. They were then cached on the beach under mounds of gravel. For many days the mounds felt soft and yielding underfoot but the meat gradually froze. This formed a store of food – a form of capital for the Iglulingmiut. The meat gradually changed to become rather like green cheese in taste, colour, and texture. It was a reserve for times of scarcity, and in small quantities was considered by many to be a delicacy – an acquired taste.

The next camp to the north was Akudneq. It was a shorter distance than from Usuarjuk to Ugliarjuk, but still a long way.

Issigaituq was returning to his family, but Johnny and another Inuk said they would like to go with us. They would be bearers of good news in the form of tea and tobacco, and also of unusual phenomena.

Reynold and Johnny carried the camping equipment and part of our load. The other Inuk and I took the rest on a second komatik. We did not expect to reach Akudneq until quite late at night. Some time after dark we became separated, and a little later we met rough ice through which we had to twist and turn to find a possible way. Eventually we came across tracks so we followed them for a very long time, wondering why we had not yet reached Akudneq. The night had been overcast but in the early hours of the morning the clouds dispersed, and the stars shone brightly in the arctic sky. They showed us we were travelling along the tracks in the wrong direction. We turned the komatik around and retraced our path.

Soon after daylight returned we saw a number of dots on the horizon ahead. As they grew larger we could see they were dog teams. We stopped to wait for them. It was an unforgettable sight. Nine teams, averaging about seventeen dogs, and each pulling a lightly laden komatik with one or two men, dashed towards us like packs of wolves. The drivers stopped their teams a few yards away, jumped off their komatiks, cracked their whips to make the dogs lie down, and gathered in a circle around us. They were the men of Akudneq, setting out to hunt walrus at the floe-edge. In their caribou clothing, their breath frosting the fringes of their hoods, and the excitement of meeting the unexpected, they carried an air of primeval vitality.

They told us Akudneq was only a mile or two away, and several of them decided the walrus could wait, and came with us. When we arrived at the camp, everyone was outside wondering why so many hunters were returning so soon. After the ritual hand-shakes with each in turn, we realized we were hungry and went into an igloo to eat. We had been travelling for twenty-seven hours, stopping only to shake out the traces and when we had met the hunters. Reynold and Johnny arrived an hour later. They had had the camping equipment and food with them, and had built an igloo to spend a comfortable night.

More people were living at Akudneq than we would find at Ig-loolik Point, where Father Bazin was staying. The leading hunters were two brothers, Aakuanuk and Qanattiaq, and it was a prosperous camp. Again all our needs were provided for and our clothing was checked, dried, and any small repairs made. We stayed only one night, getting up early on the morning of 3 February for the last stage of the journey, still with Johnny and his companion. The Igloolik winter camp was then at the southeast point of the island, about twelve miles east of the present settlement. As we drew near we could see the igloos, glowing from the light of the kudliqs filtering through their snow walls and outlining the blocks of which they were made. Among those who came outside and crowded round our komatiks was Father Bazin.

In 1931 Father Étienne Bazin, originally from Burgundy, had travelled with an Inuit family by komatik from Pond Inlet to Igloolik. Here he had established his mission and, apart from brief visits to Pond Inlet and Repulse Bay, had remained on his own ever since. Most of the Inuit at Igloolik itself had become Catholic though the other Iglulingmiut were Anglican. The father lived in a small igloo connected to one in which an Inuit family lived, and all his possessions had been brought three hundred miles by komatik by Inuit who had also their own supplies to carry. He could have had little difficulty in observing his Oblate vow of poverty. We gave him a letter from Father Clabaut, and he offered to help us in any way he could. It was a rash promise because there were so many ways he could and did help us.

We had one disappointment. We carefully unwrapped the bottle of Haig's Fine Old Scotch we had carried so far to give him, and found it had frozen and broken the bottle. We hoped we could replace it with the other bottle, which appeared intact, but it too had frozen and pushed the cork out of the bottle. The frozen liquid that remained within it had only a faint taste of whisky. Even more unfortunately we brought him a bad cold.

As Father Bazin's igloo was small, he arranged for us to stay with Ituksarjuat and Ataguttaaluk, the couple who had originally brought him from Pond Inlet. He called them the "King and Queen" because they were held in such high respect at Igloolik, where they made the major decisions affecting the camp. Their palace was a very large igloo which they shared with a married son and his family. There were two beds and Reynold and I shared one with the King and Queen, and were even given our own kudliq. They were perfect hosts, and their concern when Reynold, attempting to fix an aerial, slipped and fell through the palace roof, only turned to laughter as soon as they found he was unhurt.

As a young woman Ataguttaaluk had had a terrible experience. Late one summer, she had gone caribou hunting with her first husband in the interior of north Baffin Island. The hunting and fishing had been poor, and an exceptionally heavy fall of soft snow had both hidden their caches and made travel almost impossible. They ate everything they could, first their dogs and then the sleeping skins and spare clothing, before her husband and their three children died of starvation. Left alone, Ataguttaaluk tried to walk to Igloolik but she was too weak and the snow too deep so she returned to the igloo. Here, lying beside her dead family and waiting herself to die, she thought she heard a snowbird. She realized spring was at hand when Inuit would pass by as the igloo lay on the route between Igloolik and Pond Inlet. This gave her the will to live, though the only way was by eating the bodies of her family. She survived and subsequently married Ituk-sarjuat, a renowned hunter. Their three sons now had wives and families of their own.

Among the Inuit it was a common practice for any obviously incompetent white man to be adopted by an older woman who would make sure her adopted son was properly clothed and understood the ways of the Inuit world. Ataguttaaluk assumed this role for Reynold and me and we could not have had a more thoughtful and understanding adopted mother.

Under Ataguttaaluk's instruction we learned how to tend the kudliq. The kudliq, a large soapstone dish, was nearly half-moon shaped and about three inches deep. Pieces of blubber, the layer of fat between the skin and the flesh of a seal or any other sea-mammal, were pounded with anything handy that could be used as a mallet to release some oil, and placed in the kudliq. Three or four small cones of chopped-up moss soaked in oil were then evenly spaced along the straight edge of the kudliq, which might measure two feet. They were lit and gradually teased out along the edge to form a continuous flame, the warmth and light depending on its length. The trick lay in adjusting the wick of moss to keep the flame burning well without smoking, which produced an oily black soot. One result of living in an igloo warmed by a kudliq was the formation in one's throat of a black phlegm, known as smitch. It became lighter when away from kudliqs and disappeared in a month or so. I have no idea if it had any ill effects on health.

A kudliq kept an igloo much warmer than a primus stove as it gave out a gentle heat, whereas the hotter air from a primus quickly went out the ventilation hole, drawing in icy air from the outside. Ataguttaaluk told us that seal-oil kept an igloo warmer than oil from white whales, which gives a brighter light, and that for the whitest light a wick of cotton grass should be used. We never had an opportunity to test this, but we had great faith in anything Ataguttaaluk said.

Reynold and I could now review our situation. We had learned a lot during our journey to Igloolik. In particular we had learned that we could travel in mid-winter on our own; we had also learned that it was quicker, more interesting, and much more comfortable to travel with Inuit. It suited us much better because both of us were short on heroics and long on comfort when available. We wrote letters to Tom, to be taken by the next person going to Repulse, saying that we intended to stay in the Igloolik area and work there independently. From now on we would be on our own. Tom, to his great credit, understood our position and did not resent our leaving his expedition.

We asked the Inuit about the possibility of visiting Piling from Igloolik. This would complete the map of Baffin Island because Hantzsch had nearly reached there from the south. Little change had taken place in the distribution of the population since the time of the Fifth Thule Expedition, when Mathiassen had visited the island of Maniqtuuq in Kangirllukjuak, which he had named Steensby Inlet. This was still the camp farthest along the coast, though Inuit often hunted caribou east of there. Father Bazin said one of the hunters at Akudneq would go with us to Piling and we hoped that Issigaituq might also come.

It was always both a pleasure and an education to talk to Father Bazin. Despite a life style so different from that of his upbringing he considered himself fortunate to be living in the north and to be serving a people he admired. He was an artist and among his few possessions were brushes and oil paints with which he captured the light and beauty of a land he had grown to love. When he heard I was an archaeologist he told me about finds the Inuit had made when digging on an adjacent island called Abverdjar. He had formed a collection of these, but they were still at

Abverdjar. If I were interested, he said, I could go and get them.

The trip to Abverdjar and back took a day. In the fall the Igloolik people hunted walrus there. As it was too cold and windy to live in tents and too early for good snow to build igloos, they made houses with walls of turf, covered with skins or canvas. Towards the end of the year they moved to Igloolik Point, which was closer to the floe-edge. Here they built snow houses and hunted seal. Father Bazin's collection had been found when the Inuit were cutting turf for the walls of their houses and digging mud to shoe the runners of their komatiks. The artifacts were quite different from the material I had excavated on Southampton Island during the summer. The harpoon heads and many other pieces I could recognize as Dorset culture types. Others were new to me but they too could easily be Dorset. They were certainly not Thule.

Reynold and I would have liked to start our journey to Piling as soon as possible. We had to wait however for those who were going to go with us. In the meantime we were happy in the palace. Sometimes we would go out with the hunters. This meant a journey of two or three hours with light komatiks over the sea ice to the floe-edge. We would spread along the edge watching for a seal's head to appear. If it were shot we had to recover it using a small skin boat. Everyone gathered around the first seal to be caught, which was always opened up immediately and its liver cut into small pieces to be passed around for all to share. At the end of the day the hunters drove back with good appetites for the meat their wives had been cooking. Throughout the day the weather had to be watched carefully because an offshore wind could break off the ice and take those on it for a long and probably fatal cruise.

For some reason I was often asked for medical advice. I did my best to explain that I had absolutely no medical training. All we had was a large bottle of aspirin and some liniment, and I often found I had to provide aspirin tablets or rub limbs or chests. What always worked best however was a little tobacco.

One effect of wearing caribou-skin clothing was that it was impossible to keep free of body lice. They were much less trouble than I had expected; they tend to live in the fur and to come out infrequently to browse. Ataguttaaluk took my sleeping bag, froze it, and then beat it with a stick which is an effective method of population control.

On 3 March, about two weeks later than we had hoped, Johnny arrived at Igloolik bringing one or two boxes we had left at his camp. With him was Kutjek, a good hunter from Akudneq. Issigaituq had not been well, and could not come, but Kutjek brought another man from Akudneq named Sequtjut, who was also known as Mino.

Igloolik to Piling

6 March – 30 March 1937

We left Igloolik around noon on 6 March. Mino and Reynold had our komatik with eleven dogs, mostly our own. I was with Kutjek who had a team of fifteen strong dogs and was taking the heavier load. Kutjek seemed a quiet, capable, and rather reserved man, who would always do his best but perhaps with not much imagination. Mino was very different. He was short and plain and had no wife, no dogs, ragged clothes, a very old gun, no ammunition, and a good sense of humour. Most white men in the north would have described him as an Inuit failure. Among the Inuit he was well liked, partly no doubt because he was always cheerful and willing, and never in any way a threat. Kutjek had probably decided to bring him along as much for company as for help. Mino could speak a little English, remembered from the whalers who had once taken him to Newfoundland. They may have called him Minor for he was small and would not have been out of his teens when the last whaler left, and this was probably the origin of his name.

The wind was behind us, from the southwest, and we made good progress. After some hours we met a group of Inuit who were hunting seal where the strong currents through Fury and Hecla Strait had kept a patch of open water. They came with us to their camp on the island of Siurak, which appears on Parry's chart as Tern Island. We soon reached it and must have covered about thirty miles in all during the day. Kutjek and Mino went to one igloo. Reynold and I were taken to another where there were an older couple, a young man, a young married couple, and two children. Here we had a very good supper of bear soup, boiled bear, and frozen caribou.

We slept well and next day was a Sunday, with no suggestion of travel. All at the camp were Anglican, as were Kutjek and Mino, and the Sabbath was strictly observed. Everyone gathered in our igloo in the morning for a long service conducted by our host. It began with five hymns, one after another. These were followed by a reading from the Bible. Some passages the congregation would agree with, smiling and nodding their heads in approval. Other passages were obscure, as might be expected in a context changed from the Near East to the Far North, and there were many interruptions with everyone free to ask for an explanation. A discussion would then follow until a consensus had been reached on the meaning. In this way the reading became also a cooperative sermon. The service was concluded with another sequence of six hymns. No attempt was made to restrain the children whose play and chatter provided a family background. Now and again a mother would nurse her baby. In the meantime a large pan of bear meat had been simmering, and an older woman would sometimes ladle a few spoonfuls of fat from the top of the stew to burn in the reservoir of the kudliq below. Early in the evening a second and very similar service was held. Though I could understand only a little of what was going on, I found these services to be a real religious experience, which left me with no doubt that Christianity was a most important influence in the life of that camp.

Between the services I tried to repair the theodolite which had suffered during the journey, while Reynold walked round the island and mapped it. Mino cheerfully hummed, "When I survey the wondrous Cross," while he fed the dogs. Again we slept well.

There was a strong north wind in the morning, delaying our start until after ten o'clock. Kutjek and I now had seventeen dogs and much the heavier load. We thought we might cross Jens Munk Island, but Kutjek decided it would be easier to keep on the sea ice south of the island. After four and a half hours we were north of the Calthorpe Islands when we met a young Inuk from one of the outer Calthorpes. He said five families were living there. During the day there had been very strong drifting which cleared before we camped just past Cape Konig. Since leaving Igloolik

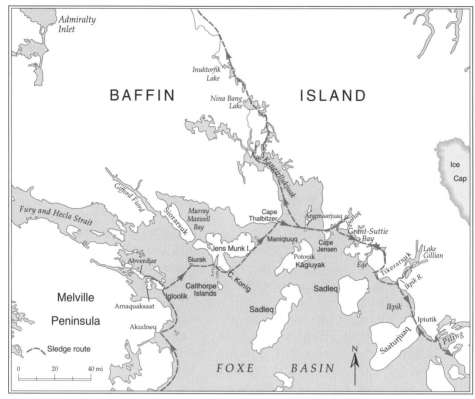

Map 5   Enlarged detail of boat and sledge routes, 1936-37, shown on Map 3
on page 24

the weather had been cold but now the temperature had risen
to 15°F.

Kutjek was very quick in building an igloo. He had brought
a small kudliq, similar in shape to the bigger soapstone lamps
but made of metal and therefore much thinner, lighter, and less
likely to break. Mino soon had it burning with a good flame. They
carried an old box lid from which to split off pieces of wood for
use as kudliq stands, pegs to stick in the snow walls from which
to hang mitts to dry, spills for lighting one's pipe, or tampers
for adjusting the wick of the kudliq if it started to smoke or if
a larger flame were needed.

Father Bazin had been very generous in giving us some of his
small stock of food, since he was planning to go to Repulse in

the early spring. As a result we could have a few beans and de-
hydrated potatoes with our bear that night. Reynold and I had
been living almost exclusively on walrus for more than a month.
There was lots of it and we always had plenty to eat, but we
felt hungry all the time for anything but walrus. Food had become
our main topic of conversation and Reynold took a masochistic
as well as a sadistic pleasure in describing favourite menus. What
he wanted most was rich plum cake and a bottle of claret. I would
have been happiest with new potatoes and, strangely, soda water,
which normally I would never have drunk. We found we had left
all plates, knives, spoons, and forks at Igloolik, but we got on
well with just our enamel mugs and snow knives.

Kutjek had brought a large piece of walrus meat into the igloo
and set it on a snow table near the kudliq, which was making
the igloo much warmer than any overnight igloo that Reynold
and I had built. We felt well fed and comfortable as we lay in
our sleeping bags, listening to the soft voices of Kutjek and Mino
singing "Abide with me."

Though we were up early in the morning nobody seemed in
any hurry. The walrus meat had thawed overnight and Kutjek
cut it into small pieces for the dogs, while Mino repaired a whip.
We could see the logic of thawing the walrus meat before cutting
it up but we had not expected that the dogs would be fed in
the morning, before a day's journey. This is what happened, however, not only that day but frequently, and the dogs seemed none
the worse for it.

We left late in the morning because two dogs were missing.
It became a beautiful day, calm with the temperature rising to
26°F, exceptionally warm for this area which has an average March
temperature of -26°F. We travelled slowly, looking for and eventually finding the missing dogs. The warm weather had tempted
a few seals out on the ice. Kutjek hunted one, creeping towards
it until he was within range but missing. He had broken the stock
of his rifle the day we left Igloolik and had either repaired it at
Siurak, or borrowed one there. We camped soon after four o'clock
and spent another comfortable night.

All the next day we sledged across the sea ice towards Cape
Thalbitzer. The sun was warm and we could have reached the
mainland of Baffin Island if we had not made a late start, or got
into rough ice at the end of the day. The sky was clear, and when

the sun had set Kutjek pointed out various stars to me. He said there were Inuit names for a large number of them. He also confirmed that there were two large islands called Sadleq in northern Foxe Basin. Eventually we camped on the sea ice not far from the mainland.

We made another late start next day. Our starts however were earlier than we had thought because we found our watches to be three-quarters of an hour fast by the sun. Reynold discovered he had left his pipe behind when photographing, but this did not matter much because we shared pipes as freely as we shared tobacco. Anyone who was smoking would pass his pipe around to the others on the komatik.

Cape Thalbitzer, where we arrived just before midday, was a cliff of loose gravel, sand, and boulders, about forty feet high and apparently being rapidly eroded. The Inuit said this erosion was owing to the very strong tidal currents in Kangirllukjuak, the deep bay to the east named Steensby Inlet by Rasmussen. They also said this was the reason there were so few seals in the region. We took compass bearings of any features we could see, because we were now entering the area for which there were no maps.

Soon after leaving Cape Thalbitzer we found a large "sausage" of walrus meat lying on the sea ice. It weighed about a hundred pounds, and had either fallen off a komatik or been abandoned to lighten one. Kutjek said a party from the Igloolik area had been hunting caribou along the Baffin Island coast and could have left this walrus. We were very pleased to add it to our load because we wanted as much dog-food as possible for our journey. Nearby was an old igloo. Mino's dogs broke through the wall and dashed out of the entrance, threading the igloo with their traces. The only way we could extricate them was by cutting the igloo into two halves.

We did not keep the piece of walrus long. In an hour or two we met a west-bound komatik with two Inuit. Their dogs were thin and hungry so Kutjek gave it to them. They told us an RCMP patrol from Pond Inlet had stopped at their camp at Angmaarjuaq the previous night and left for Igloolik that morning. We were sorry we had missed seeing the police. They had probably been hidden by the rough ice when we were at Cape Thalbitzer.

The going seemed rather sticky for the rest of the day because we were crossing new sea ice with little snow cover, but we reached the Angmaarjuaq camp by five o'clock. Earlier in the winter there had been two Inuit camps in Kangirllukjuak, but now they had come together and there must have been nearly forty people including children. It seemed rather a hungry camp because the kudliqs in the igloos were dim when we arrived and the large seal we brought with us disappeared very rapidly. However we were approaching the time of year when there would be many seals out on the ice and we were able to leave the hunters some needed ammunition, as well as a little tea, which made the wives very happy.

We set off about noon with a lighter load and soon crossed the narrow island of Angmaarjuaq from which the camp derived its name. After another three hours we reached the mainland six or seven miles north of Cape Jensen. The east coast of Kangirllukjuak was formed by a very straight granite edge about two hundred feet high which we found to lie almost directly north-south. Here there was a gap in the edge, providing an easy and frequently used land-crossing, little more than a quarter of a mile long and leading to a large bay.

We were now farther east in northern Foxe Basin than any other white man had been, and we had to balance our wish to map the coast against the need to hunt so that we could continue. Our party had two priorities that would sometimes conflict. For Kutjek and Mino our main purpose was to hunt caribou; for Reynold and me it was to explore and map the coast from here to Piling. Reynold, who had had some surveying experience, took on responsibility for the map.

At the head of the bay we found a deep fiord known to the Inuit as Isortoq. The wind was rising and we decided to camp on the east side of its entrance. When nearly there Mino saw a large caribou head in the rough ice at the tide crack. It must have fallen off the komatik of one of the Igloolik hunters, and it still contained the tongue with a liver frozen to it. The tongue, a delicacy, made us an excellent supper, after which we put up an aerial to try to receive a radio time signal to rate the chronometer watch we used for observing. We always had to warm the batteries gently over the kudliq before we could use the radio.

One or two stations came through but the rest were drowned by singing from some German station, and we failed to get a useful signal.

Next day Reynold remained in camp to map the nearby area and to check the theodolite because we hoped to secure an astronomical position here for the map. Kutjek, Mino, and I went caribou hunting along Isortoq Fiord which I was able to map. It was twelve miles to the mouth of a large river at the head of the fiord. Here there appeared to be an exposure of grey rock. I walked to it and found it was really very fine sand frozen together, which crumbled when touched. This rock flour is the typical deposit from rivers fed by glaciers or ice sheets. Nowhere in the fiord did we see any caribou, and Kutjek thought they had moved on to Eqe, the next inlet to the east.

Back at the igloo Reynold had turned the caribou liver into a very good pâté to go with our dinner. The sky was clear for observing, but it was only after listening for hours that I managed to get a time signal on the radio. Reynold then made satisfactory observations to give us one firm point on our map. It was three o'clock in the morning before we could crawl into our sleeping bags.

Reynold took noon observations of the sun before we set off next day. For the first and only time in the north I was bitten by a dog while I was harnessing Kutjek's team. It was not a bad bite and I was more surprised than hurt.

The weather was cold but clear and calm as we followed the coast east for three hours to where it turned south. We continued east, crossing the tide-crack onto the land, and camped at sunset. Several fresh caribou tracks, as well as day-old tracks of two wolves raised our expectations. After supper I noticed that Kutjek was reading the service for the solemnization of matrimony in his prayer book. He must have read it many times before, but the prayer book and parts of the Bible were then the only books in his language.

Eqe was a few miles farther. It appeared to be a lake many miles long and averaging about a mile wide, but it was tidal water and after three miles we found a long narrow passage leading to the sea. We had passed this outlet when Kutjek saw caribou in the distance. He and Mino set out on foot to hunt them. Half an hour later, while I was teaching Reynold the Scottish sword dance in an attempt to keep warm, Kutjek's dogs must have scented the caribou and suddenly bolted. I just managed to leap on the komatik as the team raced straight as an arrow in the direction Kutjek and Mino had taken, but I could not control them. After about a mile and a half we caught up with Kutjek, who jumped on the komatik, but made no attempt to stop the dogs. We were within two hundred yards of a small herd of caribou when they started to move. A dog then got caught under the komatik and was dragged along squealing, the caribou moved off the sea ice onto the land, the dogs followed, and the komatik got stuck in the rough ice of the tide-crack. Kutjek jumped off, took a couple of shots, and followed the caribou on foot. He was back within five minutes, having wounded one.

Reynold, who had meanwhile arrived with the other team, decided to walk back to pick up various things that had dropped off the komatiks and to take bearings because we were in a very complicated part of the bay. Kutjek and I crossed to the other side of the bay to make camp, where Mino joined us after a long and fruitless hunt. As a heavy mist was forming Kutjek and I set out, quite unnecessarily, to find Reynold, whom we met in a few minutes.

In the morning Kutjek and Mino went caribou hunting on foot, Reynold continued mapping, and I again worked on the radio. The chronometer watch had stopped and we would not be able to get accurate longitudes unless we could receive another time signal. Kutjek soon returned – the wounded caribou had died quickly and been easy to find. He took his team to collect it. That afternoon the carcass was thrown to the dogs. The result resembled a scrum in rugby football. The tightly packed mass of animals slowly moved downhill, dogs with bloody faces emerging for a few seconds before plunging back. Mino did not return until we were all in bed. He had not seen any caribou.

Kutjek's chest was hurting him and he had sprained a shoulder so we did not move next day. Both komatiks had lost part of their mud shoeing and the missing pieces had to be replaced. We also had to repair our clothing. I had managed to get faint Morse code on the radio the previous night. It was Reynold's turn to try but he had no luck. We never again succeeded in receiving useful signals so it was fortunate we had one good longitude, that of Isortoq, on which to base our map.

We expected we would resume our journey towards Piling next morning, but Kutjek's chest was still hurting. Instead Mino and I went hunting, intending also to collect a caribou that Kutjek said had been killed and cached on the coast by the Igloolik hunters who had given it to him. We set out early, went to the east end of Eqe bay and then overland towards the coast. We missed the correct route and had a difficult cross-country journey. Near the coast we began to feel the wind, and drifting snow restricted visibility. While making a steep descent to the shore we came across a mass of blue ice. It looked like a small glacier, but no glaciers were known to enter Foxe Basin and we had not expected to find one. I thought it might be a frozen cataract, though there was no sign of a river bed. As I could not see more than a few yards, I could not then try to find out how far this ice extended or how it had formed.

When we reached the coast we did not know where we were in relation to the cached caribou. We first sledged west for two or three miles but failed to find it. We turned and went east for a long way. It was bitterly cold, we could not see to hunt because of the drifting snow, and we would be coming this way again in a day or two and could recover the cache then. I suggested we were wasting our time and we retraced our path. It was dark by the time we found our way back to our camp in Eqe bay, where it had been fine all day with only a slight wind.

My diary for the next day begins, "No breakfast except a spoonful of raw frozen brains," but it was a large spoonful and caribou brains are very good to eat. We set off in beautiful weather and found a much better route to the coast, where there was again a biting wind and drifting snow. Turning east along the shore we soon passed a point called by the Inuit Tikerarsuk, and saw a large square rock with vertical sides, perhaps six feet high. It provided a cache secure from anything that could not fly, and on top, covered with a sealskin, was the caribou we had been given. There was an igloo nearby, but we did not use it and went on for another two or three miles before building our own.

We were in country known to be rich in caribou, so next day Kutjek took his dogs with our komatik to hunt while Mino went off on foot. They returned late having seen nothing. We did not move nor hunt the next day, I think because it was Sunday though we had travelled the previous Sunday. Kutjek also had to repair his komatik where the dogs had eaten some of the sealskin bindings that secured the cross-bars to the runners.

I woke early next day to find Kutjek packing snow into holes in the roof. It had been drifting for the past two days, but now there was a full gale, which had arrived promptly at the equinox. Everywhere in the igloo except the bed was covered by two to three inches of fine snow. It was of course impossible to travel or hunt. After we had cleared the snow away and made the igloo snow-proof, we resigned ourselves to a wasted day. We had noticed that Kutjek had a strange pattern marked with little holes on the lid of one of his boxes. He now produced some pegs and started to play a game with Mino. It was a variant of Fox and Geese, called by the Inuit *Nuktagaq*. Reynold and I watched carefully to learn the rules and then we played. It was as good a way as any to pass a storm-bound day. (The rules are given in appendix B for anyone caught in a similar situation.) The wind died in the evening.

Three days with nothing coming in and no progress to the east had done us no good. The dogs were fed on the little seal that remained, leaving only a piece of walrus weighing about twenty pounds, some seal blubber, and half a caribou when we resumed our journey along the coast. We stopped at the mouth of a river called Ikpik by the Inuit. Kutjek asked me to go with him and Mino to look for caribou from the top of a small knoll. This took about a quarter of an hour. Every possible place on the coastal plain was examined with Reynold's binoculars and Kutjek's telescope but with no success. To the southwest we could see a large low island, the more eastern of the two Sadleqs we had been told lay off the coast. Mino, having put the telescope away, was sitting on a rock, when Kutjek pushed him from the back. Mino put his head down and somersaulted all the way down the snow slope to the bottom. Kutjek then followed suit and they both started to laugh.

In the meantime Reynold was taking bearings about a hundred yards from where we had stopped, when the dogs, now very hungry, suddenly attacked the komatiks. Before we could stop them they had eaten almost all our remaining seal blubber and part of the caribou. Kutjek was confident we would find caribou if we went up the river valley, so we followed it to a large lake which Reynold called Lake Gillian after his wife, the only geographical feature we ever named. We travelled along the lake looking for caribou until after sunset when we came across tracks that were only a day old. We then camped on a small island.

The previous June at Chesterfield Inlet, Dr Livingstone had put what had proved to be a very temporary filling in one of my teeth. The same tooth had started to ache during the day and by evening it had become very unpleasant. I got into my sleeping bag and spent a miserable night. Four aspirin would alleviate the pain for a short time, but we did not have enough aspirin to continue this treatment for long. The tooth itself was firm as a rock. While we were preparing to move on next day Kutjek looked for caribou and saw two herds not far away. He and Mino set out to hunt them and I got back into my sleeping bag with the aspirin. I found that digging into the tooth with the blade of a pair of scissors and then with the fine wire we used to clean the nipple of the primus stove did not make the tooth hurt more, and that, surprisingly, it seemed rather better afterwards. I continued this unconventional treatment for some time.

At noon Reynold observed the sun to determine our latitude, while I recorded the numbers he called out. Reynold then walked to the top of a small hill to take bearings. When he got back he said he had seen through his binoculars what he thought must be an ice cap away to the northeast. In 1934 Pat Baird had climbed a mountain on the east coast of Baffin Island and had seen an ice cap far to the west, but nothing else was then known about this inland ice, subsequently called the Barnes Ice Cap, or how far it continued to the west.

When Kutjek returned he said he had killed five caribou, and he was soon followed by Mino who had got three. Our immediate food problem was over and we had a fine supper of caribou tongue, which I could enjoy, my toothache being much better.

Next day I went with Kutjek to collect his caribou. We saw several more but they were moving away from us, and Kutjek did not try to hunt them for long. Reynold went on a similar mission with Mino and then climbed the hill again but visibility was no better than it had been the day before. The dogs were given a whole caribou.

We could now see no reason for not resuming our journey to the east, but when I mentioned Piling next morning Kutjek said we would instead go back to Igloolik. He explained that we had very little coal oil left and no blubber, which was certainly true, and added that Mino and he could not keep their feet warm because they had worn out their boots. We said we were very sorry they would not come with us, but we were going on to Piling. We loaded our komatiks separately in silence, ours facing east and theirs facing west. They were probably in a more difficult position than we were, though we did not realize it at the time. They would be severely criticized by the other Inuit if they let us go on alone, especially if anything happened to us. Suddenly Mino took his old caribou-skin blanket – he had little else – and put it on our komatik. This was the turning point. We halved our last quart of coal oil, because Kutjek also had a primus, and made a few adjustments to the loads. Kutjek then took three of his good dogs, added them to our nine, and drove off towards Eqe. Mino, not very cheerfully, Reynold, and I headed across the lake, down the river, and back to the sea.

It was cold going into the wind but very warm in the sun with a following wind. The dogs Kutjek had given us were stronger than ours and we went faster than we had expected. During the afternoon Reynold found that his kulitak had dropped off the komatik and had to walk back to recover it. We camped soon after reaching the sea, and Reynold joined us an hour later. To the west we could see the blue ice that Mino and I had encountered, in sharp contrast to the dark rock of the cliffs. Mino seemed a little more cheerful in the igloo that night.

We could hear the wind as we crawled out of our sleeping bags in the morning, but it turned out to be a beautiful day. Before starting we cached a caribou to use on our way back. After about two and a half hours Mino saw some caribou near the coast. He went to hunt them while I built an igloo. Some hours later he returned looking very downcast. We thought he must have been unsuccessful and had possibly broken his gun, but he was having us on. He had shot five, and he and Reynold went to collect them. The dogs were again given a whole caribou. They had been very hungry, and earlier in the day had eaten part of the sleeve of my kulitak when I had left it unguarded for a minute. The dogs were so bloated after the caribou that they had to have a day of rest, while Reynold observed, I booked for him, and Mino skinned the other caribou. We went to bed very early.

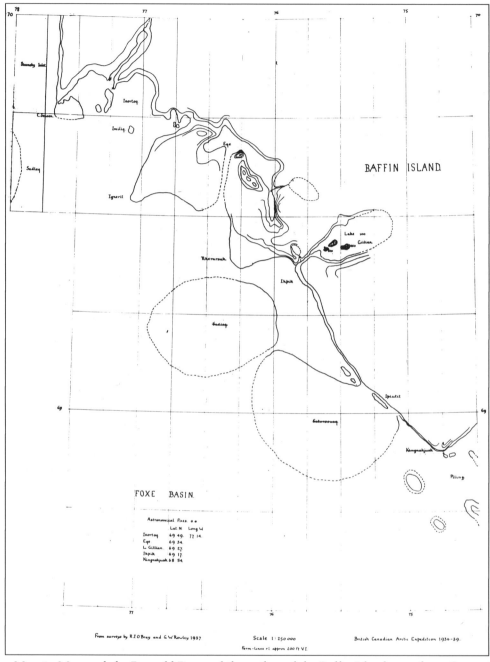

Map 6   Map made by Reynold Bray and the author of the Baffin Island coast from Cape Jensen to Piling

Our early night was followed by an early start. With a heavier load the dogs were moving slowly and I was walking ahead to encourage them when we came to the fresh tracks of three polar bears, presumably a mother with two cubs. The dogs raced along in pursuit like different animals until we had to give up because the tracks were taking us too far south. During the chase we had broken three of the komatik's cross-bars. We got back on our route and came to Ipiutik, the Inuit name for the isthmus, most of it a lake, of a great peninsula the Inuit call Saaturjuaq. The coast along the shore was so low and flat that it was indistinguishable from the sea ice. We realized we were on land only when we saw a few stones half hidden by snow. Saaturjuaq itself was so low as to be almost invisible.

We camped on the isthmus and were up early in the morning to another beautiful day. Reynold walked to the top of a cliff to take bearings while Mino and I packed up, loaded the komatik, and continued our journey. Reynold soon caught up to us as the dogs were very slow at first. They improved as the day progressed. In the afternoon we reached a prominent bluff, 400 or more feet high. Mino, who had not travelled along this part of the coast before, stopped, looked at a rough sketch that Kutjek had given him, and casually said, "This Piling, what we do now?" Feeling rather like the grand old Duke of York with his ten thousand men, we said we now went back again, but first we would like to camp just past the bluff, and to spend a day at Piling.

12

Return from Piling

30 March – 12 April 1937

Parry refers to Inuit from Piling visiting his ships at Igloolik in May 1823, but neither he nor Lyon learned anything about where they lived except that it was a journey of six to ten days to the east. At that time of the year Inuit could travel long distances in a day by komatik. Hantzsch, coming from the south, was within a few miles of Piling when he had to turn back in May 1911, ill with the trichinosis that killed him. The Fifth Thule Expedition had wanted to complete the map of Baffin Island by mapping from Igloolik to Piling, and Peter Freuchen was on his way to begin this when he became lost and froze his foot on the land-crossing to Igloolik. The next year Mathiassen reached Maniqtuuq in Kangirllukjuak but could go no farther east owing to an outbreak of dog disease. In 1933 ice had prevented the *Morrissey* from approaching the Piling area from the sea. Reynold and I were surprised to have reached Piling with no real difficulty and at practically no cost. We had been luckier than the others.

The Inuit name Piling means place of plenty. What was plentiful has now been forgotten and the name is applied to the area surrounding a large inlet. Sometimes Inuit from the Igloolik area would hunt caribou as far east as Piling but they did not stay for long. Oral history tells of Inuit from southern Baffin Island travelling north to Piling, but more than a hundred years had passed since the last of these journeys had ended in the starvation of a large party on the isthmus of Ipiutik. Another tragedy occurred twelve years after we reached Piling when three of a group of five Iglulingmiut starved to death there.

We camped just around the bluff at the entrance to the inlet and celebrated our arrival by having a tin of beans with our caribou that night. For many days it had been our last remaining southern food, preserved against great temptation for our arrival at Piling. The finest display of solar halos we had ever seen added to the occasion. Through a fine icy mist the low sun shone in a cloudless sky, surrounded by two concentric halos. On both sides of the sun a pair of sun dogs, each resembling the sun seen through a haze, marked where the halos touched what appeared to be arcs of reflected halos. A very bright patch below the sun contrasted with the very dark sky around it.

In the morning I set out to walk across the entrance of the inlet to some small granite islands and then along the coast for a few miles to where we thought Hantzsch must have reached, and certainly to where he had been able to see. On the way back our dogs appeared clearly at a distance I estimated to be about three miles from our camp. They vanished and I did not see them again until I was less than a mile away. Mirages are of course very common in the Arctic, especially in the late winter, and we would frequently see distant country that appeared much higher than it was and in fact lay over the horizon. The land was said to be "looming." On this occasion our dogs must have been looming, made noticeable by their movement and their contrast against the white snow. When I got back Reynold was already in bed. He had made very good noon observations for latitude and had then walked some miles into the inlet.

Our small party was in good shape. We were all fit and we had more than enough caribou to get us back as far as the Inuit camp at Angmaarjuaq. Our dogs were pulling better. It was now 31 March and the days were lengthening rapidly. The coldest part of the winter was over, and the weather was likely to be good for the next month or two. Very little coal oil remained to melt ice for icing the komatik every morning and boiling the kettleful of tea we allowed ourselves each day. We would not be able to cook, but caribou is even better when frozen than it is cooked, and we had nothing else to eat.

Both Reynold and I had cameras, but we could rarely use them because they did not work in the winter cold. We thought this was owing to lubrication in the shutter mechanism becoming stiff.

We tried keeping our cameras warm by carrying them next to our skin, underneath our atigis, but this arrangement was cold and uncomfortable and it seemed to make little difference as we could hear the shutter mechanism working too slowly. By taking special care and being very quick we were able to photograph the distinctive bluff at Piling without overexposure. Within twenty years it became the site of a station on the Distant Early Warning (DEW) Line.

The weather was beautiful for the first day of our return journey and we made a good start. Passing our last igloo on the way to Piling early in the afternoon, we were well over the Ipiutik isthmus when we camped. Reynold was suffering from snow-blindness, which he thought was the consequence of observing at noon the previous day. The sun was now high enough in the sky to make snow-blindness a constant danger, and the three of us had to wear sunglasses whenever we were outside. Reynold was able to rest his eyes the next day because it was blowing and drifting. We got ready to leave but found we could not see well enough to travel. Mino built an impressive set of snow works, presumably to shelter the house from the wind to keep it warmer.

The following day Reynold's eyes were much less painful. Visibility was good and in the distance we could see the blue ice sprawling over the cliff near Tikerarsuk. We had asked Mino about it and he had assured us that it remained ice throughout the summer. During the afternoon we left the sea ice to travel along the shore. Here we came across a small herd of caribou and Mino shot two from the komatik. After skinning and cutting them up we returned to the sea ice to camp in the igloo I had built a week earlier and which Mino now enlarged. A lot of mud shoeing had been lost while we had been on the land.

Mino patched the shoeing the next day, using the contents of the stomachs of the caribou he had shot. It was a good day not to travel as there was a strong cold wind.

Our kettle made enough tea to fill four mugs and there were three of us. We would fill three mugs every morning, and Reynold and I would watch with astonishment while Mino drank his at once and put down his mug for the fourth cup, which he richly deserved. We could never understand how he could drink tea that was so nearly boiling. On our journey to Igloolik Reynold and I had had a different problem with drinking tea. The tea leaves froze to the bottom of our enamel mugs and after three or four days had accumulated until they filled half the mug. We had, however, some very concentrated French coffee extract. Using this with boiling water thawed the top layer of the tea leaves and the mugs gradually became clean again, when we would return to drinking tea. We no longer had this problem as no tea leaves had a chance to freeze to the bottom of any mug that Mino used.

The two caribou Mino had shot made our load heavier when we set out next morning, and during the day we picked up the caribou and some other things we had cached at our old igloo near the mouth of the river at Ikpik. We were getting nearer to what we hoped would be a glacier, but that morning Mino enlarged on what he had said earlier. He told us that not only was ice there in the summer but also water in the winter. Reynold and I were walking ahead and discussing this when we realized that a warm spring could provide water in the winter which would continue to flow and freeze to build up enough ice to remain throughout the summer. When we reached the blue ice we scrambled to the top of the cliff and found there a lake covered with mushy ice from which a light mist was rising and on which there were shallow pools. Water was running over the edge of the cliff and freezing to form a mass of blue ice a hundred yards or more wide, several feet thick, and extending to the base of the cliff over a hundred feet below. I was able to kneel down and enjoy a long drink, a pleasant change from the snow that had been our main source of water since we had parted from Kutjek. Reynold was not so fortunate. He had let his beard and moustache grow long and so much ice had formed around his mouth that he could not reach the water in the pools.

Mino soon arrived at the foot of the ice with the komatik, and Reynold could scramble down the cliff to get a mug and our kettle to fill with water. We camped where Mino had stopped, with the luxury of having a supply of water without having to use our almost empty primus to melt ice. More mud had been lost during the day and it would have to be replaced before we could continue.

Mino decided to use moss for repairing the shoeing, while I spent the next day in feeding the dogs, getting water from the spring-fed lake, and carrying out general maintenance of our equipment. Reynold mapped the coast towards the entrance to Eqe bay. The previous day had been bitterly cold, but now we could really feel the warmth of the sun. We went to bed early so we could be off in good time in the morning.

We were rewarded with a beautiful day. From Tikerarsuk to the end of Eqe we had to follow a much more circuituous route than before to avoid stones that would break our fragile mud. Where we cut across our old tracks we saw one or two wolves had followed us. We had heard them howling from time to time but had never seen them. At our old igloo in Eqe we found Kutjek had built a new igloo nearby on his return journey. In it he had left a caribou head and a little fat for us. Half-way along Eqe bay we camped after ten hours travel. There were now only a few hours of darkness each night.

Progress was excellent the next day when the weather was again perfect. Our dogs were pulling more strongly since we had been able to feed them better, and the sound of the komatik gliding over the snow – between a creak and a hiss – was music to our ears. On the land-crossing from Eqe to the Isortoq region there were very fresh wolf tracks, and we found a recently killed caribou that had been partly eaten by wolves. Perhaps we had disturbed them at their meal. At the end of another ten-hour travelling day we camped in the large bay that leads to Isortoq.

We hoped to reach the Inuit camp at Angmaarjuaq by the next night although it seemed a very long way around the many islands in the bay to the short land-crossing near Cape Jensen. Eventually we saw the igloos in the distance but no sign of any inhabitants. When we reached the camp site we found the people had deserted it the previous day. We followed the tracks of their komatiks leading west, and it was still just light when we saw their new camp, presumably moved to be closer to where they were hunting seals on the sea ice. We felt we were returning to old friends and were soon enjoying our first cooked meal in many days.

We were being really lazy the next day when we heard somebody shouting that a komatik was coming. The traveller was Jack Turner, the Anglican minister at Pond Inlet, on his return journey after a long parochial circuit to Arctic Bay, Igloolik, and Repulse. He brought us a note from Joe Ford, the HBC manager at Repulse. Pat had been to the *Polecat* to get some equipment and had returned to Repulse just as Turner was leaving and had had no chance to write. Joe's letter told us that Tom and Peter had gone to Wager Bay in February. They had not yet returned to Repulse, but Joe had heard on the radio that Tom had visited Chesterfield Inlet.

Jack Turner was seven years older than I. He had gained a reputation in the north as a good and experienced traveller. On his circuit he had been accompanied by a man who lived on the Foxe Basin coast of Baffin Island, and who was now about to return to his family. As nobody from the camp was keen to go to Pond Inlet at that time, Turner had been expecting he would have to travel on his own. The route was used every year by Inuit on their way to trade at Pond Inlet, he had covered it himself a year earlier, Mathiassen had indicated it on a rough map, and the RCMP patrol had already followed it and would have left tracks. Jack said he would rather not travel alone, and asked if either Reynold or I would be able to keep him company.

We had not really thought much about what we would do after returning from Piling, except that we would like to go to Agu, on the coast of north Baffin Island to the west of Fury and Hecla Strait. From there we might try to map Hall Island which appeared on the official map of Canada as a separate island but we thought was probably the same as Crown Prince Frederik Island. Before then we would certainly have to visit the HBC post at Arctic Bay to buy supplies and equipment for the summer. Reynold was intending to spend the spring collecting birds in the area around Fury and Hecla Strait, so it made more sense for him to go back to Igloolik. It would also be a rather shorter journey and he was again being troubled by snow-blindness. I said I always liked to go somewhere new so we agreed that I would accompany Turner to Pond Inlet and Reynold would return to Igloolik with Mino. We would both then go to Arctic Bay and try to meet there in about a month.

Jack Turner had timed his arrival well the next day being a Sunday. He held two services, each with innumerable hymns which he led while accompanying them on a concertina. He also provided hard ship's biscuits and tea to his congregation of all those at the camp. Nobody appreciated them more than Reynold and I.

The weather was fine on Monday, and Reynold and Mino left first. Five travelling days would probably take them to Igloolik or Akudneq at that time of year, even with our tired dogs. They had a good load of caribou, which would make them very welcome.

13

Across Baffin Island to Pond Inlet
12 April – 26 April 1937

Jack Turner led the camp in a final hymn before we headed north in mid-morning. Two large packing cases were on his komatik but they weighed very little and our load looked heavier than it was. Jack expected it to be a quick journey and had based the amount of food we took for ourselves and the dogs accordingly, adding that we were sure to see some caribou if we ran short. The Lord would provide.

To my surprise we stopped to feed the dogs two or three miles from the camp, possibly to avoid a fight with the dogs there. Jack's team was not responding to his commands at first, but they improved as we went along. The day was pleasantly warm and we did not stop till eight o'clock when we were well into Kangirllukjuak. Jack built an igloo but the snow was very poor. By the time we had finished it, the sky to the northeast was beginning to lighten.

The dogs went much better the next day. We had nearly reached the land at the head of Kangirllukjuak when we discovered we were in the wrong arm of the inlet and had to turn the komatik round and go a long way back. It had been another warm day and, rather than build a snow house, we spent a comfortable night sleeping in the open by the komatik.

In the morning we found the correct arm of the inlet, though we had some trouble getting through a band of rough ice along the tide-crack. We soon came across the tracks left by the RCMP patrol from Pond Inlet and followed them until we came to an igloo they had built. After a hot and tiring day, which took us little nearer to Pond Inlet, we were happy to camp in it.

Jack thought there was a better route than the one the police had used, so we left their tracks in the morning. Our dogs were very slow as they were hot and the sun was making the snow soft. At midday we decided to rest and set off again when the sun was low and the snow would be harder. There was no longer any real darkness but in the half-light that night we lost the route we were following. Eventually we came to a large lake leading in the direction we wanted. Near the end of this lake we saw a mound that had apparently been pushed up when water below the surface of the land had expanded on freezing. It looked rather like the pingos of the Western Arctic but was only a few feet high.

We continued to pick the best way we could across very uneven ground with low ridges and valleys and small stony plains until noon, when we stopped for a rest and to shake out the traces. Jack walked ahead to see if he could find an easier route but progress remained slow. After we iced-up, it was my turn to go ahead and I had the good luck to come across the police tracks again. We followed them to the head of a valley, where we found good snow for an igloo.

My tooth had started to ache again after leaving the Inuit camp. Jack said he had had some experience in pulling teeth and would try his hand on mine. He even had a pair of tooth extractors and some novocaine on the komatik. That night he tried very hard to pull the tooth out but it was adamant and I was glad of the novocaine.

When we resumed our journey we soon lost the police tracks and had to go back to pick them up again. It was particularly difficult to follow the tracks when crossing lakes because the snow was harder there, and finding them on the other side could mean a long search. We camped by a small lake. The snow was troublesome and it was very late when we turned in. We had made much less progress in the first week of our journey than we had hoped.

As the next day was Sunday, travel was out of the question. Jack held rigid views on observing the Sabbath and the literal accuracy of the Bible. Like Father Bazin, he admired and had an unbounded affection for the Inuit, but they saw their vocations in completely different lights. It seemed to me that Father Bazin recognized and tried to strengthen the virtues of the Inuit people, while Jack believed he should not shrink from his duty to identify and correct their sins.

Though the great majority of the Inuit were Anglican, many more Roman Catholic missionaries worked in the Eastern Arctic. The parish Jack had carved out for himself included four posts where there were permanent Roman Catholic missions. Ecumenical was a little-known adjective in those days, and Jack probably thought that, when outnumbered, attack was the best defence against what he believed was his opposition. I remember his telling me that he could not understand how it was that Father Cochard, one of the priests at the Pond Inlet mission, seemed to be such a nice man and to have such good ideas about the Inuit. It did not occur to him that Father Cochard really was a very nice man and did have good ideas. The conclusion he had reached was that he was being tempted to like him, and he did not have a long enough spoon to sup with him.

Keeping in touch with his parishioners by dog team meant that Jack had to travel the whole winter in order to spend a single day each year at most, but not all, of their camps. Much of his summer had to be devoted to hunting for dog-food. It was a hard life, but he relished it because of his burning faith, which was absolute. When the weather was fine, the dogs fit, and all was going well, he thanked God for his blessings. If the weather was foul, the dogs had eaten their harnesses, he had lost his way, and there was nothing left in the food-box, he was confident that God was testing his faith, and he thanked God for thinking him worthy of so severe a trial. Such rationalization put both Jack and God in a "no lose" situation. Many of his decisions were influenced, if not directed, by the Daily Light, the passage in the Bible selected by his church to be read that day. It might seem that travelling with Jack would be a harrowing and possibly hazardous undertaking. In fact his faith in divine intervention was complemented by his experience and ability as an arctic traveller. At the same time, his readiness to discuss issues, without changing his own views in the least, and to talk freely about his experiences and beliefs, combined with his open, friendly, and generous nature, made him a most congenial companion.

We resumed our journey on Monday morning, following a valley and skirting high ground to the east. By noon we reached a large lake, which was obviously that named Nina Bang Lake on Mathiassen's map. A part of the river flowing out of the lake was open, as it had been when Mathiassen passed by. The Inuit say the river here remains open even in the depth of winter. We took the opportunity to ice the komatik runners and boil a cup of tea before crossing the lake. On the north side of Nina Bang Lake we came across the police tracks again which was reassuring, but as before they proved impossible to follow.

High mountains lay to the north between us and Pond Inlet. To avoid them, we had to go west to Phillips Creek, the valley of which provides a practicable route through comparatively low country to reach the sea ice in Milne Inlet. If we went too far west we might miss Phillips Creek; the watershed of north Baffin Island is not well defined here and it would be easy to follow the wrong valley. Inuit usually find their way on long overland sledge journeys by heading towards some distinctive land mass in the far distance, but I did not then know this, nor what feature to use as a guide. We had only the sketch-map of the route published by Mathiassen and it was little help. We soon lost our way and made a shelter in the snow by the side of the komatik, roofing it with a tarpaulin. It was very small but not uncomfortable.

We had now to find a chain of three lakes which would, according to Mathiassen's map and Jack's memory, lead us in the direction of Phillips Creek. This took some time because the first lake was farther west than shown by Mathiassen. At the end of this lake we rested in order to resume our journey late in the afternoon when the snow would be harder. We then continued along the second lake to the third lake, called Inuktorfik, meaning "where people were eaten." It was here that many years earlier Ataguttaaluk, who had been so kind to us at Igloolik, had endured and survived her terrible winter. By noon we had reached the end of Inuktorfik where we stopped. Jack slept for a few hours while I walked ahead. There was no sign of the police tracks, but I found what seemed to be a good route leading in the right direction. At the end of the afternoon we continued our journey, climbing gradually to a limestone tableland where there were many fresh caribou tracks. Here we could not agree on the route. I suggested one way while Jack wanted to go in the opposite direction. Eventually we decided to follow my way first, not that I was confident it was right, but rather because I was sure his way was wrong. To my relief we very soon came across recent tracks left by two komatiks, which we followed. Our dogs had been poor for the past few days because we were getting short of dog-food, but they now set a good pace. Later we found we were following the old police tracks as well. It was a cold night and, when we reached an abandoned igloo around midnight, we chose to camp in it.

We were short not only of dog-food. We seemed to have very little food left for ourselves, and much of that was a good piece of caribou that Jack had been intending to preserve as a present for the Reverend Maurice Flint, his colleague at Pond Inlet. I thought Jack might want to stop to hunt, but this could have taken some time, with no certainty of success.

When I mentioned to Jack that we seemed to be short of food, he pointed to the two large boxes we had been carrying on the komatik. He explained that at Repulse Bay he had stayed with Joe Ford. He had been given cereal for breakfast and had remarked how good it was. Joe had replied that neither he nor Henry Voisey liked breakfast cereal and Jack could take away as much as he could carry. They had gone to the storehouse where Joe had started throwing him packets of cereal from the loft, asking him to say when he had all he wanted. He had taken this literally and when there were none left in the loft he had packed all he had been given in the two large boxes we had with us.

They now became our main source of food. There was good variety, so far as it went: Shredded Wheat, Post Toasties, Puffed Wheat, Puffed Rice, Puffed Barley, Corn Flakes, and so on. Without milk or sugar however they left much to be desired as a sledging ration. An empty packet every few miles marked the rest of our route. Maurice Flint's present became an increasingly tempting alternative, but Jack was experienced in resisting temptation.

The dogs were pulling better when we set out next day. We had reached Phillips Creek and were following it towards the sea where we hoped to arrive around six o'clock that night. By five o'clock we thought we had another ten miles to go. At ten o'clock we came to an old igloo and paused for a mug-up. Jack said we still had another three miles to the sea. In fact we travelled throughout the night. The broad, gravel-filled valley of Phillips Creek seemed interminable. To the northeast the Krag Mountains rose high and showed no sign of ending. The dogs found the night as tedious as we did, and walked slower and slower with their tails dragging in the snow. It was eight o'clock in the morning when we finally reached the sea ice at the head of Milne Inlet. We had hoped to find an Inuit camp here but there was no sign of one.

Jack was tired after a long day and night and slept by the side of the komatik till noon when we resumed our journey along Milne Inlet. We were now in much more dramatic country, with cliffs up to a thousand feet rising steeply from the wide fiord. At six o'clock we reached an old igloo where we stopped for a meal, after which I succeeded in sleeping in my sleeping bag lashed to the komatik as we continued across the fairly level sea ice. I woke when Jack had to stop owing to poor visibility – he did not want to miss the narrow gap between Ragged Island and the coast of Baffin Island. Going round the island would add several hours to our journey. Jack slept until it started to clear a little.

As soon as we could see the gap we headed towards it. We passed through, between high cliffs on both sides, but there was no indication of any Inuit camp and recent drifting snow had covered any tracks. The dogs were becoming very tired and we decided to camp near Cape Hatt, a feature that was shown for many years on the back of the Canadian two-dollar bill. The snow on the ice was too shallow for us to cut vertical blocks and we had to cut them horizontally from the surface, resulting in a small and strangely shaped igloo. While we were building, the wind increased and it started to drift badly, but we were soon comfortable inside, happy that the next day was Sunday and would be a well-needed day of rest.

We did not wake until early in the afternoon. The howl of the wind and the hiss of drifting snow told us that we could not have moved whatever the day of the week. This was the first unpleasant weather Jack and I had had since our meeting in Foxe Basin. Most days had been perfect – cloudless skies and never more than a moderate wind.

We spent the rest of the day talking. Jack told me that his most difficult journey had been from Pangnirtung to Pond Inlet when he had to cross Home Bay in deep soft snow. Standing on top of his igloo one Sunday, he could see all his igloos for the previous week. He was very frank about some of his problems in explaining his understanding of the scriptures to the Inuit. He believed discipline to be good for children, quoting the Book of Proverbs on the subject, "He that spareth his rod hateth his son; but he that loveth him chasteneth him betimes." When he suggested to the Inuit that they should spank their children when they were naughty, they had answered, "But we Inuit love our children." He was still trying to think of a convincing reply.

After an early night and an early start we hoped to reach Pond Inlet without camping again; it was now 26 April and the days were long. Even after a day's rest, however, the dogs moved slowly. We had been travelling for some hours when we met a komatik with two Inuit. They were off to hunt seal, but instead gladly turned and led us to their igloo for a mug-up. Here Jack persuaded one of them to go in front of us to Pond Inlet on a small komatik. With something ahead to encourage them, our dogs followed at a much better pace, and late that night we saw the lights of the settlement.

14

Pond Inlet

26 April – 3 May 1937

Within an hour we had reached the settlement and driven up to the mission, where Jack had invited me to stay. After a warm welcome by Maurice Flint and a large number of Inuit, we were given a splendid meal. I do not remember what we ate, but it was neither corn flakes nor walrus, so it was delicious. I was then able to enjoy my first bath for a year or so, though enjoy is too weak a verb to describe the pleasure of soaking in warm soapy water after so long a time without the possibility of even washing. I did not feel that I had entered a nicer world, but rather that I had returned to a familiar one, in which old conditioned reflexes, unexercised for months, responded to situations they recognized. That night I slept like a log in a real bed.

After I shaved off my beard next morning, Maurice trimmed my hair. Jack lent me some "white man's clothing" as caribou skin was much too warm to wear in the house, and would have shed hair all over it. I also exchanged my caribou footwear for sealskin kamiks, by far the most practical and comfortable footwear in a northern settlement.

The morning revealed Pond Inlet to be, to my eyes at least, the most beautiful of places. On the far side of Eclipse Sound rose the mountains of Bylot Island, cut by mile-wide glaciers flowing from the icefield in its interior. They formed a long wall, about five thousand feet high, the ice of the glaciers shining a Delft blue in the sun and contrasting with the deeper blue of the sky and the dark grey cliffs. Though thirty miles away across the snow-covered sea ice, they seemed to be no farther than five miles in the clear arctic light. A solitary, tall, blue-green iceberg was grounded close inshore, west of the settlement. A few dogs were stirring around the houses from which smoke was rising vertically in the still air. To the east Mount Herodier stood like a giant pyramid silhouetted against the morning sky.

The Pond area had not always been as tranquil as it was that morning. Whaling ships had reached Davis Strait early in the eighteenth century, but they had kept to the Greenland side, mainly south of Disko Island, because the ice was heavier to the west and north. In 1817, however, two British whaling ships had reached Melville Bay and discovered the "North Water," an area relatively free of ice. They had then sailed to the "West Side" of Baffin Bay and found it to be rich in whales. The next year John Ross, on his first expedition to the Arctic, discovered an inlet which he thought was closed by a glacier and named it Pond's Bay after the astronomer royal of the time.

On reaching the West Side the whalers used to meet together off Button Point, and in 1854 the *Eclipse* found that Pond's Bay led into a complex of fiords and connected with Navy Board Inlet. Pond Inlet, as it was subsequently named, became such an important whaling area that in the second half of the last century it was frequently referred to as the "Mecca of the Whalers." The ships would often shelter about fifteen miles southeast of the present settlement in Albert Harbour, where there was good protection from both the wind and the ice. Some whalers established shore stations nearby in Igakjuak. The Inuit would visit the whalers to trade with them, but contact was limited by the urgencies of whaling and the anxiety of the whalers to head south before they were trapped for the winter.

The Canadian government ship *Arctic* spent the winter of 1906-07 in Albert Harbour, and exploratory journeys were made from there to Milne Inlet and Navy Board Inlet. Early in 1912 R.S. Janes, who had been an officer in the CGS *Arctic*, started rumours in Newfoundland that placer gold could be found near Pond Inlet, one of the areas being the Salmon River, a few miles west of the present settlement, and three ships sailed north in a minor gold rush. One was nipped by the ice and sank while the prospectors were looking for gold, one sailed south with disappointed miners at the end of the summer, and the third, the schooner *Minnie Maud*, wintered at Albert Harbour to trade with the Inuit. None found any gold.

Captain J.E. Bernier, who had commanded the CGS *Arctic* and later became captain of the *Minnie Maud*, had developed a keen interest in the area and its resources. During the next five years he established three posts there for fur trading, salting and exporting arctic char, and prospecting. He sold his interests to Captain H.T. Munn of the Arctic Gold Syndicate who in turn sold them to the Hudson's Bay Company in 1923.

Pond Inlet had also been the scene of the Janes murder trial. Janes, whose rumours had caused the gold rush, had become a fur trader, and in 1920 he attempted to force a group of Inuit to undertake a long journey for which they were not prepared. Believing this would endanger their families, one of the men killed him. The government decided that the conduct of the case should be a demonstration of Canadian justice. In the summer of 1923 a judge with a full supporting cast was taken in the CGS *Arctic* to Pond Inlet to hold a formal trial. During the proceedings a large herd of narwhal was reported. There were shouts of "Killelluat" (narwhal), and all the Inuit ran for their rifles. The judge is said to have misunderstood both their words and their intentions, with some loss to the dignity of the proceedings.

By 1937 Pond Inlet had become one of the larger settlements in Baffin Island with an HBC post, an RCMP detachment, and both Catholic and Anglican missions. Like the other posts in the Eastern Arctic, it now depended almost entirely on the white fox trade. Six or seven Inuit were employed in the settlement and lived there with their families. They were frequently joined by relatives from camps in Eclipse Sound and nearby fiords, who had come to the post to trade. Several of the older people combined a cheerful acceptance of current conditions with almost a nostalgia for the whaling days. One, Tom Koudnak, had obviously been a man of authority then and could speak some English.

My first visit was to the HBC post. The manager, John Stanners, was alone; his clerk had gone to the post at Arctic Bay, which had been re-established the previous year. Stanners told me that last summer the *Nascopie* had delivered some of the expedition's supplies. They included a dozen bottles of whisky and a case of chocolate. I had no hesitation in claiming half of each, which enabled me to repay some of the generous hospitality I received during my stay. Such half measures proved a mistake because no other member of the expedition visited Pond Inlet before I returned two years later; by that time the remaining six bottles of whisky could not be found, to nobody's surprise. I asked John to enquire if any Inuit were planning to go to Arctic Bay in the near future.

My next call was to the Roman Catholic mission where I saw Father Julien Cochard and Father Étienne Daniélo. Brother Jacques Volant was visiting one of the nearby camps with Constable Paddy Doyle of the RCMP detachment and I did not meet them until the next day. All at the mission were from France and, like Father Bazin at Igloolik, they went out of their way to be as helpful as possible. The three were keen bridge players and had been waiting two years for someone who might make up a four. Even I was better than no one, and I joined them several times during the next week.

Both the Anglican and Catholic missions had been established in 1929, but most of the Inuit were already Protestant having heard about Christianity from Cumberland Sound where there had long been an Anglican mission. After nearly eight years the Catholic mission at Pond Inlet had many Inuit friends but only a single family of followers. It must have been very discouraging for the fathers to work among a people they admired and loved but could not convert. They needed great faith that their soft-sell approach would in the fullness of time prove more effective than the hard-sell practices of their competitors.

I was back at the Anglican mission for supper. Since my arrival I had been eating almost all the time I had been awake. That night I weighed myself on the mission scales and found I was just 140 pounds, much lighter than I had been when I left Repulse. My appetite remained keen and four days later I had added another 6 pounds. Maurice Flint said he had put on 26 pounds since he had arrived in September, but he had had little exercise because he had to stay at the mission whenever Jack was travelling.

There was plenty to do at Pond Inlet, besides eating. My time was fully occupied in arranging to travel to Arctic Bay, making social calls, writing, and reading. Having nothing to read is in some ways like having nothing to eat or drink. I had been deprived of reading for a long time, and at first it did not matter much what I read, just as any food is good when one is hungry enough. During the winter I had spent a night in an igloo where the walls were lined with advertisements from the *Saturday Evening Post* of

several years back, and I read all of them. I can still remember
one that offered a new Packard for $1000. At Pond Inlet there
was no shortage of books, and there was a radio with news from
"the outside."

John Stanners told me that two young men, Arnaviapik and
Arnatsiaq, were willing to take me to Arctic Bay early the next
week. I bought all we needed for the journey at the store and
arranged how they would be paid. John helped me prepare food
for the journey by cooking beans with salt pork. To do this on
the trail would take too long and use too much fuel. We poured
the cooked pork and beans into shallow pans to a depth of an
inch or two and left them outside to freeze. They were then easy
to break into small blocks with a hammer. All we had to do was
to pack the pieces into bags. On the journey we could heat up
as much as needed in a few minutes.

Constable Doyle of the RCMP was a popular member of the
community. He had been in charge of the patrol that Reynold
and I had just missed in Kangirllukjuak in March, and he had
then gone to Igloolik and the camps near there. He said he had
found no serious hardship. The camp at Angmaarjuaq had not
been as well off as the others, and the patrol had been able to
get only a little seal for their dogs there. I remarked that their
dogs must have been pretty hungry by the time they reached Igloolik, but he replied that they had been lucky. Two Inuit had
caught up with them and had a large piece of walrus. This had
made all the difference. I did not tell him where the walrus must
have come from.

I am not implying that the RCMP should not have accepted the
walrus. All arrangements for feeding the dogs would have been
made by the Inuit special constables who were driving the dogs,
and who would not have taken anything that they thought could
not be spared. It is, however, an illustration of the way the Inuit
would put the needs of visitors above their own. It was only in
the summer that I discovered that Issigaituq had been down to
his last walrus when he had fed our dogs so generously during
the week Reynold and I had stayed with him on our way to
Igloolik.

On Friday night, after supper at the HBC, I went to a dance
at the RCMP post. It was like those on Southampton Island – square
dances to tunes played by a woman on an accordion – but with

rather more of a Scottish character. This was probably because most of the whalers who had visited northern Baffin Island had come from the United Kingdom, whereas the whalers in Hudson Bay were mainly American and usually wintered in the north. Almost all the population was present and I did not get to bed until after three o'clock. It was light throughout the night, with the sun just sinking below the mountains of Bylot Island, and time of day had lost much of its meaning.

The service in the small wooden Anglican church on Sunday morning was followed for me by roast caribou for lunch at the Catholic mission, where Paddy Doyle was also a guest. It seemed a great pity that there was so little communication between the two missions; together they might have achieved much more towards the welfare of the Inuit than they could separately. Late in the afternoon the Anglican bell announced a second service at the little church, which was again crowded with all ages. The small children were playing, crying, laughing, and running from pew to pew throughout without distracting the attention of the worshippers, or lessening the dignity of the service.

That night I had another reason to be grateful to Jack and Maurice. With a combined effort they managed to pull out the tooth that had given me so much trouble over the past year. Maurice, who had learned a number of useful skills in preparation for coming north, also filled one of my teeth, with more lasting success than I had enjoyed before.

I had intended to start the next stage of my travels by leaving from the HBC at nine o'clock the following morning, 3 May, but it was half-past ten before I was ready, and Arnaviapik and Arnatsiaq arrived soon after. John Stanners was still asleep, as was Paddy Doyle. Both had said they planned to see me off, but they knew better than I the earliest time of day that a journey would start in the long days of spring.

By half-past twelve the komatiks were loaded, we had had another cup of coffee, and everybody in the settlement was present. After shaking hands with all, down to the smallest babies in their mother's hoods, who early learned to stretch out a tiny hand, we set off for Arctic Bay.

15

Pond Inlet overland to Arctic Bay
3 May – 13 May 1937

We had two teams, one of eighteen dogs and the other of twenty-one. They seemed rather small and young, but we more than made up in numbers what we forfeited in weight. There were certainly many more dogs than we needed, though several had probably been included just to give them experience. The loads were light because we were carrying only our camping equipment, food for a few days for ourselves, and two seals for dog-food. At this time of the year it was safe to rely on hunting if we should run short of food. As we harnessed the dogs, we could see several seals lying on the ice in Eclipse Sound, asleep in the sun.

Before we left, a number of Inuit gave us letters in syllabics to deliver to people living near Arctic Bay. Syllabic writing had been developed by the Reverend James Evans, a missionary, for the Cree language. Adapted to Eskimo last century by John Horden and E.A. Watkins of the Church Missionary Society it had spread throughout the Eastern Arctic. While quick and easy to learn, it was not precise because different words could be expressed by the same symbols. The meaning was usually, but not always, clear from the context. Though none of the Baffin Island Inuit had ever been to any school, most of them were literate in syllabics and used them to keep in touch with their relatives and friends, as well as for reading the Bible and prayer books. Anyone travelling in the right direction became a convenient postman.

The day was warm, softening the snow on the sea ice, and we moved rather slowly despite our thirty-nine dog-power. When we had covered about twenty-five miles we camped on the sea ice, pitching a tent for the first time that year. This was much quicker than finding good snow and building a snow house. It was becoming obvious that my companions were experienced and efficient, as well as friendly and forthcoming.

We were up at half-past seven but were in no hurry. The day was beautiful at first and the snow was again soft and slow. Shortly after noon however the wind rose, and in a few minutes it was blowing exceptionally hard from the west. The soft snow began to drift almost at once, making visibility very bad and forcing us to camp after only a few miles. As the tent would not have stood up in such a storm we had to build a snow house, and it was much nicer to crawl into its quiet calm than to endure the wild flapping of a tent.

The wind had died down by morning, but soon after we started it was blowing almost as fiercely as the day before. The storm had improved the going by packing the soft snow into hard drifts, and we made good progress. After we reached the channel between Ragged Island and the mainland we found some shelter, and had a mug-up. This was near the site of a camp where Arnaviapik had spent much of the winter, and he knew the route well. When we continued we could occasionally make out through the drifting snow the sheer black cliffs of Ragged Island which we tried to follow in order to find the very narrow gap at the west end of the channel. This led us into one cul-de-sac, but it did not delay us seriously.

On reaching the gap we saw two komatiks approaching us from the west. I soon recognized the people Reynold and I had stayed with at Angmaarjuaq, now on their way to trade at Pond Inlet. While stopping for a mug-up together, they gave us some caribou meat, and we provided them with cigarettes, tea, and tobacco. We were told that Qanattiaq from Akudneq was ahead of them and must have missed us the day before, probably when it was drifting so strongly. They added that his load had included two boxes he was carrying for Reynold. This puzzled me at first because Reynold and I had had little left of what we had brought from Repulse. I concluded that one box was probably our radio, which had stopped working when we were on our way to Piling, and the other our theodolite, which was of very limited value without radio time signals for longitude determinations. Reynold must have decided to send them to Pond Inlet to be shipped south on the *Nascopie* next summer.

We camped that night in an igloo Qanattiaq had built. It was an architectural masterpiece, with large blocks almost identical in shape spiralling smoothly to the key-block at the top. There was now no darkness and the daylight, filtering through the walls, outlined where the blocks joined. To lie in a warm sleeping bag admiring so perfect a structure rising above one was an aesthetic delight.

Qanattiaq's igloo was comfortable as well as beautiful; it had not iced up, probably because he had spent only a few hours in it. A seal-oil lamp usually warms the air in a snow house well above freezing point and the snow of the blocks that form the walls and ceiling starts to melt. In a new house the soft snow soaks up any water like blotting paper, but when the house is deserted the air inside quickly falls to sub-zero temperatures, making the damp walls icy. Next time the house is warmed, the ceiling soon begins to drip. Dripping can be stopped on a temporary basis by putting a handful of soft snow on each of the points where the drips originate. This absorbs the water. The snow has to be replaced frequently, and the penalty for forgetting is the sudden fall of a very wet snowball, probably on the bed. For this reason Inuit would frequently build a new snow house rather than re-use one that had been lived in for a few nights and then abandoned.

Dripping was really an indication of an affluent society. Reynold and I had never been troubled by it when we were travelling on our own. The igloo had never been warm enough for the walls to begin to melt if it were a new house that I had built, or for the walls to start to drip if we were using an old igloo with walls that had become icy. In snow houses that were to be lived in for some time the Inuit usually arranged a lining of skins or canvas, often covered with illustrations from old papers. A lining both made the house warmer and kept it drier.

The following day was sunny and warm. The two Inuit hunted seal, while I read. They returned in mid-afternoon. The snow in Milne Inlet had been rather too soft for good hunting, but Arnatsiaq had gone up Eskimo Inlet, where his family had spent the winter, and had killed a seal there. Neither had taken snow-glasses and their eyes were beginning to trouble them. I had some pieces of stiff cardboard and we were able to improvise a rough substitute by cutting the cardboard to the correct size and shape, and making a narrow horizontal slit in front of each eye. By next morning Arnatsiaq was badly snow-blind, and we were further delayed because the dogs had eaten many of the sealskin lashings on the komatiks while we slept, and they had to be replaced.

It was afternoon before we left Qanattiaq's old igloo and we soon stopped to hunt a seal, which Arnatsiaq shot despite his sore eyes. We started again but had not gone far when we saw two more komatiks in the distance. They proved to be the people from Siurak, with whom Reynold and I had stayed the first day after leaving Igloolik. Meeting people one knew gave an extra pleasure to travelling, and because Inuit live by the sea and we had travelled so much along the coast, I had already met almost everyone from the Igloolik area. We had a mug-up and a smoke with them and then continued, passing several abandoned snow houses before we camped, very late and in a rising wind, at the head of Kudluktuq, the bay where several Inuit families had spent the winter.

The wind had fallen by the morning and before leaving I looked at the recently deserted igloos. Most were snow houses but one appeared to be an old stone, turf, and bone Thule house that had been renovated for modern use. This seemed to indicate more continuity between the Thule people and the Inuit of today than suggested by Mathiassen's theory. He believed them to have been two distinct peoples, the culture of one having completely replaced that of the other. I began to doubt whether this was correct.

We were now starting to cross the land between Milne Inlet and the head of Adams Sound, a fiord running into Admiralty Inlet. Our main problem would be finding the head of a valley that would lead us down a passable route to the end of the sound. To guide us we had a rough sketch of the land drawn by an old man at Pond Inlet.

As Arnatsiaq's snow-blindness was worse, I drove his team all day. Twenty-one dogs was a bigger team than I had been used to handling, and there was little weight on the komatik. At times I felt as if I were following a pack of wolves, but most of the time I was too busy to feel anything. Fortunately it was not a difficult route; we were climbing steadily up a valley with few steep inclines and not many rocks to snag the traces.

When the snow melts in the sun and refreezes later in the day it can form points as sharp as needles, which may cut the dogs' paws. The first sign of this is a stain of blood in the tracks left by the dogs. The cuts can be prevented by dog-boots, which are pieces of sealskin with holes cut for the claws, that have to be tied round each foot. We watched their tracks anxiously. The prospect of putting on 156 dog-boots every morning, many of which we would have to make from two old sealskins we were carrying, was daunting. They would have to be taken off again every night or they would quickly be eaten. We were lucky – only once did a dog cut its foot.

Next day the going was better; we seemed to be climbing very gradually across what was almost a plateau, with no steep slopes and with good snow. Arnatsiaq's eyes were improving, the weather was fine, the wind was light, we could camp quickly in our tent without having to build an igloo, we had ample food, my companions were light-hearted, and they seemed to be enjoying the journey as much as I was.

The third day of the land-crossing was not so easy. The wind became quite strong during the morning and I believe we digressed from the best route. Several steep climbs led us to what must have been the watershed and was probably between fifteeen hundred and two thousand feet high. We then descended a very steep snow slope into a narrow valley. Red cliffs towered above us on both sides as, descending rapidly, we made our way through deep soft snow while trying to avoid patches of bare stones. We were following the bed of what in a few weeks would become a torrent fed by snow melting on the uplands we had left. Around midnight we camped, hungry and tired out, but confident we were in the right valley.

We did not continue our journey until very late the next day. The valley soon became wider and less steep, and after an easy and fast downhill run of two and a half hours, we reached the sea ice at the head of Adams Sound. Here we stopped for a meal, to rest the dogs, and to ice the runners, before leaving at about seven o'clock at night.

The snow was hard on the sea ice and the dogs galloped for most of the next thirty miles. Early in the morning we rounded Holy Cross Point, which almost cuts Arctic Bay off from Adams Sound, and saw the red and white buildings of the Hudson's Bay Company on the far side. Behind them the ground rose to nearly two thousand feet at the summit of King George v Mountain,

silhouetted against the morning sky and dominating the pictur-
esque bay. The dogs sensed we were approaching the post and
raced along; it seemed only a few minutes before we were there.
Nobody was moving so early in the day. I walked into what was
obviously the dwelling, opened the first door I saw, and found
Reynold asleep in bed.

16

Spring at Arctic Bay
13 May – 15 June 1937

My arrival had disturbed the other occupants of the house and I soon met them all. Alan Scott, the post manager, was from Peterhead, a small town on the east coast of Scotland north of Aberdeen that had been the home port of many of the whalers in the British whaling fleet. Alex Stevenson, his clerk, had spent a year at Pond Inlet before moving to help open the Arctic Bay post. During the depression years, the HBC had been under pressure to find their staff in Canada rather than continue the tradition begun more than two centuries earlier of recruiting largely in Scotland. Alex, a Montrealer, had been one of the first to join under this new policy. It had given him an occupation he enjoyed and interests that absorbed him throughout his life. The interpreter, Ernie Lyall, had been born in Labrador and was the third generation of his family to work for the HBC. Like Henry Voisey at Repulse Bay he was happiest when outdoors, preferably hunting with the Inuit.

Reynold said Mino and he had had a good trip from the camp in Kangirllukjuak to Igloolik and Akudneq, where they had been acclaimed as "Pilingmiut" – men of Piling. Mino found he had achieved minor celebrity status. This was not, I am sure, for having got to Piling, but for having got Reynold and me there. It was certainly an unusual but not unwelcome role for him to play. They had then sledged to Arctic Bay, arriving a few days before me. Reynold had been lent three strong dogs at Igloolik and had made a much quicker journey than expected. He had intended to start back to Igloolik with Mino that day, and had written me a letter outlining his plans.

He did not think there would be time for us to do anything at Agu before the birds arrived near Igloolik where he would spend the summer. As soon as travel was possible next winter, he might sledge from Igloolik to Repulse Bay and then Churchill, but he could see little purpose in planning far ahead when there were so many uncertainties.

When Ernie Lyall said he knew of several old stone houses in and around Arctic Bay, I decided I would study the relationship between the Thule and the Dorset cultures at these local sites because no archaeologist had worked here. Reynold would need all the supplies our dog team could haul to Igloolik for his stay there throughout the summer and winter. I could sail south in the *Nascopie*, joining her at Arctic Bay at the end of the summer.

Reynold told me he had already made a preliminary map of the Foxe Basin coast from our observations on the way to Piling and back. It showed the coast ran southeast, not east, from Kangirllukjuak to Piling and continued southeast, not south, from there. This change made the area of Baffin Island about two thousand square miles greater than it appeared on most maps then in use.

Mino was as cheerful and easygoing as ever. He was still wearing the old, tattered caribou-skin clothing he had had when we first met. Though even old caribou-skin clothing was far superior in the winter to anything then imported from the south, it was much less satisfactory in the summer. Caribou skin is difficult to dry and loses its hair very quickly when wet, and sealskin is stiff and uncomfortable to wear next to the skin. It was a real pleasure to go to the store with Mino and buy him new woollen clothing for the summer, something I am sure he had not had for a very long time.

Reynold and Mino did not leave until the evening in order to take advantage of the harder snow. They had a heavy load but the first 150 miles would be south along the sea ice of Admiralty Inlet. Knowing Reynold, I was sure that their load would be much lighter by the time they began the easy land-crossing at the end of the inlet. He combined an ability to live on the most unattractive and unappetizing food with a complete inability to resist the temptation of eating the nicest food first. Any luxuries intended for the summer would be gone in the first two weeks, or earlier if he stopped at many Inuit camps on the way, where he would be sure to follow our normal practice of sharing all our food with our hosts. Alone in the summer he would throw the carcass of every bird he skinned, from snow buntings to sea gulls, into the frying pan, to cook whenever he felt hungry.

I would miss Reynold. There is no better way to get to know a man than to travel with him, night and day, for weeks on end, meeting the same problems, surprises, successes, and disappointments. The longer I was with Reynold, the more I enjoyed his company, and the more I grew to like him. We had discussed almost everything and had few secrets left. He was completely natural, uninhibited by any convention or affectation, and often impulsive. Of course we did not always agree. I am sure I had habits that must have irritated him, and I did not appreciate the way he always packed the arsenical soap, used for preserving skins, in our food-box, usually in the tin we kept for butter or other luxuries. This was his way of making sure it would be safe. What we found we shared completely was an admiration for the Inuit and their attitude to life. I would miss Reynold's company, but I knew we would not have seen much of one another in the summer even if we had been in the same area. We would both have been so busy, he catching and skinning birds, and I digging houses, probably several miles away.

Arctic Bay has a shorter history of contact than Pond Inlet. In 1872 Captain Adams of the British whaling ship *Arctic* had entered Adams Sound and found the well-protected bay that was named after his ship. It does not seem to have been used by later whalers, but the Canadian government expeditionary ship, CGS *Arctic*, which bore the same name and had wintered in 1906-07 at Albert Harbour, was based at Arctic Bay for the winter of 1910-11. The ship's complement of thirty-six men included a small scientific staff and had made several exploratory journeys from there. A number of Inuit were then living in the bay, and they and the expedition were able to help one another in many ways.

In 1926 the HBC opened a trading post at Arctic Bay under the name Tukik, meaning the moon, but it was closed the next year because the government was enforcing a policy of excluding new trading posts from the area that had been designated as the Arctic Islands Preserve. Tukik was not reopened until the summer of 1936. Two years earlier the company had taken a group of Inuit, mainly from Cape Dorset, to establish a post at Dundas Harbour on Devon Island. It had not proved a success and they had then brought the Inuit to Arctic Bay. Prominent among them was Kavavau, who was employed by the company, and his oldest son Takulik. Most of the local Inuit lived in small camps elsewhere in Admiralty Inlet, and the post hoped to attract some of the Igloolik trade as well. Arctic Bay was no nearer to Igloolik than were Pond Inlet and Repulse Bay, but the journey was easier and quicker.

After two days Arnaviapik and Arnatsiaq left on their return journey to Pond Inlet. As the land was still covered with snow and the ground frozen there could be no possibility of excavating for at least a month. I would have liked to cross Admiralty Inlet and Brodeur Peninsula to visit Port Bowen in Prince Regent Inlet, where Parry had spent the winter of 1824-25, but it was getting late for overland komatik journeys. It was also a very good time of year to hunt seal, and it would not have been easy to persuade any Inuit to stop hunting and come with me. In any case the area had been mapped by the officers of the CGS *Arctic* far better than I could have done. I remained at the post most of the time, helping with the chores, hunting ptarmigan and hares now and again, talking to Alan, Alex, and Ernie, sometimes playing cards with them, and reading their books. We had one unexpected visitor when a wheatear flew into the house. It was an uncommon bird there and 20 May was early in the year for a migrant.

Towards the end of May I went with Kavavau and Ernie Lyall to hunt seal and to retrieve a boat that had been left on the far side of Admiralty Inlet the previous fall. This would give me an opportunity to see some of the old houses that Ernie knew. We crossed overland to Victor Bay and then sledged north for several miles along the east coast of the inlet before starting to cross it. There were plenty of seals up on the ice. Along one crack there must have been nearly fifty.

High vertical cliffs line both sides of Admiralty Inlet. We sledged close to those on the east side, which were spectacular. Rising over a thousand feet straight from the sea, they were composed of thick horizontal bands of sandstone and limestone. Each band had its own colour which was enhanced by the bright sun shining in a deep blue sky. The cliffs seemed like a giant curtain of Madras cotton woven with stripes of yellow, green, brown, red, and mauve.

"RINGED SEAL ON SPRING ICE" BCarter

We were nearly half-way across the inlet when we met a party of Inuit. They had already found the boat and had brought it with them, so we transferred it to our komatik before returning along our old tracks. We camped together on the sea ice not far from where Strathcona Sound leads into Admiralty Inlet.

Next morning we went into Strathcona Sound to camp by some of the old houses Ernie had mentioned. The two nights we spent there allowed me to look around the site at my leisure, while Kavavau and Ernie hunted seals. There were nearly twenty houses clustered in a slightly sheltered stretch of coast on the north side of the sound, very close to its entrance. They seemed typical of stone, bone, and turf houses found throughout the Eastern Arctic.

I had been back only a day from this trip when I went away again, this time to go fishing with Kavavau, his wife, his oldest daughter Nipisa, a pretty girl who later became Ernie's wife, and two sons, Napatsi in his early teens, and Takto who was about four. We headed south along Admiralty Inlet, and a long day brought us to Iqalulik, a favourite fishing place, where a river runs into the sea. After supper, Kavavau, Napatsi, and I followed the river inland for about a mile and a half to a lake and tried fishing for an hour without success. We did however see some geese and my first flower of the year – a purple saxifrage. Back at the camp we found the women had arranged the tents and we could turn in after a last cup of tea.

I was surprised next morning to see Napatsi take soap and a towel and go to the river to wash before breakfast. With a very

slight sense of shame I thought of Reynold and me, and how
Napatsi had adopted a good habit that we had so quickly
abandoned.

After breakfast all the family walked to the lake to fish, while
I went to look at some old houses, just south of the mouth of
the river. Five or six lay in a line about forty yards from the shore,
with a single house just behind them. Another forty yards farther
back from the sea and to the north was a solitary house which
appeared much older. They all seemed to be Thule and in one
there was a piece of whalebone sled-shoeing with a drilled hole.
A cairn stood on the cliff above. There was nothing in the cairn
but on replacing a stone I saw scratched on it ⊲σ 14, which
I was disappointed to find only meant June 14.

"KAKIVAK" B Cat

I walked up to the lake to rejoin the family and started fishing
with a *kakivak*, which is a kind of leister with a spike in the centre
to spear the fish, flanked by two larger flexible pieces of antler
with barbs inside to hold it. I spent the rest of the day watching
for an unsuspecting char in the clear water, with a kakivak ready
in my right hand while jigging a lure of a small ivory fish suspended by a line of plaited sinew with my left hand. On the few
occasions I saw one I missed, defeated by the speed of the fish
or the parallax which made it appear to be in a different place.
Towards evening we heard dogs, and on returning to the camp
found we had been joined by a party of Inuit including Ivalak,
a well-known hunter who was the leader of a camp nearer the
head of Admiralty Inlet.

The new arrivals spent only one night with us, since they were
on their way to trade at Arctic Bay, except one man who remained
to fish. Kavavau speared six more char to add to the eleven he
had caught the day before and also shot a goose. None of the
rest of us got a thing.

I was sorry we had to return to Arctic Bay next day after such a very enjoyable trip, and before I had acquired much skill in this kind of fishing. We stopped to see Ivalak camped not far from the post and he and Kavavau exchanged komatiks for some reason. Ivalak would have been a splendid man to travel with and had a very good dog team but the well-being of his whole camp probably depended on his ability and leadership.

During the next week I arranged with Takulik that he and his wife and family would come with me to excavate at the two sites I knew were in Strathcona Sound. They had two small boys, aged perhaps eight and five, and a four-week-old baby. While they were getting ready I walked to Uluksan, a point at the western entrance to Arctic Bay, where Inuit often camped and where there were several old houses. The site had been occupied recently and was very disturbed. I decided any work there could be left until the end of the summer since I would have to be near the post for the arrival of the *Nascopie*. We were all prepared to leave when the weather turned too cold for the children to enjoy the journey. As there was still a lot of snow on the land, we waited at the post for a warmer spell.

17

Excavating in Admiralty Inlet

15 June – 31 August 1937

We set off by komatik on 15 June for Strathcona Sound, Kavavau and Napatsi coming with us to help with the load and to hunt on the way. After crossing the sound we camped at Avartoq, the name of the site I had visited at the entrance to Admiralty Inlet. Deep snow still covered the old houses so in the morning we followed the north shore of Strathcona Sound a few miles east to a second group of houses.

Kavavau and Napatsi left early next day. Takulik and I shovelled snow and ice out of the houses, with diminishing enthusiasm when fresh snow began to fall in a rising wind.

The snow and frozen ground made digging slow and dull, and after a day or two we were pleased to welcome our first weekend visitors. Ernie, Napatsi, Alex Stevenson, and one of Kavavau's daughters arrived late on the Friday night. Hunting occupied the next morning, and Alex then helped me excavate for an hour or two. It turned into a warm and sunny afternoon, too early in the year for mosquitoes. A stream near the camp had started to run and Alex and I decided to have a quick bathe. It was a very quick bathe.

Our visitors left early on Sunday morning and the following week we worked on the site and sometimes hunted, the hunting proving more rewarding than the digging. Many flowers were coming into bloom and we saw our first butterfly. At the end of the week Kavavau returned bringing his daughter Nipisa, Alan Scott, and Ujaraaluk, a young man originally from Pangnirtung, who said he would stay and help us dig when they left two days later.

The weather was warm enough for me to bathe two or three more times, but the site was proving disappointing. Rather than a winter settlement, it appeared to be where people had camped for a few weeks in the fall before there was enough snow to build igloos, and where they had raised circles of stones and turf with some sort of roof of skins probably around their tents. I was coming to the conclusion that there was little to learn there, especially when I excavated a rusty umbrella frame in what had seemed the oldest and most promising part of the site – where I had hoped to find evidence of the Dorset culture. Nor could it have been interesting to Takulik and Ujaraaluk to be digging up artifacts so similar to what they themselves might have thrown away. I decided we would move to Avartoq, the first site we had looked at in Strathcona Sound, which should now be nearly free of snow.

The sea ice was still solid, so on 2 July I asked Takulik to move our camp while I walked to Tukik, as the post at Arctic Bay was still usually called. The weather was poor but it was an easy day's walk, and there is always so much to see in the north when the

"COLLARED LEMMING" BCarter

earth wakes from the long winter sleep – the flowers, birds trying to lead one away from their nests, lemmings running to hide under the rocks, the views with no trees to get in the way, and of course the constant search for signs of people who had lived there in the past.

When I reached Tukik I was told about a completely unexpected event. Two white men had arrived from the south by komatik to prospect in the area and were camped by the shore a few hundred yards away. They were Jack Tibbitt, a young geologist, and Finley McInnes, who had retired as a corporal from the RCMP. I went to see them in their tent and heard the story of their amazing journey.

A syndicate in Toronto had noticed the mineral occurrences, especially of platinum, described in the report of the activities of the CGS *Arctic* in the winter of 1910–11, and had asked Jack Tibbitt to look at them and to stake any he thought worthwhile. He had had little experience in the north and Finley McInnes, who had served for many years in the Eastern Arctic and had a well-deserved reputation as an excellent traveller, was engaged to accompany him. The season for geology in the north, as for archaeology, is the late spring and summer when most of the land is free of snow. This meant they had to start the long journey to Arctic Bay from railhead at Churchill during the winter.

They had left Churchill with two Inuit and nine dogs on 15 March. Conditions were difficult and they had to walk by the side of the komatik all the way to the HBC post at Chesterfield. Here they were delayed because of some misunderstanding about their letter of credit. By the time this had been sorted out, spring had reached Chesterfield and again they had to walk most of the way from there to Repulse where they arrived on 12 May in time to listen on the radio to the coronation of King George VI. Here they had been lucky because our old companion Kutjek had come to trade later than the other Iglulingmiut, and they were able to go with him, again walking rather than riding, on his way back to Igloolik, where Kutjek said he would continue to help them on their journey.

There was little snow where they walked across Baffin Island and Jack had been able to stake two or three claims there. On reaching the head of Admiralty Inlet, they found the sea ice to be still sound, and from there to Arctic Bay they enjoyed their first good ride since Churchill. Up to that time they must have walked over a thousand miles often through soft wet snow. I had missed Kutjek, who had had to return immediately to Igloolik to get home before the ice broke up in Fury and Hecla Strait.

They had seen Joe Ford at Repulse Bay, but both Pat and Peter had been away when they passed through. They had left a letter from Tom with Reynold, whom they had met near Igloolik, and they gave me a note from him. Reynold's note enclosed a letter Peter had sent to both of us, which had been brought to Igloolik by some Inuit who had been to Repulse to trade. Peter and Tom had both travelled to the post at Wager Bay in January. Peter had broken his komatik so he had remained at Wager to map the inlet, while Tom had gone on to Chesterfield and back to make astronomical fixes along the coast. Peter had then returned to Repulse direct and Tom had set out towards Back River which he had not been able to reach because of lack of dog-food.

Reynold's letter also said that some Inuit who had been trading at Repulse had brought mail from England for both of us, but he had not had mine with him when he saw Mac and Jack, and it would have taken him more time to get it than they could spare. I was surprised how little I minded. It was from a different world, I was happy in the world I was in, and one world at a time seemed enough.

Mac and Jack belonged to my new world. Mac had served at many posts in the Eastern Arctic, including five years at Pond Inlet, and everyone liked and respected him. There he had invented a harpoon gun that could be set above a seal's breathing hole in such a way that it would be triggered by the seal when it came up to breathe. This fired a harpoon to kill and secure the animal. Several of these devices, made by modifying old guns, were in use in Baffin Island. His ingenuity had increased the productivity of hunting, while releasing many Inuit from the icy vigil of waiting motionless over a breathing hole for hour after hour.

I was at first a source of some concern to Jack. He had heard I was doing something with a spade in Strathcona Sound. This was where the CGS *Arctic* had reported the most promising indications of minerals, and he must have suspected that I too was a prospector and had gone there to stake claims ahead of him. He was relieved to find that I knew as little about prospecting as he did about archaeology.

I had intended to spend only a night or two at the post but it started to rain too heavily for me to enjoy the walk to my new camp. While I was waiting for the weather to improve, a hunter came to the post with a narwhal he had killed. Kavavau, Napatsi, and Ernie decided they would go whaling next day. As a result

I could ride with them because my camp at Avartoq would be
on their way.

We reached Avartoq in the afternoon. Takulik, his family, and
Ujaraaluk had pitched our tents close to the site. Several other
Inuit families were camped nearby. Next day was too wet to dig
but we made a start the following morning. That evening the
whale hunters returned from farther along the inlet, happy but
very tired after killing, cutting up, and caching four narwhal, and
they spent the night with us. The sea ice at Avartoq was still
firm, though it looked as if it might soon break up.

Next morning we awoke to cries of "Killelluat" and we heard
a hissing noise. Rushing out of the tent we witnessed a most
unusual sight. Ice still covered Admiralty Inlet to the horizon but
there were a number of long leads a yard or two wide where
Strathcona Sound ran into the inlet. Along these leads more than
two hundred poles appeared to be sticking vertically into the air.

"NARWHAL" BCarter

They were narwhal tusks. The animals must have been scared
by killer whales which had driven them under the ice. Killer
whales have a large dorsal fin which prevents them from following
their prey in the ice. The narwhal were safe from the killers but
needed air to survive. They had had to swim many miles to find
these leads and were exhausted. With little room in the narrow
leads the only way they could reach the air they needed desperately
was to raise their heads in the water, balancing the heavy weight
of their long ivory tusks by keeping them vertical. This display

lasted only a few minutes while the narwhal were restoring the oxygen level in their blood.

Whenever I described this episode in the south I was greeted with so much scepticism that I found I was beginning with, "You won't believe this but . . ." My self-assurance was restored the day that a Greenlander replied that he too had once seen narwhal behaving in just this way.

Next day the ice had almost disappeared, and the narwhal had presumably moved farther up Admiralty Inlet. Seals were seen close by the shore and later in the day I understood why. I was walking on rocks by the sea where the water was deep when a killer whale charged by very close to the rocks. It reminded me of standing on the platform of a small railway station when an express train sped through. All other sea mammals are terrified when killer whales are in the vicinity, and seals will even come ashore to avoid them.

"KILLER WHALES" B Carter

The next day Aiula, Takulik's eldest son, was in bed with a sore leg. He was a quiet boy, who had always been cheerful, active, and healthy, and it must have been hurting badly to keep him in the tent. He felt worse in the morning and his leg and much of his body were covered with painful blisters. As we had no boat Ujaraaluk walked to the next camp with a note for them to take to Tukik asking for ointment.

We continued to dig, usually at night to avoid mosquitoes and slept during the day. The site had been disturbed and little of interest was turning up. My memories of the next few days are of worry about Aiula, of reading Shakespeare from the complete edition I had found at the post, and of eating a lot of *muktuk*.

The flesh of the narwhal and the white whale is not much liked and is usually kept for the dogs, but the skin, called muktuk, is very popular, that of the narwhal having a rather nicer flavour. Some say it tastes slightly of walnut. It is eaten either raw or boiled for a long time. Either way it is chewed until one is tired of chewing and then swallowed.

In three days a boat brought ointment for Aiula. This seemed to give him some relief. The bad patches of blisters were dressed about three times a day and were much better by the third day. We thought that he would now recover quickly, but next day he had a pain in his stomach. The day after it was very much worse. Ujaraaluk and I set off to walk to a camp some distance up Strathcona Sound where there was a boat. From here we were taken across the sound. The boat waited for us while we walked many more miles across to Tukik, where we roused Ernie. He brought a medical kit and we all walked back to the boat.

A long time had passed since our last meal. Some birds were flying near the boat and Ujaraaluk threw a stone at them, killing one which he skinned and we all ate. Seeing, killing, preparing, and eating our meal took only two minutes.

We sailed straight back to Avartoq, where we found Aiula weaker. Ernie thought he might have a blocked bowel and we tried an enema, repeating it as it was not successful. I went to my tent to sleep and it seemed only a short time when Ernie came to tell me that Aiula had died.

I have no idea what caused his death. Everybody else was and remained in good health, so it could not have been infectious. We had all been eating the same food. Eleven days had passed since his leg had kept him in bed, and only two since he had complained of a pain in his stomach. A coffin was made immediately from any pieces of wood we could find, a simple service was held, and he was buried that day. After a short rest Ernie took Takulik and his family back to Tukik.

Ujaraaluk and I remained behind to clear up the excavation and pack up the camp. Kavavau and Alan Scott came for us on 17 July in the post's motor boat and we left next day for Tukik. We were not sorry to leave.

We did not know when to expect the *Nascopie*. She had an unusually full schedule and would arrive at Arctic Bay as early as possible and sail the moment she could. I decided to stay close to Tukik and camp at Uluksan by the entrance to Arctic Bay where Takulik, Ujaraaluk, and I could excavate the old houses, and from where I could not miss the *Nascopie* entering the bay.

On 5 August we brought our equipment over to Uluksan by boat to set up camp. We could walk from there to Tukik along the shore in less than an hour. On our fourth day at the new camp Ernie arrived in the motor boat, with Mac and Jack who were going to prospect in Strathcona Sound. He picked up Takulik, Ujaraaluk, and me so we could look at some houses near the entrance to Adams Sound, which were on their way. They left us there but returned for the night as they found the water too rough in Admiralty Inlet. They were able to resume their journey in the morning. The houses did not seem interesting or old, and I was pleased that the boat was back the next day to return us to Tukik.

The sea was dead calm as we skirted the high cliffs, where the Inuit said ivory gulls nested. Numbers of fulmars were feeding, gliding slowly only a few inches above the still water. Every twenty yards or so they would strike the glassy sea with the tips of both wings, and resume their glide, concentric ripples spreading from where their wings had touched. They repeated this two or three times before flying up or settling on the water. I assumed they were preventing stalling by raising themselves a little higher to increase their speed.

"NORTHERN FULMAR" B Carter

From Tukik we walked back to Uluksan. We were not alone there because several Inuit families were camped close by. One day I watched a raven flying low over the Inuit camp, heading into the wind. Chasing after it were about twenty dogs. The raven decided to rest and alighted on a large rock, ignoring the dogs dashing towards it. When the leading dog was only about three yards away, the raven turned its head toward them and gave a single baleful squawk. All the dogs stopped dead, turned round, and trotted back to the camp like sheep. The raven rested a few more minutes before taking off again into the wind.

I was coming to the conclusion that Uluksan, a site where people often camped and was therefore very disturbed, would not provide any information on the Dorset culture. I had found only Thule culture in what appeared to be the oldest of the houses and in the lowest layers of the middens. After a few days Ernie and Alex arrived in the motor boat on their way to collect Mac and Jack, and Takulik went with them to hunt.

By now the *Nascopie* was expected daily. The later she was, the more the captain would be in a hurry. The ship could not know that I would be a passenger, so I decided I had to be ready for her and moved all my things to the post. I could still walk over to Uluksan every day to dig and Alex and I could wander over the hills, looking for berries while exchanging our thoughts on how much we liked the north and admired those who lived there. Once or twice we swam in the icy sea. The nights were rapidly getting longer and darker, and summer was nearly over. At noon on 30 August the *Nascopie* steamed into the bay.

18

South on the Nascopie

31 August – November 1937

Leaving Arctic Bay was made easy because so many of my friends there were embarking on the *Nascopie* with me. They included Kavavau, Takulik, their families, Alex, Ernie, and Mac and Jack. This exodus was largely because the *Nascopie*'s next task was to establish a post near Bellot Strait, which bounds the most northern part of continental America. Kavavau, Takulik, and Ernie were moving to this new post, which would be called Fort Ross.

The HBC's plan was for their schooner *Aklavik* to come from the Western Arctic to meet the *Nascopie* in Bellot Strait. Here the *Nascopie* would transfer some supplies to the *Aklavik* and take aboard the *Aklavik*'s fur. This exchange would constitute the first commercial use of the Northwest Passage. It would be on a very small scale to demonstrate feasibility, but in future years it was thought such transactions might be increased as a way of supplying the eastern part of the Western Arctic. Freight could probably be delivered there through Fort Ross at a much lower cost than by rail through Edmonton to Waterways in northern Alberta, barge along the Mackenzie River route, and then small coaster or schooner from Tuktoyaktuk.

The *Nascopie* had been built as a sealer before the First World War, her hull was well strengthened, and she was about 2000 gross registered tons. Her holds carried the annual supplies for all the posts on her itinerary, and her cabins had to accommodate almost everyone coming to or going from the Eastern Arctic where most places saw no other ship. There were three main groups on board: employees of the HBC on their way to, from, or between posts as decided by the district manager, who was on board; RCMP who were being moved, and their superintendent who inspected each detachment; and the government's Eastern Arctic Patrol, coordinated by Major D.L. McKeand, the secretary of the Northwest Territories Council. The Eastern Arctic Patrol represented the government's presence in the Arctic and consisted mainly of scientists gathering what limited information they could during short visits to so many places. Most of the other passengers were adventurous and well-to-do tourists enjoying an unusual cruise, but there were also a few missionaries and individuals like me who did not fit into these categories.

We sailed at first light on 31 August. The weather was clear, and when we reached Lancaster Sound we could see across it to the snow-capped mountains of Devon Island. There was a little loose ice in Lancaster Sound and as we turned into Prince Regent Inlet in the evening we were faced with a belt of pack ice, but the lookout in the crow's nest was able to guide the ship to an easy route through it. At one point both the water and the ice seemed alive with harp seals. The ice cleared before morning as we ran down the coast of Somerset Island, its steep cliffs outlined by grounded ice along the shore. By early afternoon we had reached the eastern entrance to Bellot Strait and anchored close to Brown Island, a low-lying ridge of limestone. Clouds were hanging over the high hills on both sides of the narrow strait which appeared dark and even menacing. A few pieces of ice were being carried out of it by the current. There was no sign of the *Aklavik*.

A boat was lowered and sent ahead to sound with a handline. She returned in a few hours having found a safe passage to Depot Bay, a small sheltered bay on Somerset Island which was being considered as a possible location for the new post. The captain decided to move the *Nascopie* there at daybreak. He had been fortunate in reaching Bellot Strait so easily, and he was well aware of the danger of ice moving in and imprisoning his ship for the winter.

During the night the lookout reported he had seen a flare to the southwest. Two or three weeks earlier a Russian aircraft flown by S.A. Levanevskiy, the USSR's most experienced arctic pilot, had disappeared during an experimental polar flight from Moscow to Fairbanks, and a search was being mounted for him. A message was sent by the *Nascopie*'s radio, suggesting, rather irresponsibly, that the flare might be a signal from the missing Russians. This was picked up in Europe, reported quite widely in the press, and caused some excitement. No trace of Levanevskiy was ever found.

In the morning the *Nascopie* proceeded cautiously into Depot Bay where she dropped anchor shortly before noon. Within fifteen minutes we were joined by the *Aklavik* which anchored off our starboard bow. Her captain, Scotty Gall, came aboard and said that Lorenzo Learmonth, who was to be in charge of the new post, and D.G. Sturrock, his clerk, were investigating the coast by canoe looking for Inuit camps and a suitable site for the post. Learmonth was held in such well-deserved respect in the company that he was always referred to as Mr Learmonth or L.A., his initials, and a nickname for him was unthinkable. Few knew his Christian name, so out of keeping with his Scottish background and bearing.

In the afternoon a site was selected for the post buildings and unloading began. It was nearly midnight when Learmonth arrived in a canoe. He said he had been responsible for the light seen from the *Nascopie* the previous night. He had lit a gasoline flare, hoping to attract the *Nascopie* to where he had found an excellent site for the post on the other side of the strait. It was now however too late to consider a change.

Everyone helped the carpenters in erecting the post. Most of the company men on board were experienced in this sort of construction and could tell the rest of us what to do. The eighteen Inuit who had come with us were camped with their thirty-seven dogs on the shore and were suffering from the annual ship's cold, which had immobilized our party on Coats Island a year earlier. The symbolic exchange of cargo was made and recorded by every camera on the ship and, with due ceremony and a speech or two, a wreath was thrown into the sea in memory of Sir John Franklin and the crews of the *Erebus* and *Terror*. One of the tourists found a cairn and a record left by Leopold M'Clintock on a Franklin search expedition. One morning I went to see some old houses, which were obviously in the Thule tradition. The two or three foxes I saw paid little attention to me. Foxes could often be seen and photographed eating a dead seal on the beach.

On 6 September Learmonth fell from the ratlines of the *Aklavik* onto her deck and hurt his back. He was in considerable pain and the district manager was very worried about leaving him at

Fort Ross, with no possibility of medical assistance for at least a year. A heavy snowfall that morning was a warning that the *Nascopie* would have to sail as soon as possible or risk being frozen in for the winter. Fortunately good progress had been made in building the post. The house was finished, and next day a fire was lit in the stove and the HBC flag raised on the flag pole. The warehouse was almost complete, and its roof was being shingled. Learmonth, who was very keen to stay, said he felt much better and it was decided to leave him at Fort Ross when the *Nascopie* sailed.

The captain had planned to get under way early on 8 September but that morning we could not even make out the shore owing to heavy drifting snow. By noon conditions were improving a little and visibility had increased enough for two caribou to be seen from the ship. We were able to say goodbye to those remaining at Fort Ross and to receive a final favourable report on Learmonth's progress.

The snow stopped late in the afternoon and we sailed at seven that evening, leaving this most remote of HBC posts, which had been planned to link the Eastern and Western Arctic. In fact Fort Ross did not prove the success that the company had expected. Heavy ice in Prince Regent Inlet prevented supplies from being delivered in both 1942 and 1943 and the staff had to be withdrawn by air in November 1943, following a parachute descent by a USAAF officer to locate a place where their Dakota aircraft could land and take off. Reopened in 1944, the post closed again after the *Nascopie* ran aground and sank at Cape Dorset in 1947. It was replaced by a new post at Spence Bay on Boothia Isthmus, which was supplied entirely from the west, and the Inuit we had brought to Fort Ross in 1937 moved there.

Scotty Gall had joined the *Nascopie*. He was going to Scotland on furlough, and could leave the *Aklavik* in the capable hands of Patsy Klengenberg, who had been his mate. Scotty, Jack Tibbitt, and I shared a cabin at the stern.

One of those in the Eastern Arctic Patrol was Dr Livingstone, whom I had last seen and felt at Chesterfield. I did not tell him about the subsequent history of his filling and my tooth. There were also two physiographers, David Nichols of the Geological Survey of Canada and P.G. Downes, a young American, who had travelled extensively by canoe with Indians and who later wrote an arctic classic, *Sleeping Island*. When we were sailing near enough to the coast they would point out to each other characteristic features of the landscape, and explain to me how they had been formed.

As we left Fort Ross we could see ice to the south but a gentle north wind was keeping it there, and Prince Regent Inlet was open to the north. The stiff head winds that faced us in Lancaster Sound were said to be the strongest the *Nascopie* had met since leaving the St Lawrence. She pitched sharply on our way east, with the wind howling in the rigging. The storm was blowing itself out as we skirted the north and east coasts of Bylot Island to anchor in the sheltered waters of Pond Inlet.

We spent only twenty-four hours at Pond Inlet. I knew everybody there, but I could only greet them and then keep out of the way because they all had so much to do. Two of the busiest were Jack Turner and Maurice Flint. They had told me they considered some of the government restrictions on killing wildlife were unfair to the Inuit, in particular those relating to geese, which the Inuit could kill legally only after the geese had already migrated to the south. They believed such legislation encouraged the Inuit to break the law and that they should not be put in this position. In the spring the two missionaries had therefore taken ten snow goose eggs each, reported this to the RCMP, and insisted on being charged. During the day a court was convened by Major McKeand, who was a magistrate, and their cases were heard. Each was fined ten dollars, but they had made their point.

At Salmon River, a few miles west of the settlement, an outcrop of coal was being mined by the HBC to burn at their posts at Pond Inlet and Clyde River. The *Nascopie's* scows brought bags of government coal from the ship to the shore to be unloaded by the Inuit for the use of the RCMP detachment. The same scows were being loaded by the same Inuit with bags of HBC coal from Salmon River to take from the shore to the ship for the company's use at Clyde River. This must have puzzled the Inuit, who then knew little about how government operated.

From Pond Inlet we sailed to Clyde River. The weather was clear but we had to keep too far out to appreciate fully the spectacular scenery of the east coast of Baffin Island. After a stay of eight hours at this small post we left for Pangnirtung. Again we had to keep well offshore, and we ran into a southeasterly gale, followed by rain and drizzle with such poor visibility that at times we could not proceed owing to the danger of hitting one of the many icebergs we could see when the weather cleared a little. Conditions improved as we turned into Cumberland Sound, the clouds soon parted, and the sun was shining on the mountains when we entered the striking Pangnirtung Fiord to anchor off the settlement on the afternoon of 16 September.

We were nearly three days at Pangnirtung, where the HBC had established a post in 1921 and which had subsequently become the largest settlement on Baffin Island. There was much more cargo to handle here than elsewhere. We were also delayed because the *Nascopie* had picked up at Lake Harbour a patient with a throat tumour to take to the small Pangnirtung hospital where he was operated on by Dr Livingstone.

Pangnirtung was our last call in Baffin Island, leaving only Port Burwell on our northern itinerary. As we crossed Hudson Strait in snow flurries and mist, a flock of tired ptarmigan alighted on the deck. We spent a day at Port Burwell, which had been the most northern Moravian settlement until the brethren withdrew in 1924. Tom cod were plentiful in the harbour; any number could be caught from the ship with a line, and they made us a good dinner that night. While at Burwell I was given a message from the Roman Catholic mission vessel *M.F. Thérèse* that she had succeeded in reaching Igloolik and was now at Wakeham Bay on her way south with Reynold aboard.

After we rounded Cape Chidley the voyage was uneventful. We faced a series of equinoctial gales from the southeast through which the *Nascopie* slowly pitched and rolled her way south. When visibility was good, we could only just see the Labrador coast. Whenever the wind dropped, it was replaced by fog. The weather was no better after we had passed through the Strait of Belle Isle and begun to see other ships. Nobody was sorry to dock in Halifax early on the morning of 28 September.

Most of the passengers going to Montreal and Ottawa caught the afternoon Maritime Express, but I wanted first to settle my account with the Hudson's Bay Company for everything I had bought at Pond Inlet and Arctic Bay as well as on the voyage. I had been able to send a message through the *Nascopie*'s radio to my mother in England asking her to arrange for some money to be cabled to me in Halifax. By some mischance it had been sent to the wrong bank. However I received a letter my mother sent me care of the *Nascopie* in which she had, on an inspired impulse, enclosed a £5 note. This was the first actual cash I had handled since leaving Churchill, and with it I initiated enquiries about the money I had requested and bought a pair of very cheap shoes. I had been able to make myself look unremarkable in other ways, but knee-length sealskin boots are not satisfactory for walking on the hard and slippery streets of a town and seemed out of place in the Lord Nelson Hotel. By the end of the day my money was located and I was able to look the HBC accountant in the eye. Until then he had been keeping a pretty close eye on me.

With my debts paid and a bed that neither pitched nor rolled, I enjoyed a good night's sleep. Next afternoon I caught the 3.15 train to Ottawa, arriving there late on the last day of September.

I went to see Dr Diamond Jenness as soon as I could, taking with me Father Bazin's collection from Abverdjar. Dr Jenness was extremely interested in it. He examined each piece carefully and confirmed that the collection was exclusively Dorset culture. There were about four hundred artifacts. Not one of them was Thule. Most were of types that he had assigned to the Dorset culture. The remainder were new to him but appeared to be of the same age, had no drilled holes, and were without doubt also Dorset. It was becoming clear that Dorset was both a distinct and a well-developed culture.

A few days later Reynold arrived in Ottawa with his wife Gillian, who had come to America to meet him. He told me the *M.F. Thérèse* had brought Father Bazin back to Igloolik together with Father Trébaol, a Breton. There would now be two priests at Igloolik. The *Thérèse* had also left lumber to build a church and house. Mino, better equipped than ever before, had killed nine walrus during the summer and had married a blind woman at Akudneq. He was now well set up with our komatik and dogs, a rifle, a tent, and many other useful things that Reynold had given him. Reynold was pleased with the birds he had collected, and he and Gillian were going to an ornithological meeting in the United States before returning to England.

Reynold then said he was sorry about my winter mail. He had not had it with him when he had met Mac and Jack, because he had cached it near Akudneq. Unfortunately some dogs had broken into the cache and had eaten everything in it. I replied that it was not his fault in any way. It could not be helped and I would probably never know who had written to me. Reynold then suggested that I should ask him questions about my mail. I asked him what he meant and he explained that after he had read his own mail he had read mine of course as he had nothing else to read. He had found it rather more interesting than his own and might be able to remember some of it.

Our dialogue then continued in the following sort of way:

"Was there anything from a man named Rodney?"

"Yes, I think so. Was he in the army?"

"Yes, he was."

"He went to India, and I think he is now engaged to a Canadian girl."

In this way we reconstructed some of my mail. Reynold had a good memory and a splendid imagination and I suspect his accounts were often more entertaining than the originals had been.

About the middle of October Pat Baird also joined us in Ottawa. In the spring he and an Inuk had visited Wales Island in Committee Bay. He had then joined Tom and Peter at the *Polecat* in late May to prepare her for the summer. Both Peter and Pat had to return to England owing to deaths in their families, and they had hoped to reach Cape Dorset before the *Nascopie* called there. The *Polecat* was in the water by the end of June, but ice, packed tight into Frozen Strait, had prevented them from crossing to Southampton Island until 2 August. Owing to the ice, they could make only slow progress along the north coast of Southampton Island, and on 14 August Pat and Peter had had to start to walk to Coral Harbour, leaving Tom to continue on his own. They reached the post to find the *Nascopie* had left three weeks earlier. By early September it was clear that no other ship would call at Coral Harbour that year, so John Ell had taken them in his whaleboat to Chesterfield where they were able to arrange for another boat to come from Churchill to pick them up. They had arrived at Churchill on 6 October and travelled south from there by train. Peter had had to go direct to Montreal and was already on the Atlantic.

I completed all I had to do in Ottawa and booked a steerage passage on the *Empress of Britain* from Quebec City at a cost of twelve pounds. Before I went to bed on my last night in Ottawa

I telephoned from the boarding-house where I was staying for a taxi to take me to the station early the next morning. I asked the driver to make sure I was there in time for the train to Quebec City or I would miss my sailing. I rarely oversleep but I woke next morning to find a strange man shaking me. The taxi driver had remembered my words, discovered which was my room, gone in, and found me still asleep. While I dressed, he packed my bag. Without his initiative and assistance I would have missed the train and the ship.

The passage across the Atlantic was quick and comfortable. The *Empress* reached Southampton in little more than half the time the *Alaunia* had taken on the much shorter voyage from Southampton to Halifax. I enjoyed the company of the two others with whom I shared a cabin. One was a man who had recently retired and was beginning a nostalgic visit to the place where he had been born. The other was a young wrestler hoping to make his way in Europe, who gave me the impression of being too polite and gentle to succeed professionally in that occupation. I was no longer keeping a diary so I do not know the date we docked or when I arrived home, but it must have been in the first half of November.

PART TWO

19

Return to Repulse Bay

6 August – 2 September 1938

I spent most of the next few months at home or in Cambridge, working on the material I had excavated and picking up the threads of my life from nearly two years earlier. When Reynold returned from America I went to stay with him and his wife for a few days at a house they had been lent in Sussex. Together we wrote an article on our travels for the *Times*, and he told me that he was missing Igloolik as much as I was. He was thinking of returning to Piling to continue his ornithological work in Foxe Basin as soon as he could. My only other contact with arctic Canada was seeing Scotty Gall in London. He had met a Scottish girl on his furlough and they were on their honeymoon before beginning the long journey to the Western Arctic.

Television began many years earlier in England than in America. Unfortunately I was out of the range of Alexandra Palace, then the only television station, when Reynold was shown wearing his duffle parka in a simulated igloo and demonstrating how to light a soapstone lamp. I think he used lard in place of blubber and a cotton-wool wick.

I was not finding it easy to settle down to living in England. I realized I had made a wrong choice at Arctic Bay when I decided to spend the summer there looking for evidence of the Dorset culture. I had failed to excavate anything except much more recent material. Had I known the *M.F. Thérèse* was planning to call at Igloolik that summer, I would have returned there with Reynold and Mino to investigate the site on Abverdjar Island where Father Bazin's collection had been found. I still wanted to go back to Igloolik and excavate at Abverdjar, but I doubted that I could afford to spend another year or two before starting to earn a living.

I made up my mind on the spur of the moment and at the last possible minute. I do not know what was the deciding factor though an unexpected grant of £50 from Cambridge University was certainly an encouragement. It may have been simply that I had realized it had become now or never. On a Wednesday early in August I decided I had to go. On Thursday I went to Manchester to book a passage on the *Empress of Britain* and to arrange a letter of credit from my bank. On Friday my mother and I took a train to London. That Saturday I said goodbye to her on Waterloo Station, caught the boat train, and sailed from Southampton.

I had another smooth, quick passage. This time I was travelling tourist class because there was nothing cheaper. It had the advantage that I could use the swimming pool and squash court, which I did every day. We took the northern route, through the Strait of Belle Isle, in fine weather very different from when I had sailed through aboard the *Nascopie* in mist and wind the previous September. We docked at Quebec City before noon on 11 August. Less than a week had passed since I had booked my passage in Manchester.

I chose to go to Winnipeg by the Canadian Pacific Railway since I had already made the journey on the Canadian National route. I could again buy a very cheap colonist-class ticket to Churchill because Quebec City was a port of entry. The train from Quebec to Montreal arrived there several hours before the Transcontinental was due to leave for the west. As the afternoon was fine, warm with a cool breeze, I decided to take one of the long line of open horse-drawn carriages outside Windsor Station for a drive to the top of Mount Royal. Recognizing a girl who had been on the ship and was waiting for the same train, I invited her to join me. The views along the St Lawrence and north to the Laurentian Hills and a pleasant companion made a memorable reintroduction to Canada.

The seats on the colonist car were hard, but the journey to Winnipeg was only two nights and one day. I found that by careful timing I could have leisurely meals in the much more comfortable dining car and watch the lakes and woods of northern Ontario pass by. I did not have to stop in Ottawa as I had cabled my intentions to the Northwest Territories administration and secured its approval, and my permits to excavate and to kill game in the north were still valid.

In Winnipeg I checked in and had a bath at the Empire Hotel and then went to see the HBC Fur Trade Department. I was planning to travel in the company's schooner *Fort Severn* to Repulse Bay, and I learned she would not sail from Churchill until after the next week's train had arrived there. This gave me nearly a week in Winnipeg to decide what supplies I would need and to arrange for them to be shipped on the Churchill train with me. My bank had written to the company guaranteeing my credit up to what I thought would be an adequate sum, and I handed the envelope to the appropriate officer so that he could write a similar letter to the HBC posts in the north. When he opened it he found my bank manager had neglected to sign his letter, but this was straightened out before I left.

It was a Saturday and too late to start shopping, so I telephoned friends who had been kind to me when I was in Winnipeg before. Throughout the week they filled most of my spare time with interesting things to do such as canoeing on the river and seeing Lower Fort Garry. Trans-Canada Airlines had just started to fly across the country and one evening we drove to Stevenson Field to watch the silver Lockheed Electra arrive on its mail flight from the east.

I also telephoned Mr Greenaway, the representative of Cadbury chocolate, whom I had met before. He was very interested in the Arctic and asked me to his house where I described what Reynold and I had done in Foxe Basin. When I told him about my plans he said his company would like to provide fifty pounds of chocolate, which I accepted with alacrity.

I had left England so hurriedly that I had not had time to have my teeth checked. Not wanting to repeat the experience I had had before, I went to see a dentist the Empire Hotel recommended. I told him I was going to the Arctic for a year or more, and asked him to fix anything he thought might give trouble during that time. He put in two small silver fillings and a much larger gold one. When I asked, with some apprehension, what I owed him, he replied, "Would five dollars be too much?" I paid him at once; he then suggested that, as it had been a hot day, we should have a drink at his club. We spent an hour or so there and had supper before I had to go back to the Empire Hotel to pack. Until that day I had never felt entirely happy about visiting dentists, whom I had subconsciously classified as adversaries. This experience

changed my attitude completely, and the fillings he put in lasted
for years. I was free of any dental worries until long after I left
the north.

The next morning I made a final visit to the Hudson's Bay
Company before catching the train to The Pas. Mr Greenaway
very kindly came to see me off and to make sure the chocolate
had been put on the train. We left on time but during the night
there was a long delay at Hudson Bay Junction, making the train
several hours late at The Pas.

The scheduled journey on the Hudson Bay Railway in summer
was much quicker than during the rest of the year. Trains left
The Pas at least once a week, and there was more than one train
crew so the journey was completed in one day instead of three.
In addition the train did not leave The Pas until after the arrival
of the daily train from Winnipeg, avoiding the need to spend a
night there. I had such good memories of The Pas that I would
have been happy to stay longer. As it was I had time only to wash
and shave, to buy a pair of moccasins and some beads, and to
talk with the line superintendent, whom I had known in Churchill,
before the train left in mid-afternoon. Both Tommy Jack and
Newsy were on the train and their stories and meals were as
good as ever. Newsy's cooking was much appreciated by a very
thin boy who was returning from harvesting. While supper was
being prepared, he was talking to me about his work and how
little he had earned to take home. He looked so hungry that I
got even more satisfaction from buying him his supper than I
did from eating my own.

We were held up at Wabowden for part of the evening because
an engine had run off the track between our train and the water
tank. It had to be moved out of the way so that our engine could
take on water. The passengers were able to fill in the time in
much the same way by having a drink or two in the little hotel
that, with the station, seemed to be most of what there was of
Wabowden. Our next delay was during the morning when our
engine burst a pipe that had to be repaired before we could continue. However we were only a few hours late when we arrived
at Churchill during the evening of 21 August.

I checked my luggage as it came off the train. Everything had
arrived safely except the chocolate. When and where it had gone
was, and remains, a mystery. I then walked to the quay to reassure

myself that the *Fort Severn* was there. In the cabin I found Buster Brown, the manager of the HBC Nelson River district, who had so kindly lent us the Revillon Frères house at Repulse. The *Fort Severn* was really part of his district, carrying much of the freight, exchanging personnel, and taking him to inspect his posts. He told me the *Fort Severn* would sail as soon as the weather allowed so I took my things aboard and slept there.

A storm next day prevented our sailing and gave me an opportunity to buy some caribou skins for my winter clothing and to have a meal with Bill Kerr, the RCMP corporal I had met at Chesterfield two years earlier. I knew that Reynold and Pat were also returning to Foxe Basin and had preceded me to Churchill. I now learned they had sailed ten days ago in the *Thérèse* bound for Igloolik, and might already be there. They were intending to continue by whaleboat to Piling, where they planned to establish a camp for the winter. The day before they left, Reynold had received a telegram from his wife telling him he had become the father of a daughter. The *Thérèse* was carrying everything necessary for a HBC post at Igloolik, which would be included in Buster Brown's district.

I also heard that ice conditions in Frozen Strait had remained difficult all the previous summer and Tom had had to winter on Southampton Island. Early in August he had managed to sail the *Polecat* across Foxe Channel to reach Cape Dorset the day before the *Nascopie* had called, bringing his fiancée. They had been married on the ship next day. The best man had been Johnny Buchan, the son of the governor general, who had joined the HBC and was now the clerk at Dorset. Tom and his wife Jackie had left Cape Dorset in the *Polecat* for Foxe Basin a day or two later.

After another night on board I walked to the station to see the train off and to make sure the chocolate had not been found. The *Fort Severn* sailed soon after I returned. The water was rough at first but the sails steadied her markedly as soon as we were out of the river. The *Fort Severn* was a sturdy two-masted schooner of under seventy tons with an auxiliary engine and had originally belonged to Revillon Frères. The skipper, Captain Barbour, was a Newfoundlander while the mate, Eric Carlson, was a well-known Churchill character. Two engineers, an excellent Belgian cook, and two or three Chipewyan and Cree seamen formed an ideal crew. I got to know them well as I slept in the fo'c'sle, and

I never heard anybody complain or appear out of humour. Apart from Buster Brown and the crew, the only others aboard were Geordie Anderson and his wife. They had just married and he was taking over the company's post at Tavani.

We anchored off Tavani, a small and lonely post, the next afternoon and went ashore. Mrs Anderson had her first look at her new home, which was very different from what she had expected. I heard Buster Brown consoling her and promising a new house next year, which must have seemed a very long time ahead. Here I met Jean Gabus, a Swiss anthropologist, who was making ethnological collections. Our discussions about the Inuit were cut short when we discovered that one of us had knocked over a three-pound tin of molasses that had been left open in his tent on a sewn-in tarpaulin floor. I was very sorry not to see Louis Tapatai, who had moved from Repulse Bay to Baker Lake where he was working for the RCMP. He had just been into Tavani and was nearby hunting walrus for dog-food.

After a night on shore we went aboard early in the morning. In place of the Andersons we had four new passengers. Tommy Crawford was being transferred to be post manager at Repulse Bay, and was travelling there with his wife, a sister of Henry Voisey, and Lewis, a small boy they had adopted. The fourth was a very pleasant and amusing Roman Catholic priest. It was rough away from land and we had to seek shelter near the Morso Islands, where we spent two days and played a lot of bridge. The radio told us the *Thérèse* was having difficulty getting through the ice near Cape Penrhyn on her way to Igloolik.

The sea had moderated when we pulled out early on 27 August and we made good time, reaching Chesterfield Inlet that night. Joe Ford and Henry Voisey, both of whom had moved here from Repulse Bay, came aboard and unloading began. I knew that Buster wanted to sail as soon as possible and I might not get a chance to go ashore, so I was not sorry when, at the height of the tide, Joe stranded the scow used for discharging cargo. This gave me a day to spend in the settlement. Joe, who had been on furlough, had brought back a wife, and they asked me to lunch. I was pleased I had heard at Winnipeg about their marriage and had remembered to bring a wedding present for them. Joe told me Henry Voisey was returning to the Repulse post and was getting ready to join us on the *Fort Severn*. I was able to buy a few more caribou skins at the HBC, giving me enough for my winter needs.

In the afternoon I went to the hospital to see Father Cochard, one of the friendly priests I had met at Pond Inlet. About a month earlier he had become seriously ill at Arctic Bay, where his church was planning to build a mission. Fortunately the *Nascopie* had left a radio transmitter there on her way to establish Fort Ross, and Alan Scott had been able to send a message to the bishop at Churchill, saying Father Cochard was suffering severe pain and his temperature had reached 105°F. A church aircraft on floats, piloted by Father Schulte, "The Flying Priest," was at Churchill at the time. Bishop Clabaut, for our old friend Father Clabaut from Repulse Bay had been consecrated assistant bishop of Hudson Bay the previous summer, asked his help. In the first "mercy flight" in the Eastern Arctic, Father Schulte flew to Arctic Bay, picked up Father Cochard, and took him to the hospital at Chesterfield Inlet via Igloolik and Repulse Bay. Father Cochard was making an excellent recovery.

Father Schulte had had to return to Igloolik a few days later to bring another patient to the south. Ukumaaluk, a son of Ituksarjuat, the "King of Igloolik," had been accidentally shot in the thigh. He was also in the Chesterfield hospital making good progress. I told him I was on my way to Igloolik and he would have liked to come to Repulse and Igloolik with me, but the doctor decided it was too early for him to travel.

Though I had missed Tapatai, his ten-year-old son Felix was in Chesterfield. He had spent a lot of time in our house at Repulse and his visits had always delighted us. He watched everything we did and would sometimes draw pictures of us. Seeing him made me feel I was coming home.

Repulse was the next call on the *Fort Severn's* itinerary and two days should have taken us there, but we ran into bad weather again. Some of our cargo was for the Wager Bay post so Buster decided to land it on the south side of the bay at what was known as Laddie Harbour, where Wager Dick, who ran the Wager Bay post, would collect it in his Peterhead boat. The tide was against us at first in the Narrows, and even with the engine and the sails set in a good breeze, giving us a speed of over eight knots, we made less than half a mile along the rugged shore in an hour. The first sheltered bay we tried was the wrong one but in the next we found Wager Dick already waiting for us.

We lay up at Laddie Harbour for a day and a half, transshipping cargo to Wager Dick's Peterhead. He had brought us some caribou meat and also had a beautifully beaded miniature dress which I would have bought had not Buster got it first for the HBC museum in London. Buster, who had once been post manager at Wager Bay, was an old friend of Wager Dick and their conversation was fascinating. I remember Wager Dick describing one official with whom he had travelled: "I met many white men but all better than him." When travelling the same official would eat Inuit food, but with obvious distaste, and kept a supply of his own, which he did not share with his hosts. One day, irritated by his fastidious attitude, his companions put a small amount of hare droppings in his plate of stew. His expressions of horror and disgust were met with the disarming reply, "You no eat shit? plenty shit good. Only man shit, seal shit, dog shit no good."

The weather had cleared by the time we were ready to sail. We waited for the tide to help us, and left Wager Bay for Repulse Bay in the afternoon on 1 September.

The Second World War is often considered to have brought radical changes to the north. Our voyage to Repulse Bay in 1938 had seemed much like any other fur trade voyage over the past twenty to thirty years, but there were indications of what was beginning to happen. The two new managers we took to northern posts both had wives with them, and at Chesterfield Joe Ford was now married. Our freight for Repulse Bay included a radio transmitter that would be able to send messages in Morse code to the south. As we sailed north in Roes Welcome Sound, a small float plane flew low over us and dipped its wings. It was Father Schulte returning, as we discovered later, from carrying out ice reconnaissance in Foxe Basin for the *Thérèse* through skies where no other aircraft had ever flown. These were early signs of revolutions in the social life, communications, and transportation of the north that would end its isolation and change its character for ever – revolutions that were accelerated rather than initiated by the Second World War.

As night fell we entered the calmer waters of Repulse Bay and we could soon make out a light far in the distance. It guided us in the dark and for a long time seemed to come no nearer. Several hours passed before we anchored off the post very late that night.

Waiting at Repulse Bay

2 September – 19 December 1938

At Repulse Bay I was greeted by Big Boy, The Bouncer, Father Massé, Father Lacroix, and many Inuit whose faces I could remember much better than their names. The mission now had a radio and the fathers had heard that the *Thérèse* had failed to get through the ice to Igloolik and was returning to Repulse. She was held up in Frozen Strait but expected to arrive in two or three days. Reynold and Pat had been landed near Winter Island with all their supplies and an old whaleboat they had bought in Churchill.

The Hudson's Bay Company's plan to establish a trading post at Igloolik depended completely on the *Thérèse* because she was carrying everything for it, as well as the needs of the mission. I had arranged with the company to buy all I wanted at their new post and to pay any Inuit I employed with credit there. Life at Igloolik would be much more difficult if there were no post.

I spent my time helping unload the *Fort Severn* and writing letters to go south with her. Buster Brown, who understood radios and had pioneered their introduction in the northern fur trade, installed the transmitter and the wind-charger for the batteries that would power both the radio and a modest amount of electric lighting. Early next evening the *Thérèse* was seen, and she anchored at nine o'clock. We all went aboard to get her latest news. We were told that Reynold and Pat had been landed in good spirits and expected to make their way to Igloolik in their whaleboat in a few days. The captain was rather concerned at having left them so much on their own, and I promised to send him a message over the new Repulse radio if I received any news of them. Among those on board the *Thérèse* were the two HBC men who were to have been the manager and clerk at Igloolik and who had been looking forward to opening the post.

There was still a possibility the *Thérèse* would again try to reach Igloolik if there were strong winds from the north or west, which would clear the ice in northern Foxe Basin. I was ready to sail in her with my supplies but the next two days were calm. On 5 September the captain decided it was too late in the season to make another attempt because he was short of fuel, and the crew began to unload the cargo that had been intended for Igloolik. I moved into the HBC house to become the grateful guest of the Crawfords, and the *Fort Severn* sailed for Churchill with the Repulse fur and the disappointed pair who would have staffed the Igloolik post.

Unloading the *Thérèse* occupied three days in all. During this time I saw something of the Oblate fathers who were travelling in her, two of whom were keen botanists. They said they had been given some three thousand archaeological specimens when the *Thérèse* had been at Igloolik the previous year, but had no record of where any had been found. The night before the *Thérèse* sailed, Henry Voisey and I paddled his canoe out for a final visit and a drink with the captain. After talking for some time we said goodbye and went on deck. We looked for our canoe to find that it had broken loose and drifted ashore. As it was late and we did not want to disturb anybody, we spent a cold night in the galley on the deck until first light, when we were taken ashore in a whaleboat. We watched the *Thérèse* raise anchor to sail south and then went home to sleep. When I awoke I had a very stiff back, either from moving cargo or trying to sleep in the icy galley. This stopped me from doing anything active for the next two days, and I could review my plans.

Now that the ships had sailed for the south, life was simpler. My starting point would certainly be Repulse, and I would have to rely on what I could carry with me. I wanted to reach Igloolik as soon as I could but that would not be until winter travel was possible and I could persuade some Inuk to take me. I had neither dogs nor dog-food and in any event had no intention of attempting such a long winter journey alone. With luck I might arrive at Igloolik in February but it could be much later if I had to wait until an Iglulingmiut family came to Repulse to trade, as these journeys did not usually begin until early in the spring. I would not be able to excavate until towards the end of June when the ground starts to thaw. I might therefore have several weeks I could spend in exploration from Igloolik.

Reynold and I had completed the coastline of Baffin Island, but the interior was scarcely known. Though Inuit often went inland to hunt caribou, European travel had been limited to three or four routes across the island. I myself had followed that between Igloolik and Pond Inlet. The highest mountains of Baffin Island lay to the south, where the next crossing was from Cumberland Sound to Nettilling Lake and then along the Koukdjuak River to its mouth in Foxe Basin. Half of Baffin Island lay between these two crossings. Reynold and Pat were hoping to find a crossing from Piling to Clyde Inlet. I had a rather similar plan.

Franz Boas, a well-known anthropologist, had spent the year 1883-84 in Cumberland Sound and had asked the Inuit about the journeys they made. His report contained a rough map of the routes they knew, and showed one that led from Kangirllukjuak, (now Steensby Inlet) in northern Foxe Basin northeast to the head of Anaularealing, a long fiord that entered Davis Strait about halfway between Clyde Inlet and Pond Inlet and had been named Cambridge Fiord. The Inuit told me they had heard of this route but nobody now alive had crossed Baffin Island there. I thought I would try to find this old, almost-forgotten route and visit Pond Inlet again, before returning to Igloolik by mid-June to begin my excavations.

I had been expecting to use the HBC post at Igloolik as my base for any exploration as well as for excavating in the summer. I would now have fewer supplies, and I would not be able to replace anything I used, broke, or lost once I left Repulse. I would have to rely almost entirely on local resources but Igloolik always had plenty of walrus. This would not be an exciting diet but it would do me no harm. Any Inuit who helped me, I could pay with credit at Arctic Bay, Pond Inlet, or Repulse because they would still have to go there to trade. I could see no compelling reason for changing my plans.

After two days my back felt better and I was able to start on some of the things I could do before the beginning of winter. Naujan, the archaeological site Mathiassen of the Fifth Thule Expedition had excavated in 1922, was only a mile or two east of the Repulse Bay post. Here he had found the artifacts that led to his definition and description of the Thule culture. I walked there the first afternoon I could. There had been no snow and the ground had not yet frozen, so I could compare the site with Mathiassen's description of it, and look at any ground where he had started to dig but had not had time to finish excavating. I found a few artifacts and several small pieces of native copper. This might indicate a close connection with the Coppermine area over 700 miles to the west. I thought there could still be time to do some useful archaeology, and I walked to Naujan many times during the next two or three weeks. Though the weather remained unseasonably mild, it was always too windy or too wet to excavate before the snow came. My only serious digging was in fact for my spade, which became buried in our first heavy snowfall after I had carelessly left it on the ground. It took me two days to find it.

September at Repulse Bay was a good time for hunting from canoes with outboard engines, particularly for seals and white whales, and occasionally I accompanied the hunters. Most of my hunting however was for much smaller game. I usually took a .22 rifle with me when I went to Naujan and was sometimes rewarded with a hare. They turned white before the snow came and stood out against the rocks at that time of the year. The ptarmigan arrived later than usual but by the second half of September they were plentiful, and a walk of an hour or two would usually produce several. They were ridiculously easy to shoot and often a flock would not fly away when approached or even after one or two had been shot. Inuit would sometimes kill them with stones or a whip. Oldsquaw duck were massing in the small bay near Naujan. I estimated there were three thousand one afternoon, but they never came within range.

The fall brought frequent gales, usually from the southeast or northwest. Northwest winds cleared ice away from the bay and southeast winds brought some of it back again. A northwesterly gale began on 14 September, blew hard for three days, and was followed by a day or two of calm weather. It must have provided just the conditions that the *Thérèse* had been wanting. While hunting one day I saw a whaleboat with two men coming under sail from the east. I raced down to the beach thinking they might be Reynold and Pat, but they were two Inuit visiting from a camp along the bay.

The old skis I had taken to Churchill two years earlier had been sent to Repulse. I tried them out for a day or two and found them of little use as the snow was packed into hard drifts by the winds. They would have been much more satisfactory in the spring. I helped with some work that had to be done on the post buildings, including installing the two or three electric lights the batteries could supply. A small addition was being made to the house and insulation packed on the inside of the walls. This was complicated by the fact that when Captain Cleveland was building the house, he had installed all the windows inside out, over the protests of his clerk. Work of this sort and indoor painting was done when the weather was bad, and could be continued into the winter.

When the ice on the lakes was about six inches thick, it was time to secure the winter supply of drinking water. A long saw was used to cut ice blocks about three feet long by two feet wide, which were then pulled out of the water, sledged to the post, and stacked outside the house. In the sitting room was an old forty-five gallon oil drum full of water, which was ladled out as needed. Pieces of ice from the stack were added to this drum from time to time and slowly melted to replace what we used.

Towards the end of September, unexpected but very welcome visitors arrived. Two men and a youth walked in with pack dogs from Qiqitarjuk, a camp in Lyon Inlet where the Inuit from Gore Bay had now moved. One of the men was Kutjek, whom I had not seen since we parted company on the way to Piling. He had been to Repulse with his family to trade in the spring, but the snow on the land had melted unexpectedly early preventing him from returning to Igloolik. He had had to spend the summer at Qiqitarjuk. We had a long talk and in due course I asked if he would be willing to take me to Igloolik as soon as travelling conditions allowed. He said he would and that he could return to Repulse to pick me up around the middle of December. This solved one of my most important problems.

The north was such a self-contained world that what we heard of events from "the outside" usually held little interest, but the days immediately after Kutjek left to return to Qiqitarjuk were

an exception. The news on the radio had been very disturbing
for some time, and I had decided that if war broke out I would
have to sledge south to Churchill rather than north to Igloolik.
On 27 September we heard the British fleet had been mobilized,
but next day news reached us that the Munich agreement had
been signed. Though reception on the radio was very poor at
the time, all we heard seemed to indicate that the immediate threat
of war had been removed, and our world contracted again to become only the north.

The weather remained warmer than usual in the fall. On 15
October very heavy freezing rain covered any exposed metal with
nearly an inch of clear ice and brought down the aerials. A violent
wind soon after blew the wind-charger from its base, shattering
a blade. The aerials were soon put up again, and a spare blade
was found for the wind-charger which was easily repaired. On
calm nights a little ice would form on the sea, but it would break
up quickly and did not persist until 21 October.

We saw the priests from the mission almost every day, and one
or two evenings a week we would get together for bridge. The
fathers made a good wine out of raisins. One evening they produced a bottle of brandy they had been sent. This was a new
experience for Henry, who thought he was drinking wine and
remarked, as he walked rather erratically back to the post, that
the fathers' wine had been very good that night. Our attempts
to brew beer were much less successful. We bottled our first brew
too soon, when the yeast was still working, and the result was
mildly explosive. The little we could recover both looked and
tasted rather nasty. Our next efforts were a little better.

Early in November we heard the *Northern Messenger* on the radio,
and from then on we gathered together every Friday night to
listen to it. This programme, then broadcast from KDKA, a station
in Pittsburgh, was the only way that messages from "the outside"
could be sent to people at isolated posts in the north. Once a
week northerners would gather round the radio, thinking there
might be a message for them and hearing the messages intended
for everybody else. This increased the "insideness" of the north.
Though you might never have met the clerk of some post, he
did not seem a stranger when you knew from the *Northern Messenger*
that his father had had a heart attack, his sister had had twins, and
one of his cousins had just graduated in engineering from McGill.

One message the mission received was that Father Schulte had a new and larger aircraft. The fathers thought he might bring it to Repulse and ferry supplies to the mission at Igloolik. He might even bring me back from there next year as the plane would be light on south-bound flights from Igloolik. However we heard no more of this and Father Schulte never returned to Repulse.

Our numbers varied a little. Mrs Crawford never participated in our evenings since she had Lewis to look after and bridge was considered a male occupation. Henry was away hunting for the second half of October, and the day after he returned Father Lacroix left to spend two weeks at an Inuit camp to prepare a family for baptism. On 17 November a new member joined our circle. Father Clabaut had gone to Churchill in the summer of 1937 and his place at Repulse had been taken by Father Frans van de Velde, who had just arrived in Canada from Belgium. In April he had gone to Pelly Bay where he spent the summer. An Inuit family from there was travelling to Repulse and they had brought him with them. His enthusiasm for the north and its people and his friendliness made him a most popular addition.

The radio transmitter the *Fort Severn* had brought made little difference to our lives. The normal practice at HBC posts was for the clerk to operate the radio. At Repulse Henry Voisey hated the radio with an intensity that made him incapable of learning the Morse code. The conditions of the transmitting licence obligated the station to serve the whole community, but the prospect of sending messages reduced Henry to such a state of nerves and misery that nobody had the heart to initiate any without a very pressing reason.

Of course Father van de Velde wanted to let both his family and the bishop know where he was. It took Henry a long and harrowing time to tap the messages to the Department of Transport at Chesterfield, where their much more powerful station relayed them in clear to Churchill. We happened to hear Chesterfield transmitting to Churchill that night. Somehow the two messages had become combined into a single message addressed to the bishop. "My parents arrived safely in Repulse Bay, van de Velde." The only message I sent from Repulse was to my mother in mid-December to say I was leaving for Igloolik.

The time before Kutjek was due to return passed quickly. I had one or two archaeological books to read and the post had a substantial though very mixed library. As well as bridge, we played chess, dominoes, and any other game we could find. Henry came back from his hunting trip with five caribou and an ample supply of char, so we ate very well.

Like Joe Ford, Tommy Crawford did a little trapping on foot, more for exercise than for profit, and sometimes I would keep him company. He trapped to the west of the settlement in order to avoid the Arctic Islands Preserve, where trapping was restricted to native people and which included all the District of Franklin, but not Keewatin. The boundary between the two ran through Repulse Bay, though nobody there knew exactly where.

Near the end of November Ivalak, who had helped Reynold and me with our load when we set out from Gore Bay two years earlier, sledged into the settlement with some other Inuit from Qiqitarjuk. He offered to take two big boxes for me as far as there. This delayed him a day while he put mud on his komatik runners owing to the extra weight, but it meant I would be able to leave Qiqitarjuk for Igloolik with a full load.

I had to get ready for my journey to Igloolik in such ways as deciding what to take, and making food and primus boxes with sliding lids so their contents could be reached without unlashing the komatik. Winter clothing was most important, and The Bouncer took some of the caribou skins I had brought, softened them, and soon made me an outfit that set me up for the winter.

Not wanting to overburden The Bouncer I gave some skins to a man from a nearby camp and asked if his wife would make them into a sleeping bag. I explained in my best Inuktitut, as the language of the Canadian Eskimos is now called, that I felt the cold more than the Inuit and therefore I wanted to have a double bag, one with the fur inside to fit within the other, with the fur outside. He said he understood and that his wife would certainly make the bag. Within a week he returned. As he unrolled my bag I saw it was a single bag and then that it was very much wider than I had expected. He smiled as he said, "Big enough for two, plenty warm now." I probably blushed as I explained that this was not exactly what I had meant. The bag he had brought would do very nicely for my inner bag, but I would like another one to go outside it. He laughed, took some more skins, and returned in a few days with an outer bag.

Late on 17 December Kutjek arrived with his son, Panikpakut-tuk, who was about ten years old, and three other men. We decided to start for Qiqitarjuk on the 19th, which should get us there before Christmas. Next day was spent on the inevitable last-minute preparations. I also wrote a number of letters because there was usually some way for mail from Repulse to reach Churchill during the winter. From now on I would not be able to send mail until the next summer. In the evening I was given a farewell party by the Crawfords, which the three fathers attended, and I was able to thank everybody, wish them all a Merry Christmas, and say goodbye.

21

Christmas in Lyon Inlet

19 December 1938 – 4 January 1939

Kutjek decided we could carry much more food than I had expected and packed, so we did not leave Repulse Bay until late in the morning of 19 December. An older man who was going in the same direction kept us company. The air was so calm that it seemed almost warm though the sun scarcely rose above the horizon. After four or five hours we reached a small camp, and decided to build an igloo and spend the night. One reason was that the family living there had been lent one of Kutjek's dogs and wanted to keep it. There was a long discussion, which I could not follow, leading to an agreement that Kutjek could have the dog back again in exchange for one that was not as good.

Nothing could have tasted better than the frozen caribou we had for supper, and Kutjek then made bannock before we went to bed. We were not using a kudliq and the igloo had become cold as I pulled off my clothes and crawled into my nice new double sleeping bag, gathering it around me. I then saw that the older man had neither sleeping bag nor blanket. There was only one thing I could do. A few minutes later Kutjek remarked that his caribou-skin blanket was rather small to cover both himself and Panikpakuttuk – far smaller than my now single sleeping bag. Again there was only one thing I could do and I shared it with Panikpakuttuk. Throughout the winter there rarely seemed to be enough bedding and this became a frequent sleeping pattern. The man whose wife had made my bag knew what he had been talking about. I was plenty warm, and I had learned my lesson. Two in a single bag are just as warm as one in a double bag, and it is easier and lighter to carry.

The weather remained fine the next day as we left the sea ice and began to cross the land between Repulse Bay and Lyon Inlet. We reached a long narrow lake before we camped. While supper was being prepared, Panikpakuttuk was making complicated string figures with a length of plaited sinew. I could recognize some from illustrations in anthropological accounts, but rarely could I complete one. The night was short as Kutjek was up and making breakfast by four o'clock. Feeding the dogs, repairing harness, replacing any lost mud, icing the runners, and packing up always took a long time and it was after nine o'clock when we resumed our journey.

We soon came to an igloo where a family was camped. After a short stop we continued in a rising wind which made the snow drift badly, and visibility became so poor it was difficult to follow old komatik tracks. A rock we failed to see broke a lot of mud off one runner, we became separated from the other komatik, and somehow we diverted from the correct route. It was late when we decided to camp and the drifts were so shallow we had to use the slow method of cutting horizontal blocks of snow to build the igloo.

We must have got back near a recognized route because we had not finished the igloo when a komatik arrived, coming from the direction we were headed and attracted by our light. Two men were with it and they stopped and came to meet us. In the light of our lantern I saw to my astonishment that one was Pat. My first words were, "Where is Reynold?" He replied that he was dead, drowned on the way to Igloolik. The Inuit were already making a second igloo, so close to ours that the two igloos over-lapped and theirs used part of our wall. When both were finished the common wall was cut away, forming a single wide igloo in much the same shape as a compressed figure eight, so we could all spend the night together. Here Pat told me what had happened after he and Reynold had left the *Thérèse*.

They had spent three days on shore, sorting their supplies and waiting for the ice by the coast to loosen up, before they were able to start their journey. Wind, snowstorms, and ice delayed them from time to time, but most days they were able to move a few miles along the coast, and some days much farther. Their greatest problem was that their boat leaked. Every two hours, and sometimes more frequently, they had to bail her, and to sleep well they had to beach her and prop her up. Rough weather and frequent beaching made the leaks worse the farther they went. She had an outboard engine which was another source of trouble. By 13 September they had reached an Inuit camp, only about fifty miles south of Igloolik. Reynold knew many of the people there, and they told him where the other Iglulingmiut were intending to spend the winter. Pat thought one good day's sail would take them to the mission, where Father Bazin was arranging for a family to go with them to Piling.

Next day brought a strong wind from the northwest, as we had had at Repulse the same day. The wind was offshore clearing away any ice, so they left the Inuit camp early, sailing north in the lee of the coast and hoping to reach Igloolik that day. After two or three hours the engine was running poorly so they ran in close to shore, anchored, took the engine apart, and started to clean the carburettor. As it was a convenient time to make tea, Pat waded ashore with a kettle for fresh water. He had to walk some distance to a lake and the better part of an hour may have passed before he returned. Either the tide had risen or the anchor had dragged because the water had become too deep for his hip-length waders. He called to Reynold to row a line ashore in a little folding dinghy they carried. He soon realized Reynold was in difficulties. He had taken only one oar, could not make any headway against the wind, and was being blown out to sea. For some reason he had not tied a line to the boat.

Pat was able to wade out to the boat, the water coming up to his waist, but he had to remove the outboard engine, raise the anchor, replace the rudder, and hoist the sail. By the time he had the boat headed downwind there was no sign of Reynold or the dinghy among the broken waves. Pat searched the area as long as he could but found nothing. The boat was filling with water, the sea became rougher the farther he went out from the coast, and he was swept overboard but managed to drag himself back. Eventually he had had to sail to the shore and beach the boat.

Pat then walked back to the Inuit camp, where the people then helped him take the boat to Igloolik. Reynold and he had hoped to establish a base at Piling that fall, but this was now out of the question. He decided to carry on with a modified plan but his first priority was to reach a radio transmitting station to send news of Reynold's death to his wife. The Inuit advised him that he would be able to travel to Repulse earlier than to Arctic Bay.

He had spent the fall with the fathers at the mission, making short journeys from there. Qanattiaq, who lived at Akudneq and had a first-class dog team, agreed to take him to Repulse as soon as long journeys became possible. They had left Akudneq early in December and expected to reach Repulse in another day or two. After informing Reynold's wife of the tragedy, Pat planned to return to Igloolik with Qanattiaq, continue on to Piling with an Inuit family, try to find a way across Baffin Island to Clyde River post, and follow the coast north from there to Pond Inlet. In the summer he would explore Bylot Island before returning south in the *Nascopie*.

Kutjek was making breakfast by four o'clock and again we did not start until several hours later. Pat and Qanattiaq, who had only a light load, left at a gallop for Repulse. We too made solid but less spectacular progress. Despite the drifting snow we were able to keep to the route, following a long lake and then a wide river to the sea. After dark we travelled on the sea ice for hour after hour until we came to the island of Qiqitarjuk where there were seven houses built of snow and turf. There was also an eighth structure, a curved wall of ice blocks. It gave protection from the wind and dogs and was the camp latrine.

Everyone came out to help us unload and I recognized several men whom I had seen much closer to Igloolik, including Cleveland's Johnny, who had been our host at Ugliarjuk. We went into Kutjek's igloo where I met his wife. There we ate, talked, and smoked until I fell asleep in my clothes on the bed. It had been a very long day, saddened by memories of Reynold. I was now in a setting that would have provided him with the peace of mind he had described as making him incredibly happy at all the Inuit camps along this coast where we had stayed and been treated so well.

I knew that Kutjek and Qanattiaq would want to travel north together. It would be several days before Pat could reach Repulse, send his messages, and return to Qiqitarjuk, so I could look forward to spending Christmas, and possibly New Year here. I would enjoy this. My only worry was the effect that a long stay including Christmas would have on my supplies, which would have to last me for several months. At least our load would be much lighter when we left, and the extra food that Kutjek had said we could take from Repulse would no longer be a burden.

As at Gore Bay, Qaunnaq had the largest house, where religious services and the major social events took place. I visited each family in turn, starting with his. The community seemed prosperous with plenty of food and numbers of happy, healthy, and inquisitive children. Several of the women could play the accordion and there were dances the first day I was there. Each dance would last half an hour or more and dancers would drop out if exhausted and be replaced. We were dancing in a house with a snow roof and there was much laughter when a cigarette lighter, lost by one of the dancers before the house had been built, was seen embedded in one of the blocks that formed the roof.

I was of course staying in Kutjek's igloo. I told him that, once I had reached Igloolik, I was intending to try to find the old Inuit route across Baffin Island to Anaularealing. To my surprise he said he would like to continue with me when I went on this journey. I was delighted because he was a capable hunter and traveller, had good dogs, and was always helpful. Even more important was the fact that we had already travelled together, so neither of us would be dealing with an unknown.

Next day was Christmas Eve and it brought much larger, longer, and more crowded dances. At one time there were eight couples on the floor and six were common. It was the first Inuit square dance I had attended where somebody was calling. This was usually Cleveland's Johnny and he used a mixture of Inuit and English. "Pissukpose" for Promenade, followed by "Swing your partner." After two or three hours there was an interval, not because the dancers were tired but because the ice floor was beginning to melt. It soon refroze and the dancers returned for two more hours. Dances in the whaling days must have been like this.

On Christmas Day the custom was to shake hands with everybody one met and say, "Christmassy." Qaunnaq held a long service in his igloo which I did not attend because no one told me about it. While it was in progress I made up little packages for each igloo, containing a plug of tobacco, a number of cigarettes, a bar or two of chocolate, chewing gum, and some candies, with a rather larger package for Qaunnaq's igloo.

The church service was followed by a feast for everybody. We started with a traditional dish which I had read about but never

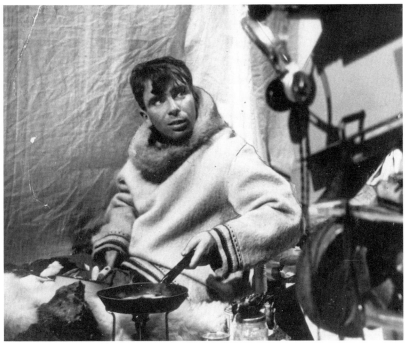

Reynold cooking
bannock in the TV
studio, Alexandra
Palace, London, 1938

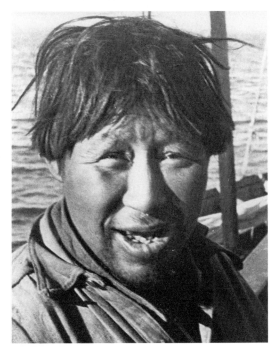

Mino

The Roman Catholic mission at Igloolik

Memorial cairn and stone. The syllabic inscription reads: "Umiligaarjuk died here. We will always remember him."

Albert

A recent photograph of Buchan Gulf, looking towards Anaularealing

Air photograph of route across Baffin Island showing ravine and heart-shaped lake

A recent photograph of Buchan Gulf, the Mitres

Air photograph showing route followed across the Baffin Island watershed

Faces cut in antler, and two ivory figures excavated at Abverdjar. Scale is
indicated by the ivory figures, which are about two inches in height.

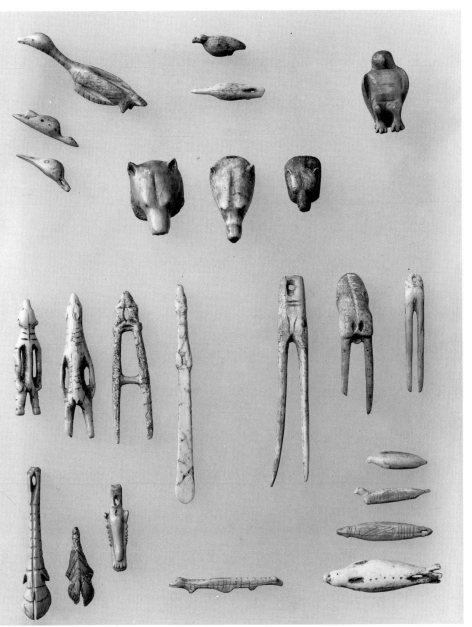

Ivory representations of animals and parts of animals from Abverdjar, many with holes for suspension. Their size is indicated by the middle bear's head, which measures 1 5/16 by 5/8 inches.

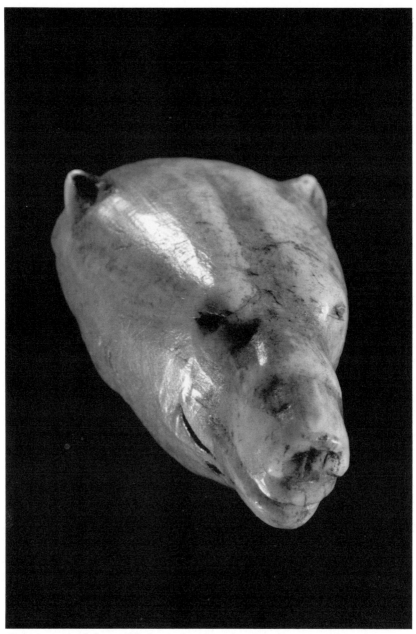

Enlargement of the middle bear's head on the preceding page. It is carved from a bear's tooth.

Inuit whaleboats visiting at Abverdjar

Excavation at Abverdjar showing flat stones

Aipilik and Panikpakuttuk climbing mast of visitors' boat

Aipilik on makeshift raft setting net

Kutjek's adopted daughter and Mino's new stepdaughter satisfying their curiosity about the author

M.F. *Thérèse* southbound

seen before, consisting of caribou fat already chewed up with berries by the women. It was followed by boiled rice and bannock. Then came tea and ships'. biscuits, which were my contribution. After a short pause, frozen caribou appeared in large quantities, and then frozen char and more tea. We finished with a salad – the contents, mainly lichen, of the stomachs of several caribou. There may have been other dishes, but these were the only ones I ate. During the meal Ivalak passed me a piece of paper on which he had written ENOOET 45, the number of people present, which I am sure was everybody in the camp. I have had many Christmas dinners since then, but this remains my most memorable.

We returned to our igloos after the feast, and the exchange of presents began. So far as I could make out everybody in the camp gave everybody else a present. The children from each family would arrive carrying something for everyone in the igloo, and they would be given something to take back to distribute to their families. I know that I received four dog harnesses, some dog traces, the promise of a dog, some line made of bearded sealskin, a pair of caribou-skin mocassins, a pair of kamiks, a cigarette holder, a whip, sealskin for replacing worn-out boot bottoms, a lamp trimmer, and many objects collected from old houses. I had great difficulty in finding suitable and adequate presents in return. Tea and plug tobacco were a great help. The Inuit often had the same problem and many presents changed hands several times during the day. I saw Kutjek, faced with having to find two presents at short notice, divide a pack of cards he had been given into two and and give half to each.

Between Christmas and New Year was a time for feasting, dancing, and visiting. In an Inuit community anyone walks into any igloo at any time and is made welcome. Kutjek went out one day to collect a cached walrus, and when he returned our igloo was soon full of people helping us to eat it. At one igloo I had narwhal muktuk that had obviously been saved for Christmas. Some igloos had caribou, some fish, and some seal. On two days the snow was drifting so badly there was little visiting, which helped to preserve my rapidly dwindling stock of tobacco.

The children also came visiting, not usually with their families but in their own groups of friends. Panikpakuttuk's normal companion had a very pronounced stutter. He would always use Panikpakuttuk's full name. This often took a long time, but it caused him, and everyone else, amusement rather than embarrassment.

I was of particular interest because I was new and different. I had a few books with me which the children and often their parents enjoyed, particularly *Birds of Canada* and Jenness's *The Copper Eskimos*. They watched everything I did, insisted on lighting my pipe for me, and probably imitated and exaggerated my mannerisms to amuse themselves. I found some of them brushing their teeth with my toothbrush every morning. They liked trying to speak a few words in English, writing down numbers, and playing new games. They had minds that wanted to learn and needed only a sensitive and innovative educational system to be able to meet the challenges that change would bring.

There were of course dances on New Year's Eve. For one of the dances that night, partners were chosen in a different way. The men circled the women and each threw a dishcloth around the neck of the girl he chose. The next dance it was the women's turn to use the same technique for choosing their partners. I was lucky both in securing one of the prettiest girls with my dishcloth and in being chosen by Qaunnaq's wife.

New Year's Day was in many ways a replay of Christmas Day, except that the greeting was "Happynewyear" instead of "Christmassy." Again there was an extended interchange of presents. Among mine were two pieces of caribou skin decorated with beadwork for my atigi, one was a pocket and the other an edging, about an inch wide, for the hood and the bottom. They were soon sewn on and I found that the beads were not only decorative. The weight made the atigi fit better and helped to prevent it blowing up to expose one's bare back to the wind and drifting snow.

As soon as Qanattiaq and Pat returned we could set out for Igloolik. The Inuit had expected them to be back soon after Christmas, because there was little dog-food at Repulse. New Year's Day had been stormy, but the next days were better and some of the Inuit left to hunt. I went for a few short walks and continued visiting igloos. In one a small girl was playing with two sharp knives and the top of a broken glass bottle. Her mother was watchful but did not interfere. The Inuit did not believe their children would learn more quickly by being frustrated. I did not mind the delay as I could always see something interesting, learn new words, and gain a better understanding of life in an Inuit camp.

22

Lyon Inlet to Igloolik

4 January – 30 January 1939

Pat and Qanattiaq did not arrive until the evening of 4 January. They had very hungry dogs. Kutjek and I were ready to leave, thinking they would want to continue their journey the next day, but Qanattiaq decided to give his dogs another feed and a day's rest.

Pat told me they had reached Repulse on 23 December but he had decided to wait until after Christmas to send such terrible news to Reynold's wife. The day after this had been done he had heard on the BBC news a very fanciful description of Reynold's accident which must have originated with somebody who had intercepted his message. To correct this he had prepared a more detailed accurate account, which he had sent himself because he found he was better at Morse code than Henry. He and Qanattiaq had then been held at Repulse by the same harsh winds we had experienced around New Year.

On 6 January the wind was much too strong for travel. Drifting snow made visibility so bad that the Inuit watched unobtrusively to be sure that neither Pat nor I went out on our own even from one igloo to the next, though they were only a few yards apart. It was like walking blindfold, and impossible to tell if one was walking uphill or down, with the howl of the wind drowning all other sound. The only way to keep direction was by carefully observing the way the wind was blowing in relation to oneself.

The wind had dropped a little in the morning, but local advice was that the drifting would be much worse on the sea ice than at the camp so again we did not travel. Two Inuit who managed to arrive back that day from a hunting trip said we had made

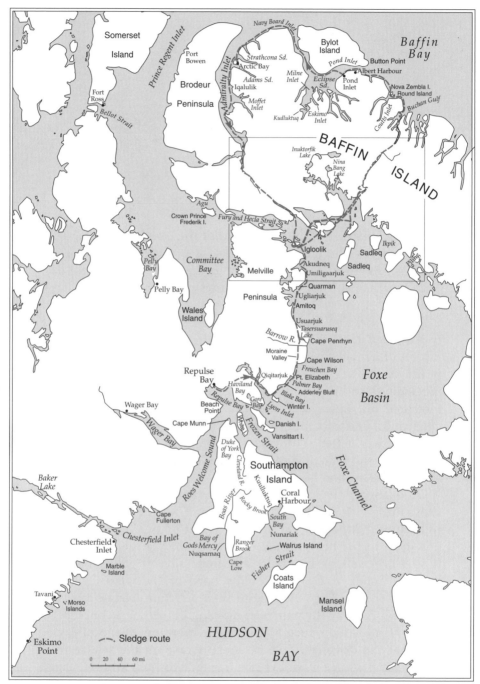

Map 7   Sledge journeys by author, winter 1938-39

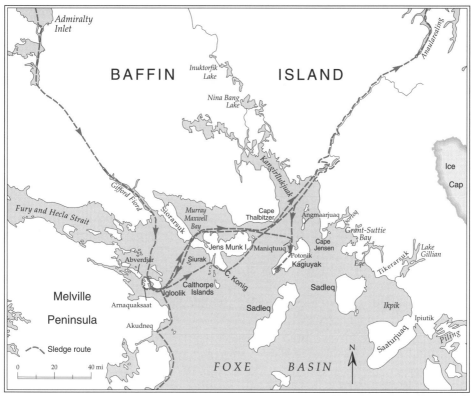

Map 8   Enlarged detail of sledge journeys, 1938-39, shown on Map 7

the right decision. The next day was a Sunday, when starting
a journey was taboo among the Anglican Inuit. Qaunnaq as usual
held a short morning service. The rest of the day Pat and I made
our final preparations for the journey, discussed our plans, and
cooked bannock to take with us.

The weather had cleared on Monday when Kutjek, Panikpakuttuk, and I set off. Our dogs went very well and it was not
until we had stopped for a mug-up that Qanattiaq and Pat caught
up with us. They had picked up some meat before leaving. We
had not gone much farther when we met a solitary traveller. He
was Amiimiarjuk whom I had known at Akudneq and he told
us he had come from Quarman, the camp south of Igloolik, where
Reynold had stayed the night before he was drowned. Amiimiarjuk

had been two weeks on the way. We travelled on after dark and camped on the land not far from the entrance to Lyon Inlet.

We were up early in the morning and left at first light. Following the coast, we mistook an inlet for the strait between Winter Island and the mainland, but a short land-crossing at the head of the inlet brought us down to the sea again. Qanattiaq had left a number of caches of walrus meat on his way south, and we picked up the first of these and then crossed Blake Bay to camp south of Adderley Bluff.

The dogs were given a large feed before we set off next morning. The ice had broken off quite close to the coast so we had to follow the shore much of the way, losing a lot of mud as a result. We camped early, about half-way across the next bay. Kutjek used woolly fur from an arctic hare to repair the mud on his komatik.

We crossed the land again at Point Elizabeth. The recent very strong northwest winds must have broken off most of the land-fast ice along this coast. Finding suitable snow that night proved difficult, and nearly two hours were spent before Qanattiaq was satisfied. He always built beautiful regular snow houses but he went about it in a very deliberate way, and he also seemed slow when preparing and lighting the kudliq. Pat and I found this rather exasperating. There was little we could do to help, and just standing around was cold and tiresome. Qanattiaq had developed a bad cold and was not feeling at all well, but we had been making good progress despite having to travel so much on land rather than sea ice.

Qanattiaq had left another cache of walrus for dog-food on a small island. We collected this before we began the land-crossing on January 13, the same day that Reynold and I had started the crossing two years before and within a few miles of where Peter Freuchen had been caught and badly frozen in a sudden blizzard exactly sixteen years earlier. Qanattiaq struck inland four miles south of where Reynold and I had, and headed rather west of north to reach a river. We followed it for several miles, Kutjek and Qanattiaq taking great care to avoid any rocks.

Next morning we crossed two lakes into Moraine Valley where we were back on our old route. The mistake Reynold and I had made in going too far east on the sea ice had probably added between five and ten miles to our journey. That afternoon the temperature dropped and when we came to the next piece of walrus that Qanattiaq had cached we found only its skin; foxes had eaten the rest. We then encountered very heavy soft snow. Instead of riding, as we had been able to do on the level, we had to walk and push all the way and were not sorry to camp that night at the end of the long lake just before the Barrow River.

We next followed a short-cut Reynold and I had missed along a little valley to the river, where there was more soft snow. The going was very slow as we proceeded downstream to the cairn that Reynold and I had assumed must mark where the river and the route parted. We had been correct, for this was where the Inuit left the river to head north. They knew a more direct way than Reynold and I had found from there to the long lake called Tasersuaruseq, which we reached just before dusk, through soft snow all the way. The lake provided rather better going and we did not camp until we were near its north end. That night we heard the dogs break into the snow annexe Qanattiaq always built to house the harnesses, traces, and dog-food, but we were able to chase them out before they did much damage.

The snow was not quite so soft as we continued to the end of the lake, up a valley to a smaller lake, and then on to a plateau. Dusk fell as we reached a valley that led down to the sea, and we camped near the coast. Qanattiaq had cached some walrus dog-food here and the dogs could eat well. A frigid wind made the igloo seem delightfully warm when we finally crawled inside.

Next day we followed the coast on the sea ice at first and then cut across an isthmus where Qanattiaq, who was leading, took us too far inland. It was bitterly cold, and our teams were shrouded in the mist formed by their breath. We returned to the sea ice hoping to reach the camp at Usuarjuk, where Reynold and I had met our first Inuit after the land-crossing, and where Pat and Qanattiaq had spent a night on their way south. A couple of hours later our dogs caught the scent of the camp and broke into a gallop. We soon reached a large igloo to find it empty. The family that lived there must have moved very recently to the north. We spent a cold and miserable night in the small entrance passage to their deserted house, which would have been even colder. It was a complete contrast to the warmth and comfort we had anticipated and that Reynold and I had found there.

Only Panikpakuttuk was cheerful as we resumed our journey north. We had no dog-food left, the dogs were not pulling anything like as well as they had been, the snow was still soft, and the wind was icy. We kept to the sea ice along the shore except where we had to go inland for a time to avoid rough ice. At night Kutjek, who was finding his heavy komatik difficult to manage in the dark among the shore ridges, suddenly decided to camp. He usually left such decisions to Qanattiaq, who was a little way ahead. Probably because we had all the food and the blubber for the kudliq, Qanattiaq stopped too and started to build an igloo so we joined him. I was sure Pat was pleased to camp. Being tall he felt the cold more than I did and he looked frozen. I thought he had often been very cold on the journey but too stoical to say so. To his diary, however, he spoke frankly of the miserable conditions. We had all been living on only biscuits and bannock for a day or two and, like the Inuit, we felt colder if we had not eaten meat. My major problem was with the cut of my hood; for some reason it did little to protect my nose, which I could not stop from freezing.

Kutjek followed a common practice in the north of carrying a large thermos type of flask to hold water for icing the runners during the day, or hot tea for mug-ups. Like us it was clothed in two layers of caribou skin, an inner bag with the hair inside and an outer with the hair outside. Next morning he produced a single oxo cube to add to the two quarts of boiling water in the flask. I never discovered how he had an oxo cube – which I had never seen in the north. He also decided to leave our heavy boxes behind when we resumed our journey. Qanattiaq, who had stronger dogs and more of them, did not reduce his load. We covered a greater distance that day because we were on the sea ice most of the time and the snow was firmer. We had crossed the isthmus at Amitoq and were well to the north of it when we camped, rather earlier than usual because the sky was overcast. It cleared as soon as we had finished building the igloo.

Our dogs seemed to pull better next day. Early in the afternoon Kutjek said we would meet Inuit before dark because his ears were ringing. An hour or so later we saw four komatiks in the distance. They turned out to be Jack Turner on his way to Repulse Bay, one of Qanattiaq's sons looking for his father, Issigaituq, who had been so kind to Reynold and me at Usuarjuk, and four or five other Inuit helping Jack with his load. The Inuit soon built two connecting igloos as it would take too long to build the size of igloo such a large party would require. The smaller one was for Jack, Pat, and me, and the larger for the Inuit. It was particularly nice for me to have this unexpected opportunity to see Jack again and to hear news of those at Pond Inlet.

Jack told us he had established a new mission at Moffet Inlet, a branch of Admiralty Inlet. He was on his way to Repulse Bay and would then go to Pelly Bay and Fort Ross before crossing Prince Regent Inlet to return to Moffet Inlet. He had not stopped at Igloolik because it was a Roman Catholic stronghold. For both ourselves and our dogs, meeting his party meant a change to feast from famine for they had plenty of meat.

We had intended to spend only one night together but we woke next morning to a blizzard and the day after was a Sunday. Though Pat did not believe in delaying a journey for a Sunday, he felt better about it when he went outside and found there was still a strong frigid wind from the northwest. The double igloo became a church for the two services that Jack held that day. It was a devout gathering because the men travelling with Jack were doing so mainly to hear more of his teaching. He led the hymns, and there were many of them, accompanying them on his concertina. The Inuit, who often sang hymns among themselves, seemed reluctant to join in so they were largely solos. Pat and I, though familiar with the tunes, did not know the Inuit words that went with them.

Some of our clothing and sleeping bags had been getting progressively wetter during the journey as our perspiration and breath condensed and froze on them. We were able to make good use of a method Jack had devised for warming an igloo enough to dry clothing. He carried something resembling a tent made of light cotton to which a number of short sticks were attached by pieces of string, each tied around the middle of a stick. It took only a minute or two to push the sticks, one by one, through the igloo wall, leaving a lining suspended by the strings. The igloo then warmed quickly and to a higher temperature without the snow walls melting, and in a few hours our clothing was much drier.

On Monday we parted, and a short day with good going in nice weather took us to the camp at Quarman, where I found

I knew almost everybody. Their only food was large quantities of walrus that had been cached a long time, to which we were able to add some bannock. I noticed they kept much of the bannock for the two or three invalids in the camp. Issigaituq, who was living here, went to collect the boxes Kutjek had cached, and some dog-food was sent to Jack Turner to replace what we had used. Qanattiaq left next day to return to his family at Akudneq but Pat, Kutjek, and I stayed for three nights. We visited all the igloos, talking or not talking because in Inuit society one does not have to talk in order to be sociable, and handing out tobacco on a scale of one plug, weighing between one and two ounces, per kudliq. Tobacco was what everyone wanted; it was easy to carry and, as in Europe after the Second World War, was almost a currency. When I mentioned that my nose had frozen sometimes on the journey, a kind woman quickly sewed a strip of dog fur round my hood. From then on I had no more trouble.

Quarman to Akudneq proved a long cold day. On the way we stopped at the cairn Pat and a number of Inuit had built in memory of Reynold near where he had drowned. It was about seven feet high, strongly made, with a soapstone plaque inscribed with his name. It stood out as the only feature on the bleak, flat, limestone shore. He would be remembered in a place where he had been content and liked by everyone, and he would be pleased that the Inuit still call the area Umiligaarjuk, "He with a small beard," the name he had been given by them.

The wind started to rise as we reached Akudneq. It looked like the beginning of what was known in the Eastern Arctic as a three-day blow, which shuts down all activity until the wind starts to weaken on the third day. The only course is to sit it out. Akudneq was a smaller camp than before but it seemed to have even more dogs. We stayed in a very large igloo which Qanattiaq shared with his older brother and another couple. Qanattiaq's oldest son had a hernia and he was planning to take him by komatik to the hospital at Pangnirtung for treatment. We suggested the Chesterfield hospital might be an easier journey, but, as it was operated by Catholic nuns and his family were strong Anglicans, Qanattiaq would not consider it. As at Quarman Pat and I visited each igloo, distributing plugs of tobacco. We had plenty of time because the wind blew fiercely for two more days, and the third was a Sunday.

There was no formal service but a lot of hymn-singing throughout the day.

We left on a fine Monday morning again. Two other Inuit were with us and I drove one of their teams much of the way. Around noon we met two komatiks headed for Akudneq. With one of them was Kutjek's father and mother and a small child. Their clothing was well worn and they looked cold. We had a mug-up together, but both Pat and I were surprised at the apparently offhand way in which they exchanged greetings with Kutjek and how little they spoke to one another, though it must have been nearly a year since they had last met.

We arrived at the Igloolik mission that night to be greeted by Father Bazin and his colleague Father Trébaol; a warm comfortable building, including both a dwelling and a church, had replaced the small snow house that had been his home for so many winters. It was 30 January, four days earlier in the year than Reynold and I had arrived there.

23

Jens Munk Island

30 January – 27 February 1939

Father Bazin welcomed us with great kindness, even though he developed a terrible cold soon after our arrival, a repetition of what had happened after Reynold and I had first met him. His knowledge and advice, freely given, were again invaluable. Father Trébaol was a young priest from Brittany who then spoke little English. I found that whenever I was at a loss for a word in French, it was the corresponding Inuktitut word that came to my mind. Fortunately his Inuktitut was already good, so he could understand what I' was trying to say. Like Father Bazin, he did all he could to help me. Because the *Thérèse* had failed to reach Igloolik in September, the mission was short of supplies, but this did not stop the two priests from pressing on me anything they thought I would need.

The mission had been built beside a stream on the west side of the large bay called Ikpiakjuk that nearly divides Igloolik Island in two and provides a well-protected harbour. Though all subsequent development has taken place here, it was not where the Inuit lived at that time. They had two camps, one on Abverdjar, the nearest island to the west, and the other at Igloolik Point, the southeast corner of the island. Both were about ten miles away. The two fathers visited them frequently and Inuit were continually coming to the mission. We were there for only one Sunday, when it seemed that everyone from both camps had come for the service. I soon saw Ituksarjuat, Ataguttaaluk, and the others I had known so well at Igloolik Point.

In the article we wrote for the *Times*, Reynold and I had described Ituksarjuat as the "King of Igloolik." The Royal Navy (RN) was then commissioning a new class of large destroyers, known as the Tribal Class. One of these ships was named HMS *Eskimo*, in honour of the people the RN had met on many naval expeditions. The *Times* had forwarded to me a letter from the officer appointed to command HMS *Eskimo* with a picture of the ship asking if I would present it to Ituksarjuat.

I had brought the picture with me and I was now able to give it to him and to try to explain the reason for the gift, which undoubtedly surprised him. I do not know how successful my explanations were, but Ituksarjuat received it with apparent pleasure. The setting was certainly appropriate; as we could see from his igloo where HMS *Fury* and *Hecla* had wintered and the RN and the Inuit had first learned to like and respect each other. Parry and Lyon would have approved and would have thought how much the ships and how little the people had changed since their time.

It was still early in the winter – earlier than I had expected to arrive in Igloolik. I thought I should wait until the days were longer and warmer before starting what could be a difficult journey across Baffin Island to Anaularealing. Kutjek's dogs also would benefit from delay. Hauling the komatik through soft snow on the journey north must have taken a lot out of them because they did not seem the same team we had had when we left Repulse Bay. I did not want to impose on Father Bazin's good nature and hospitality by staying long at Igloolik, especially as I knew that at any time Bishop Clabaut might arrive by dog team from the north on his first visit to the Igloolik mission. I decided therefore to go east to Kangirllukjuak as soon as I could. Kutjek had learned that there was dog-food there, and we could get our dogs into better shape before attempting the crossing. It would also give me a chance to look at Kagiuyak, a large island that Mathiassen had reported and named Koch Island, but had not visited.

Both Pat and I had much to do before we left, Kutjek, Panikpakuttuk, and I for Kangirllukjuak, and Pat, with a much larger party, for Piling. I had to make three additional sledging boxes, and to copy an excellent little Inuktitut grammar and vocabulary that Pat had compiled at the mission during the fall. We both had to decide what to take and to leave. We were in very different circumstances. I had only what I had brought up from Repulse on our komatik, while Pat had all the supplies for a year that he and Reynold had had in their boat. I was surprised to see how much Pat was planning to take on by komatik, which would give him a very heavy and ungainly load.

We had been at Igloolik for only a few days when a team from Arctic Bay brought Bill Ford, the HBC clerk there. He was a son of Sam Ford whom we had known as post manager at Coral Harbour. Bill had come to encourage the Inuit to go to Arctic Bay to trade their foxes. Both Repulse Bay and Arctic Bay were HBC establishments but there was always rivalry between different posts for fur, especially when, as in this case, they were in different HBC districts. I was able to get some ammunition from him, and Pat and I arranged for a sack of flour to be sent to the mission. After two days he left for Abverdjar on his way back to Arctic Bay.

In the meantime Kutjek had gone seal hunting. He returned in a few days saying, with a very satisfied smile, that he had instead eaten a lot of very good caribou and arranged to exchange some tea and tobacco for a supply of blubber. He then went to Akudneq where Panikpakuttuk had been left with his grandparents. We also saw Qanattiaq again. He had changed his mind and decided that he would send his son to the Chesterfield hospital. I arranged a credit at the HBC for him in exchange for dog-food.

My last night at the mission was 9 February. Next day Kutjek and Panikpakuttuk arrived, bringing me a new and much appreciated pair of trousers. I wrote one or two letters to go south with any traveller headed that way, and we left for Igloolik Point before dark. Here I felt that I had really returned to Igloolik life. This was probably because I stayed with Piugatuk. He was a son of Ituksarjuat and had been living with his family in his parents' igloo at the same time that Reynold and I were there.

We were accompanied by Albert, who was an older man, and his young son, when we set off in the morning. We did not have heavy loads, but it was an exceptionally cold calm day with the temperature probably approaching -60°F. At very low temperatures snow takes on some of the characteristics of sand. Even with carefully iced runners, it was like dragging our komatiks across a desert. I walked ahead to encourage the dogs, but we made very slow progress though we re-iced more than once. After about four hours Kutjek discovered his kulitak had dropped off the komatik, and went back for it. We had continued on for half an hour when we came to an old igloo in which we camped. It was so cold we had to light the primus for part of the night because Albert and his son did not have good sleeping skins.

We had finished breakfast when Kutjek returned with his kulitak at about half past eight, so we had a second breakfast and repaired some harnesses before we left. We also acquired a stray dog, which nobody recognized. The day must have been warmer because the komatik pulled much better. The sea ice was "smoking," the graphic term used in the north for drifting snow, only a few inches high, raised by a moderate wind. Late in the afternoon Albert, who was ahead and thought he knew the way, led us into some very bad, rough ice in which we lost a part of our mud. The wind was rising when we camped and blew hard throughout the night, falling to gusts in the morning. We cut up dog-food and fed the dogs before we left, still in rough ice. Soon we came across tracks which I was told would lead us to the camp on Siurak, an island where I had stayed before and usually an easy day's journey from Igloolik, but we soon lost these tracks. Later we came across different tracks which we followed. Eventually Kutjek decided to cache our heavy walrus dog-food, and after dark he walked ahead with a lamp. It was about seven o'clock when we reached the camp at the west end of Jens Munk Island, having missed Siurak.

Five families were living in the camp in two large igloos. Here I met Kinga, who was probably the last of the Sadlermiut. He had been one of the babies adopted by the Aivilingmiut when they found the Sadlermiut dying from an epidemic in 1903. He was a little above average height, but in no significant way did he look different from the other Inuit. Our host went to collect the walrus Kutjek had cached but returned instead with two seals. Part of one was eaten raw and part was boiled. For some reason I was not given any. I suppose I should simply have helped myself. As there was no more fresh seal in the igloo, I started eating some of the very old, rather green walrus. I was then offered a caribou tongue, a great delicacy, but I did not accept it in order to establish the principle that I ate the same food as they.

Albert and his son left early next day. Kutjek mudded his komatik and then went to recover the walrus he had cached, but came back empty-handed because he could not find the cache in the drifting snow. Our host checked the local traps, returned with two foxes, and then began making a harpoon for hunting walrus. The women were all busy sewing. Three more visitors arrived. It was a fairly typical day in an Inuit camp. I noticed that the women addressed few inquiries to Kutjek, but when he was out of the igloo they peppered Panikpakuttuk with question after question about where we had been and what we were intending to do.

I had been getting worried about how fast our coal oil was being used. It did not seem sensible to use a primus to make tea where there was plenty of seal-oil and every kudliq was burning brightly. A kettle suspended over a kudliq boiled water just as well though much more slowly, and the coal oil used by a primus was needed for our journey. As well as coal oil, I had the only sugar in the camp. When the tea was made with the kudliq, I passed round the sugar; when the primus was used, I forgot. This soon helped to conserve the coal oil, and we could do without sugar when we were travelling.

The wind had died in the morning and Kutjek went to collect some walrus, I believe from Siurak. I understood that this was owed to him because the people there had used his whaleboat the previous summer. The walrus we had cached was recovered for us that day by somebody else. Towards the end of the day I had an unexpected but welcome surprise when Mino drove into the camp.

Mino was the same undistinguished, unprepossessing, and unassuming character that Reynold and I had grown to like and appreciate so much. He was difficult to describe except in negative terms, but he was always cheerful, anxious to help, and well liked by the other Inuit. He was the sort of man who had learned not to expect much out of life, but was happy to make the best of whatever it offered, cast in a supporting role not as a principal. He was wearing a large pair of polar bear–skin trousers, which were uncommon among the Iglulingmiut, and he looked more prosperous and self-confident than when I had last met him. He was driving the komatik Reynold had given him with a dog team that still included one of our old dogs. Sadly his wife, who had been blind and whom he had married about eighteen months earlier, had died, leaving him once more on his own.

I soon realized that Mino's arrival was more than just a visit; he had come to join us. I thought that perhaps Kutjek had decided he would like to have a companion. There would certainly be advantages, including greater safety, in having two teams rather than one. On the other hand it would be an additional strain on our already slender resources. When they were both absent, however, two or three of the women at the camp told me, with knowing smiles, that Mino's real objective in coming with us was to look for another wife.

We resumed our journey next day, which was calm and cloudless. Our team might have improved a little, but Mino's was very slow. Late that afternoon we came to an igloo built by Pat's party and camped there overnight. The dogs pulled no better and had to be led the next day. Kutjek was no longer using mud on his komatik. Instead he had bone covered with blood which was then iced. This did not slide as well on sea ice as mud, but would be less fragile on land.

There were two Inuit camps on Jens Munk Island and we reached the second at dusk to find Pat and his party there. I stayed in the igloo of a different Piugatuk from the one at Igloolik. The best hunter and traveller in the area, he had been the last Iglulingmiut to kill a bowhead whale. He often accompanied Jack Turner on his long missionary journeys.

Pat told me he had left the mission three days after I. His party had been making very good progress, but had stopped to hunt seal to provide oil for their lamps. He was worried because they had not yet killed any seals. His party was large and included two women, three young children, and within the next six weeks a baby. They required a standard of living much higher than mine. He had just had a narrow escape while hunting when the sea ice had suddenly given way under his feet; he had managed to heave himself onto firm ice, but his caribou-skin clothing was still being dried.

We spent a day at this camp, where I was delighted to be given a pair of very warm mittens of puppy skin and a pair of boots made from the skins of caribou legs – something I had always wanted. The skin of the leg wears much better than skin from other parts of the caribou. I decided that, since our dogs seemed to be no better than when we had left Igloolik, we might as well go straight for the land-crossing, and not bother about Kagiuyak Island. Pat had let me use some of his surplus supplies while we were at Igloolik, and I was now able to give him some of my coal oil – his need seemed greater than mine. Here our paths would diverge, he going southeast to Piling, and I northeast.

My next objective was Cape Thalbitzer where we arrived early on the second afternoon and found a camp with all the Kangirllukjuak people in two large igloos. That night we spoke with two Inuit who had often hunted in the interior of Baffin Island, and they told us where they believed there would be a way across the island. I think it was one of them who drew a map in pencil on a scrap of paper and gave it to Kutjek. We were also able to acquire a large piece of fresh bearded seal meat.

Next day we set off for what we hoped would be the beginning of the old Inuit route across Baffin Island. We had been told to follow the valley of a fairly large river, the mouth of which was marked by a small dark hill. To get there we had to cross Kangirllukjuak. The crossing took three days which was not as quick as I had hoped, partly because we went so slowly and partly because Kutjek, who always got up early, never failed to make a very late start, by which time half the day had gone. In the south we consider the evening to be the time for leisure, for repairs to equipment, and similar maintenance tasks. For Kutjek it was the morning. He probably had some very good reason, though I do not know what it was. The winter days were as cold as the nights, so sledging conditions were much the same. It may have been that he wanted to give the dogs easy days to prepare them for the more difficult conditions that lay ahead.

At our second camp an Inuk arrived with some coffee and tobacco I had left at the last camp as a present but which they thought I had forgotten. Early on the third day we could make out the small hill that was our landmark and could head straight for it. Two hours later we reached an island and soon after the mainland of Baffin Island, where a river had cut its way through a well-defined old river terrace, now about twenty feet above high water. We had been told that there were many wolves around, and the first thing we saw when we reached the river was a wolf track in the snow.

It is difficult to remember what I used to think about, walking beside the komatik day after day. Frequently, of course, I thought how nice it would be to crawl into my fur sleeping bag that night, and how many hours would pass before I could do so. I seldom thought of food during the day, though I did once I was in the igloo and out of the wind. The body has its priorities. Sometimes I would recite poetry to myself and I found I could recall long passages, mainly Shakespeare and Keats, learned years before at school. Occasionally, and unexpectedly, I would suddenly feel intensely happy. I have no idea what caused such irrational and yet unbounded euphoria. I remembered part of one of Siegfried Sassoon's war poems, "Everyone suddenly burst out singing, And I was filled with such delight as prisoned birds must find in freedom, Winging wildly across the white orchards and dark green fields." The context was completely different, but the emotion was the same.

The next day was a Sunday and we did not travel. I walked to the top of our landmark hill to take compass bearings because from this point on it would be new country, and I would have to try to map where we went. On the way I shot a hare which gave us all a good supper. Tomorrow we would be able to start inland and our dogs seemed a little stronger.

24

Through the Baffin Island Mountains
27 February – 17 March 1939

Leaving the coast to make our way inland was in some ways like sailing into uncharted waters. We were going from a known coast and the familiar environment of the sea ice to enter unmapped country. From now on I would have to make the best map I could with the resources I had – a compass and a wrist watch. This meant taking bearings whenever we changed direction, and estimating our distances by timing how long the dogs walked and how long they trotted on each heading. Every night I would make a sketch-map of our day's progress.

I had wanted an early start the first day of the crossing, but we did not set out until late in the morning after a number of irritating delays. It was, however, 27 February, close enough to the equinox that each day was about twenty minutes longer than the previous one, and daylight hours were rapidly becoming less precious.

The river was half a mile wide where it entered the sea but soon narrowed to fifty yards. Though much of its surface was icy, the going was far better than over the gravel terraces through which it had cut its wandering course. We walked beside the komatiks along the river for many miles. We could not see far, partly because the sides of the terrace rose well above us and partly because of ice mist. In these conditions it was difficult to take bearings and estimate distances correctly, although we moved so slowly that there was always time for me to stop, take and record bearings, and catch up again.

In the afternoon we came to a major bend in the river and decided to save ourselves three or four miles by climbing onto the terrace and heading northeast until we came to the river again. We had entered a U-shaped valley, cut by some ancient glacier through granite hills. One side of the valley was a sheer face of dark rock in marked contrast to the snow-covered but steep slopes along the other side. The scenery was bold and dramatic, very different from the softer, horizontal, limestone country of Jens Munk Island, Igloolik, and the other large islands of northern Foxe Basin. We made our way across rocky terrain with little snow cover for about two miles to where we could rejoin the river. The snow was good for cutting blocks here so we camped. We were about ten miles from the coast, though we had travelled much farther along the river during the day. According to my pocket aneroid barometer our short cut had taken us up to 270 feet above sea level, but our igloo was 60 feet lower and the river another 30 feet below that.

As I had hoped to take a number of photographs, I had had all the lubrication in the shutter mechanism of my camera washed out with paraffin, but it still failed to work properly in the cold. I found later that part of the mechanism itself was made of a rubber that stiffened at low temperatures, making my camera useless until the spring.

We set off rather earlier next day. Visibility was poor because it was snowing, though not heavily. Descending to the river we continued northeast along it, across a small lake, and onto a large lake, which we followed to its end. Here the main course of the river lay to the northwest. We tried to follow it but we were soon in a narrow rocky ravine, an effective barrier to any dog team, and had to turn back. We could see no feasible route to the northeast where the lake appeared to be enclosed by high hills.

Kutjek now brought out the piece of paper he had been given at the last Inuit camp we had visited, and we could all study the rough map drawn on it. It showed a heart-shaped lake northwest of the lake we were on, with the river then resuming its course to the northeast. Our problem was how to get from the one lake to the other. The map was not of much help for this. The man who had drawn it probably knew the country largely from hunting caribou on foot in the summer. The most important landmarks he had indicated were the dark rock faces of some of the hills, which could be seen from many miles away, where rivers and lakes were often hidden in valleys. He must have told Kutjek there was a possible route to the upper lake, but we did not know where it lay.

We decided to try a small valley, leading into the lake we were on from the northwest, to see if we could work our way round to the heart-shaped lake on the map. Our first problem was getting off our lake. We had been moving quite well on the river and lake all day. Now we had to climb up a steep bank, with all the dogs hitched to each komatik in turn, carrying some things ourselves. The snow rarely covered the rocks in the valley and when we came to a suitable snowbank at dusk we camped. We had risen about two hundred feet above the lake.

The next day proved very disappointing. We continued along the valley, but decided it was veering too much to the west, so we tried a smaller valley leading north. It proved too steep and we returned to the first valley. By the end of the day it was taking us southwest towards the coast, the opposite direction to what we wanted. While we were camping I walked to the top of one of the hills, a thousand feet or more in height, and away to the northeast I could see the heart-shaped lake that was our objective. There was no easy way to reach it.

In the morning Kutjek set out on foot to look for a possible route while the rest of us loaded the komatiks. When he returned he took us up a very steep valley. We then crossed a watershed at a height of 640 feet by my aneroid, but I think it was higher. We continued to the north and then to the east down another steep and rocky valley. The going was very difficult and we were not sorry to camp when we reached a small lake, knowing the steepest part of the valley was well behind us.

Though the way ahead looked easier, our prospects of completing the crossing of Baffin Island had become rather slim. At the end of the fourth day we were little farther from the Foxe Basin coast than we had been at the end of the first day. We had used up an appreciable amount of our supplies and dog-food, and it was poor consolation to think that this had made our loads lighter. I knew the distance from Foxe Basin to the general trend of the coast in Baffin Bay was about 150 miles, but the crossing could be up to 50 miles shorter than that if we reached the sea near the head of one of the long fiords that penetrate the coast. We had covered less than a tenth of the land-crossing. When we reached the sea there would be at least another 100 miles along the coast to Pond Inlet though there was sure to be an Inuit camp somewhere on the way.

The following day gave us an easy mile or two descending about a hundred feet from our camp to the heart-shaped lake we had been trying to reach, and in not much more than another hour we had crossed it to rejoin the river. We then came to a chain of very small lakes leading north-northeast followed by a short stretch of river through what appeared to be a small moraine. The river probably ran fast here in summer because ice had built up along its banks. A larger lake then took us six or seven miles in the same direction and we camped after another mile of river. The day's journey had been much more satisfactory and we had progressed some thirteen miles in the right direction. That night the dogs broke into the snow annexe and ate some of our walrus dog-food before we could get them out. This was not a real loss; the food simply reached its destination sooner.

Another mile or so of river brought us to a longer lake. Kutjek headed across it towards a valley that I thought would take us too far to the east. We all looked at Kutjek's map. Mino and I were sure he was wrong. Kutjek himself must have started to have some doubts because when we reached the shore he said he would walk ahead while we made a hot drink. He returned nearly three hours later, admitting he had been wrong but bringing back two hares he had shot, which made his walk well worthwhile. We had no other fresh meat left except a very small piece of bearded seal.

We continued along the lake which ran slightly west of north to its end, where a large river entered from the northeast. Here we camped. Though we had not gone far that day we were much more confident we were on the route that Kutjek had been advised to follow.

The valley we entered next morning was all we could have wanted. The river connected a succession of long rather narrow lakes all heading northeast and providing splendid going. The character of the country had again changed. We had risen to a plateau about a thousand feet above sea level. The lakes ran between low hills, with none of the towering dark cliffs and short steep valleys that had provided dramatic scenery and difficult sledging during the past six days. It was a Sunday but there was no suggestion of making it a day of rest. It seemed the Sabbath was observed more rigorously at a camp than on a journey. I thought the bitter wind was blowing from an ice cap, of which we could see no sign. We spent a long day walking by the side of the komatiks, and had covered more than twenty miles, our best day yet, before we camped on a long lake. While we were building the igloo, Panikpakuttuk saw a hare, which Kutjek shot. We had finished our last meat at breakfast, apart from very old walrus, which had been intended for the dogs but had become the major part of our diet. We still had a few pounds of flour, rolled oats, and beans to provide variety.

The going was even better next day, with the valley continuing in the same direction. The dogs started to trot a little, something they had not done for days, and we crossed the tracks of a few caribou. The cold wind had abated and, late in the afternoon, Kutjek stopped, convinced that there were caribou nearby, though I do not think he had actually seen any. The light was failing when he and Mino walked ahead. Panikpakuttuk and I saw something moving on the slope of a nearby hill. It was too small for a caribou and I think it must have been an unusually dark wolf or a wolverine, which are rarely seen in Baffin Island. Some time later we heard two shots and four caribou dashed across the lake ahead of us. We could only just restrain the dogs from charging after them. Kutjek and Mino returned a few minutes later, having shot two of six caribou they had seen. We were a happy and satisfied group in the igloo that night.

This seemed a good area to replenish our larder so a day was spent in hunting. Kutjek and Mino set out after caribou, Kutjek going ahead to the next large lake. I walked in the area near the camp, where I came across Mino. He had not got very far before sitting down for a smoke. Though the hills were becoming higher and much of the ground was stony, there was more vegetation there than at lower altitudes and signs of animals were more frequent. Ptarmigan were plentiful and I saw a hare but no caribou. I have good eyesight, but I always found that Inuit could detect caribou at far greater distances than I. Kutjek returned at dusk, having killed five caribou. Our situation had improved greatly over the past five days. We were more than fifty miles closer to our destination, we had plenty of food, and our dogs were in better shape.

In the morning we moved on to where Kutjek had shot the caribou. It seemed a land of plenty. We saw a blue fox, which Kutjek shot, and two white foxes. We disturbed two or three flocks of ptarmigan and were continually crossing caribou, wolf, and fox tracks. We camped by the side of a large lake where there was good snow for the igloo. The night was cold and clear.

It was still dark when Kutjek shook me awake. I lifted myself up and hit my head on the snow house roof. When I had fallen asleep it had been three or four feet above me. The whole house was sagging in. We dressed as quickly as we could in the small space left, cut our way out of the house, and started removing our equipment from it, beating the snow carefully off the sleeping bags and other skins. Everything was melting and as the sun rose it seemed like summer. We packed snow around the runners of the komatiks to protect the mud and ice shoeing from thawing in the direct sunlight and dried anything that was wet, while Panikpakuttuk made our breakfast in the open. There was a slight breeze and the sky was still clear. In an hour or so it began to grow colder and by noon everything was freezing hard. The temperature must have risen and then dropped at least 50°F within twelve hours. We were back in midwinter, but with a thin crust of ice on the snow.

I do not know what could have caused such a sudden, short, and very marked change in temperature in the middle of Baffin Island at an altitude of at least 1000 feet on the night of 8 March, and I have heard of no comparable occurrence. In some way a bubble of warm air may have moved several hundred miles north from the North Atlantic. The nearest station where the temperature was read daily was Pond Inlet, about 150 miles to the north, and nothing unusual was recorded there. On that day Pat reached Piling, 150 miles south of us, and wrote in his diary that a cold northwest breeze sprang up in the evening, a wind that continued strong the next day. We were in the foothills of the range of mountains that form the east coast of Baffin Island, with heights often well over 5000 feet, and we had had no strong winds.

Fortunately, the thaw had not lasted long enough to have had much effect on the going. Pulling the komatiks through a thick crust would have been very hard on the dogs. In two hours we reached the end of the lake, above which was a much smaller lake. The river entered this lake from the southeast, which would lead us away from the sea, so we all tried to find some way of continuing to the north or northeast.

I walked to the top of a small hill but all the country appeared to be difficult. While there I found I was in the middle of a congregation of arctic hares. Wherever I looked I could see several despite their snow-white colour. I counted forty without moving my head, and shot two for supper. After returning to the komatiks, I built an igloo. Kutjek and Mino came back later, still uncertain of the route we should take.

Early in the morning Kutjek set off on foot and some hours later returned saying he had found a way that would lead us to the sea. A strong cold wind had sprung up and we decided to spend the rest of the day where we were. Kutjek went on another walk in the afternoon to determine which was the better of two possible routes he had found. He returned with a hare and said he thought the sea might be only two or three hours away. I was surprised as well as excited because we had not yet crossed the watershed between Foxe Basin and Baffin Bay.

We continued our journey in the morning going up a valley that passed near the hill where I had seen so many hares. We then crossed the watershed to the head of a terrible valley, steep, full of stones of every size, and with hardly any snow. All the rest of the day we toiled down it, always thinking we might be able to see the sea once we got around the next moraine. We had covered about four miles along the valley when we camped, wondering whether we should have kept on a little longer. Kutjek was rather quiet. We had been travelling for several hours and our field of vision was still limited to the steep sides of the valley, and the boulders that lay ahead. There was always the possibility, which at times seemed very real, that our route would be blocked completely in some way, such as by a precipice, and we dreaded the thought of having to return up this horrible valley.

We made an early start next day and soon came to a more open area. From here we could see a wide and deep valley far below us. Within it a frozen river ran northeast and could lead only into Anaularealing or one of the other fiords that would take us to Baffin Bay.

We had first to make our way down an almost perpendicular slope, partly covered with snow, to reach the river below. At the worst part we threw the caribou meat over a cliff to lighten the

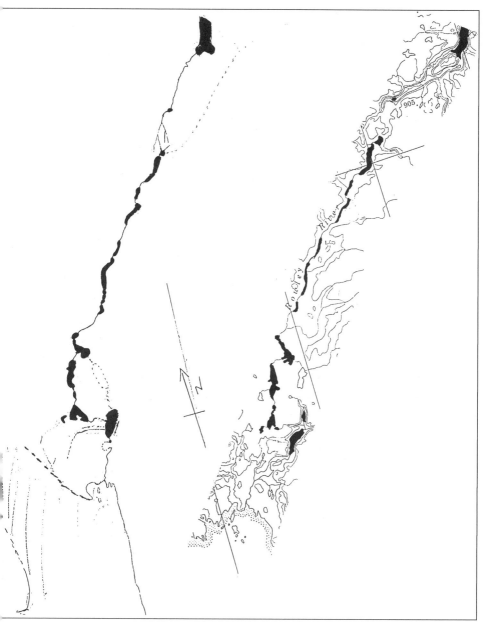

Map 9   Comparison of map made by author with compass and watch on journey across
Baffin Island and modern map made from air photography

komatiks and watched it drop freely and then roll safely to the bottom. We treated our sleeping bags and anything else that was unlikely to break in the same way. We then took everything off Mino's komatik, turned it upside down, and let his dogs pull it that way to preserve its mud shoeing. Our dog whips were wound round the runners of the other komatik, which had bone shoeing, to act as brakes. Even then the komatiks kept overrunning the dogs and pulling them along rather than their pulling the komatiks. In this way we descended the slope in a series of traverses, the komatiks coming to a halt every few yards, and we scrambling down after them. To our surprise and great relief everything survived this treatment, and we retrieved all we had thrown over the precipice.

After travelling four or five miles along the river we reached a small lake, crossed it, and continued for about another seven miles before we camped, still without reaching the sea, but thinking it must be very near. We had descended over 1600 feet from the watershed, according to my barometer.

Terraces lined both sides of the valley, which became much broader next day and was filled with gravel through which the river meandered from side to side. To preserve our komatik shoeing we had to keep to the river though it was frustrating to follow large bends for perhaps half a mile in order to advance to some point only fifty yards or so farther down the valley.

Well into the afternoon we finally reached the sea ice at the head of a long fiord, which looked like a Scottish loch and was undoubtedly Anaularealing. We were again in the known world, and we laughed as we looked ahead over the smooth ice, back to the valley and mountains we had just left, and then at one another. We were all enjoying the satisfaction and relief of accomplishment.

25

Anaularealing to Pond Inlet

17 March – 23 March 1939

The dogs seemed as happy as we were to be back on the sea ice, which had only a thin cover of hard snow giving excellent going. For the first time in days they broke into a trot and their tails, which had been dragging in the snow so long, rose and began to wave in the air, while we were able to ride on the komatiks again. After more than two hours we saw a small piece of old ice that had frozen into the fiord, in the lee of which we found the snow drift to be about a foot deep. Here we could cut horizontal blocks for the igloo that Kutjek soon built.

We were relaxed and happy that we had succeeded in finding a way across Baffin Island. I would be able to put one line across more than 50,000 square miles of Baffin Island where only the coasts had been mapped. My companions would have tales of an unusual journey with a strange fellow traveller to add to the local folklore. It was just the sort of story that Mino would enjoy telling. We must have followed the traditional but long-disused Inuit route most of the way, but we had probably gone wrong twice, once on the second day when we could not find the way out of the first long lake, and again where we had crossed the watershed. Both these sections of the crossing had been much more difficult than anywhere else, though there may well have been no easier way.

In the nineteenth century, whaling ships had sometimes sailed into the fiords of the east coast of Baffin Island, but what they had found did not appear on any chart. It was not until the summer of 1937 that an expedition from Cambridge University had visited this part of the coast in a Norwegian sealer and mapped the fiords, including Anaularealing, which they had provisionally named Glenroy Fiord. They, like me, had been struck by its resemblance to Scotland. I had brought a copy of the excellent map they had made from the deck of their ship, and I had no difficulty in finding our position on it.

As we continued northeast along the fiord next morning the character of the country changed. The hills became more rugged, and the steep shores and high terraces on both sides gave way to vertical cliffs, their height increasing as we progressed. On top of the cliffs, patches of blue glacial ice began to appear.

After about twenty miles Anaularealing turned north and the scenery became still more spectacular. The fiord, little over a mile wide, was lined with cliffs of three or four thousand feet rising sheer from the sea ice. Glaciers hung down steep valleys and sometimes reached the sea. We were cutting right through some of the highest mountains of the east coast of Baffin Island. The fiord we were following had been carved by ice from a long-vanished ice sheet over north Baffin Island and, alone among the fiords of the region, cut right through the high coastal range. We had seen no ice caps or glaciers during our crossing of Baffin Island and until we were well along Anaularealing.

Kutjek's dogs were now in better shape than they had been since leaving Repulse, and Mino's were not far behind. In the afternoon Anaularealing widened to a gulf into which other fiords entered, and we came across komatik tracks. After another mile or so we saw a team and raced forward to meet it. The driver must have been greatly surprised when two strange komatiks appeared coming from Anaularealing. His name was Inuya and he led us to his camp where there were two igloos. Almost all the other men were away hunting or travelling, but they had left the camp well provided. There was certainly no shortage of seal-oil as the lamps were burning brightly and the igloos seemed very warm to us. We slept late our first day here and the women dried our clothing and sleeping skins.

The people in this area were closely related to the Iglulingmiut, many of whom they met each spring when both groups went to the post at Pond Inlet to trade the foxes they had trapped during the winter. Life at their camps was much the same, the men hunting and trapping when they could, and the women tending the kudliqs and the children, while always softening or sewing skins.

The children played and learned by watching. One game I saw at several camps always made me uneasy. A teenager, usually a boy, would loop a piece of skin-line around his neck and tighten it until he became light-headed. I never saw a boy tighten a loop about another child's neck, or lose complete consciousness, but I was always apprehensive that this could happen when no adult was present.

That night the wind rose and next day was blowing hard with drifting too severe for travel. Inuya said we would run into both soft snow and rough ice on our way to Pond Inlet, but our dogs had improved so much that we were not worried and the wind that was holding us at the camp would harden the snow. Before we left Kutjek told me that, despite what had seemed a disproportionate number of women at this camp, Mino had not succeeded in finding a wife.

The next camp in the direction of Pond Inlet was a long day away. Around midday we converged with another team. The driver, whose name was Merqusaq, was on his way from his camp north of Clyde River to visit his father at Pond Inlet. Late in the evening we reached three igloos sheltered in a small bay in what is now known as Buchan Gulf. This too seemed a prosperous camp with plenty of meat and skins. Seal were abundant in these fiords where they were killed at their breathing holes. Several hunters were using the harpoon guns devised by Finley McInnes, who had been the RCMP corporal at Pond Inlet some years before he and Jack Tibbitt had made their long walk from Churchill to Arctic Bay. After a very good supper of seal liver I fell asleep while everybody else was still talking. Every woman in the camp seemed to have a husband, so we would again be a party of four, three men and a boy, when we left.

I woke early and looked around the igloo, realizing for the first time that I was not in a normal snow house. I could see some large stones that were cantilevered to support the roof. The walls must also have been stone but they were lined with skins and canvas as in many large snow houses. Nor had the house appeared any different outside, being almost drifted over. Looking around, I thought I could well be in the Thule culture. In Milne Inlet, two years earlier, I had seen a Thule stone house which had been occupied the previous winter, and I had begun to doubt the then commonly held theory that the modern Inuit were a different people from the Thule Eskimos. I became more confident they were the same people, a view now generally accepted.

From this camp we drove below the magnificent cliffs on the north side of Buchan Gulf as they gradually changed in alignment from northeast to northwest, bringing us out of a complex of deep fiords and into Baffin Bay. Continuing along this spectacular coast lined with vertical cliffs rarely less than two thousand feet high, I realized how lucky we had been to find what must have been one of the very few places where it was possible to descend to the sea. We could easily have come to a slope too dangerous to attempt and have had to retrace our tracks across Baffin Island.

During the afternoon Merqusaq, who had left later than we had, caught up to us. He brought our kudliq and one or two other things we had forgotten. We knew there was rough ice off Nova Zembla Island so we decided to keep to the coast and go inside Round Island and Nova Zembla. This would take us into the entrance of Coutts Inlet, where the ice was believed to be easier. Merqusaq was taking the shorter but rougher route outside Nova Zembla, so we parted before camping.

We camped in rough ice but it was smooth between Nova Zembla and the mainland, nor was the snow as soft as we had been warned. The sun was now making us warm in the middle of the day though it became much colder as the afternoon wore on. We had to camp before dark because we had broken our lamp and had no candles. By then we were well out of Coutts Inlet.

We set off early in the morning again running into rough ice at first, but we found tracks that led us along a good route and gave us a nice dog whip that had fallen off somebody's komatik. In the distance we could make out the mountains of Bylot Island. When we camped we hoped the next day would take us to Igak-juak, a camp just east of Pond Inlet, where most of the Inuit in the area lived.

We were getting ready in the morning when Merqusaq appeared. He was faster than we were but he had not travelled the day after we parted – a Sunday. We drank tea together before he left. We followed but soon found ourselves in rougher ice than we had anticipated and had to re-ice the runners twice in the first hour or so. The strait between Bylot Island and Baffin Island was notorious for storms, and as we approached it in the afternoon we could feel the wind rising. When we saw an old snow house we decided to camp early rather than face strong winds at the end of the day.

It was blowing a gale when we left next morning. The wind was quite warm, but became terrific when we reached the narrowest part of the strait. The dogs could scarcely move and we had to lead them in visibility of two yards at best. I had never tried to travel in such a storm, and I kept getting blown away from the komatik. We were continually losing Mino and his team and, as we could not see well enough to follow old komatik tracks, found ourselves again in rough ice. I was wondering how much longer we could keep on and where we would camp, when conditions began to improve. An hour later we passed Albert Harbour in a dead calm.

Beyond the foot of Mount Herodier we reached Igakjuak where there were two or three wooden shacks, a legacy of the whaling days, in addition to several snow houses. Kutjek found one of his sisters was living here with her family, and we spent the night in her igloo. Fortunately we still had plenty of caribou left for the family reunion. In the morning we soon covered the remaining few miles to the settlement of Pond Inlet.

Pond Inlet to Igloolik

23 March – 16 May 1939

We reached Pond Inlet on 23 March, more than a month earlier than I had arrived two winters before, from the opposite direction, and again to the surprise of those who lived there. Kutjek, Mino, and Panikpakuttuk had friends to stay with, and I went to the Hudson's Bay Company. The post manager was now Alex Smith who seemed to have an intuitive understanding of everything I wanted. He invited me to sleep at the post, produced a bottle of rum, and asked the three other white men in the settlement to share it. They were Constable Len Corey, of the RCMP, and my old friends Father Daniélo and Brother Volant from the Roman Catholic mission. Constable Earnie Leach was away on a patrol to Arctic Bay and Igloolik.

It did not take long to learn the changes at Pond Inlet since my previous visit. Both members of the RCMP detachment were new. The previous summer Father Cochard had been at Arctic Bay planning a new mission when he had been taken ill and had been flown to the Chesterfield hospital by Father Schulte. Maurice Flint was on a long winter journey, taking a sick boy from Pond Inlet to the hospital at Pangnirtung, so the Anglican mission was empty. I was very sorry to learn that I would not again see Tom Koudnak, who could remember the whaling days better than anyone else and had remained highly respected in the community. The previous winter he had come to the settlement to say that his wife had died. "She been pretty good wife to me pretty long time. Maybe now I die too." Within a few weeks he had joined her.

Alex Smith told me that as a boy he had always wanted to go to sea, so he had trained for the merchant marine in England.

His first voyage was to South America and he had been seasick all the way there and all the way back. He then decided to join the HBC because he would find the sea frozen most of the year, a change of careers he had not regretted. During the afternoon we were joined by Jack Ford, the HBC clerk, who had come back in a rising wind from a visit to Bylot Island. He was a nephew of Sam Ford, whom I had met when he was manager of the Southampton Island post and who had now moved to Clyde River. Jack had spent some time at posts in the Western Arctic and was the only man in the east who drove his dogs in a tandem hitch and secured them with a chain when they were not in harness, common practices in the west.

In such company the evening passed quickly. The small white population of the Eastern Arctic was like an extended family. Everybody knew or knew something about everyone else, and visitors would add to the pool of knowledge. It was after two o'clock in the morning when the party broke up. I understood this was the normal bedtime at Pond Inlet. I enjoyed a long and relaxed sleep.

Having been out of touch so long with what was happening "outside," I found I did not have the same intense interest as the rest of the settlement in the ominous developments in Europe being reported by the BBC. I heard that, ten days before my arrival, Czechoslovakia had dissolved and the Nazis had occupied Bohemia and Moravia. Madrid had just surrendered and within a couple of days the totalitarian forces of General Franco had claimed complete victory in Spain. It seemed a different world and a different life – one that had no immediate relevance to the north – where the situation was sure to have changed again before it could affect me personally. "The outside" did not disturb the eleven halcyon days I spent at Pond Inlet.

Rather than discussing international affairs, my main preoccupation was eating. According to the HBC scales I put on thirteen pounds, which must have replaced most of what I had lost since leaving Repulse Bay. My only problem was occasional indigestion, which was not surprising and not severe enough to affect my appetite.

Those at Pond Inlet enjoyed one another's company, and most evenings we at the HBC visited the RCMP or the Catholic missionaries, or they came to us. After a meal we usually played bridge as we listened to the gloomy news from Europe, the *Northern Messenger*, and any local traffic that was on the air. I was told there had been one or two messages for me during the winter but nobody could remember what they were, and I never found out who had sent them. We heard that Jack Turner had reached Fort Ross and listened to Cape Dorset sending a message from Tom Manning to his parents.

The trapping season was ending, and each day brought some Inuit group from nearby camps to trade their foxes. It was too early to expect the Iglulingmiut or other people from faraway places. However, a few days after my arrival Earnie Leach returned from his patrol. He said that all was well at Arctic Bay, Igloolik, and the camps he had visited. He brought no news of Pat Baird, so I thought he had probably reached Clyde Inlet and might arrive at Pond Inlet any day.

I had of course to return to Igloolik to excavate during the summer. I decided I would go first to Arctic Bay to buy supplies as it was an easier journey to Igloolik from there than from Pond Inlet. Kutjek, Mino, and I would have to take everything we needed for the summer, and possibly the next winter, from Arctic Bay to Igloolik. There were two ways to Arctic Bay. One was to cut across the land from Milne Inlet to the head of Adams Sound, and the other was to go the whole way on sea ice down Navy Board Inlet to Lancaster Sound and then up Admiralty Inlet. As I had already crossed by land I thought we would take the sea ice route. It was said to be a longer but easier way, though we should expect rough ice in Lancaster Sound.

Before I left I made a map for the RCMP of the route we had followed across Baffin Island and gave them a short account of my activities. In return they gave me a hot bath, one bringing a series of kettles of hot water, while the other scrubbed my back. I also copied the Cambridge map of the fiords between Pond and Clyde Inlet for them and the HBC, which was much more detailed and accurate than anything they had.

There was no problem in preparing for the next stage of my travels. Father Daniélo gave me about forty pounds of fish and also a large bag of frozen pork and beans, prepared by Brother Volant, who was a first-class cook. Alex Smith was also getting ready for a journey. He was going to Clyde River and we could do our pre-journey cooking together. The RCMP gave us a memorable farewell supper.

Alex and I left Pond Inlet at the same time, soon after breakfast on 3 April, but in opposite directions. Kutjek and Mino were not sorry to get away. They said so many people had arrived in the past few days with whom they had shared their food that there had been little for them, and Mino had again failed to find a suitable wife.

We soon had heavy snow and then a strong following wind. The route was well travelled, and after we turned north up Navy Board Inlet there were several Inuit camps, where we stopped to drink tea or spend the night. My most vivid memory of the journey is of a raven we saw and heard as we entered Lancaster Sound. It was circling and calling in a cold and cloudless sky, hazy with ice crystals. Black, when all else was white, raucous against the silence, it seemed to defy the arctic winter. The rough ice in Lancaster Sound was easier than we had expected and we found more Inuit camps in Admiralty Inlet. We reached Arctic Bay after eight days, one of which had been spent hunting.

There was no light in the HBC dwelling when we arrived rather late on 11 April, so I slept with the Inuit and walked over to the post in the morning. Here I surprised Alan Scott, who was reading the thermometers. The radio transmitter had made Arctic Bay an important meteorological station: it was the farthest north on the North American continent from which daily reports could be received.

Alan took me to meet his wife, a Scottish girl the *Nascopie* had brought to join him the previous summer in what was claimed by the *Beaver*, the HBC quarterly journal, to have been the most northerly wedding service ever held in the British Empire. I was glad to accept their kind invitation to stay with them. Bill Ford was away but returned during the day. It must have been a lonely winter for Mrs Scott. There were no other white people at Arctic Bay and none of the few Inuit living there spoke more than a few words of English. Alan and Bill had the interest of running a trading post, but she must have found time lying heavy on her hands. I am sure the arrival in July of the most northerly white baby in the British Empire completely changed that.

My stay at Arctic Bay proved to be longer than I had planned. I had to buy my own supplies for the summer and possibly longer, and to pay Kutjek. The going rate for a man with a dog team was then two and a half dollars a day, but it was more advantageous to Kutjek if I bought all the things he wanted and then

gave them to him. I could buy from the Hudson's Bay Company
at a substantially discounted price and the dollars Kutjek had
earned bought much more for him in this way. I forget what arrangement I made with Mino, who had travelled with us for his
own purposes, but both Kutjek and he seemed very satisfied when
we left the store.

A partial eclipse of the sun occurred on 19 April. The day was
very bright and the sun could only be viewed through several
pairs of sunglasses. We felt the temperature drop sharply as the
sun became hidden. Many days earlier I had told Kutjek to expect
the eclipse. Inuit from Agu and other distant camps were beginning to arrive to trade at the post, and I hope he gained prestige
as a prophet.

As we would need dog-food for the journey to Igloolik, Kutjek
spent several days hunting seal. Mino continued his own hunt.
A recent widow apparently met his specifications, but he may have
fallen short of hers. Most of the nuances of the situation escaped
me, and I was never fully aware of the current state of play or
of how far Kutjek's role as an advocate extended. All I could do
was wonder whether our journey would be resumed with or without Mino and with or without a bride.

Alan Scott, who was a good radio operator, sent a message for
me to my mother saying that I was well and was returning to
Igloolik.

We left during the afternoon of 22 April. There were only three
of us, including Panikpakuttuk looking very smart in a new duffle
parka. I thought this meant that Mino's search had been successful, but not long after we had camped that night he rejoined us,
still single. He had been looking for a missing dog. We stayed
in camp next day while Kutjek returned to Arctic Bay. I did not
like to inquire why, but I think he went to ask again about a
wife for Mino, who was apparently very shy. Kutjek, a respected
hunter, could plead his case for him. Mino, though in no way
handsome, was easy to get on with, resilient, loyal, and able to
make the best of any situation. He needed and deserved a good
wife. While Kutjek was on this mission we enjoyed a visit by
Ujaraaluk, who had excavated with me two years earlier.

I had expected a quick, comfortable, and easy journey to Igloolik,
but I was wrong. The next day, very cold for late April, took
us to Iqalulik. The day after brought a savage wind so we started

late and camped early. It continued to blow, though the temperature rose, and a very long day was needed to reach Ivalak's camp, where we had expected to find plenty of dog-food but were disappointed. The next day was blowing too hard to travel or hunt. I saw my first snow bunting of the year sheltering in the lee of an igloo.

Here I visited Udloriaq, reputed to be the oldest person in north Baffin Island. Her father and mother, or perhaps it had been an uncle and aunt, were said to have met Parry and Lyon during the winter of 1822-23, and all the old men remembered her as having been an old woman when they were boys. One man said to me: "She is indeed old. Even the land has grown up since she was a girl." He then explained that she had remembered when the sea came up to the igloo where her parents had lived. It had been at a site that was now half a mile inland.

Udloriaq was living with one of her many descendants and was sitting on the bed in front of her kudliq. She had a welcoming smile as she laid aside her pipe to stretch out her hand. I was told that her sight and hearing were fading, but time had touched her gently. Her eyes were bright though they seemed to be looking into the past rather than the present. I too felt I was looking into the past because in the soft light of the kudliq the wrinkles faded and I saw a serene and beautiful woman. I realized that among the Inuit the old people enjoyed love and care in full measure. She had become a spectator of life rather than an actor, and she was obviously enjoying the show.

The wind was still fierce when we left Ivalak's camp and the temperature had again risen. We had hoped to reach the next camp that day but, thinking we might miss it in the storm, we built an igloo for the night. By morning everything was thawing and soft snow was falling. In an hour or two we reached the camp, where a friend of Kutjek called Kudlak lived. Here I met an Iglulingmiut who told me that Pat Baird had not been able to find a way across Baffin Island from Piling to Clyde Inlet. He had had to turn back and follow the route to Pond Inlet that Jack Turner and I had travelled in 1937, and was intending to spend the summer on Bylot Island.

The snow had become so soft overnight that we decided to spend the day sleeping and to set off late in the afternoon when travelling conditions should be better. However by then it was blowing so hard we could not see to move and we had to wait for better light. In the morning a more serious problem faced us. The dogs had managed to get at the harnesses and traces during the night and little remained of them. We spent the day sewing new harnesses and Kudlak left for Arctic Bay to bring us some rope to replace the traces. The gloomy situation improved later in the day when Mino caught a seal and a man arrived from Igloolik who could spare us a piece of walrus and some skin-line.

We sewed harnesses for another day before Kutjek, Panikpakuttuk, and I set out at night, leaving Mino at Kudlak's camp. We had a single thick piece of rope as a central trace with the dogs attached to it individually in what was known as the Nome hitch. This worked better than expected and in two hours or so we camped where the sealing was said to be good. Here I started to make traces out of the skin-line we had been given, while Kutjek went sealing without success. The wind had risen again and next day it was blowing still harder. Snow penetrated everywhere, to melt and soak most of our possessions.

We moved a short distance to be nearer where Kutjek wanted to hunt, but again there were no seals. The next day it was drifting so badly that all we could do was sit in the igloo waiting for better weather. I had picked up a few books, mostly Jane Austen and Dickens, at Arctic Bay, intending to read them during the summer. They helped to fill up such periods of enforced idleness since I did not want to spend all the time asking what must seem to my companions to be silly questions, and I had already learned all the string figures that Panikpakuttuk knew.

Next day was fine and we continued our journey. Several seals were lying on the ice, though they seemed very shy when Kutjek hunted them without success. After we had built our igloo that night we noticed a tent in the distance, so we went to se whose it was. We found Father Cochard with one of Ituksarjuat's sons, on their way to Arctic Bay. He had recovered completely and had spent some time at the missions at Repulse and Igloolik en route. We learned we had missed Ituksarjuat and Ataguttaaluk in the drifting snow.

Asleep in our own igloo that night we were awakened by Mino who arrived very late and with an obvious air of accomplishment. He had been delayed because Kudlak had taken a long time going to Arctic Bay and back, but he had brought a box of supplies that I had asked Alan Scott to send me, two seals, and the rope, which was no longer important because we had been given some skin-line which makes better though more edible traces. Mino was suffering from snow-blindness but not badly.

The four of us continued next day, meeting more Iglulingmiut on their way to trade at Arctic Bay. The following day we reached the end of Admiralty Inlet, and were half-way over the land-crossing when Kutjek saw a caribou which he and Mino went to hunt. They did not return until noon the next day, having killed two caribou. We could afford to give the dogs two good meals, one that night and another in the morning.

Warm weather had returned, making the snow soft and the going slow, so we travelled all day and all night before camping in an old igloo. After a good daytime sleep we left at night, reaching the sea in under two hours. Early in the morning we met two Iglulingmiut and exchanged some of our caribou meat for walrus. We continued along Gifford Fiord throughout the day and had reached its end when we camped at night on the frozen sea.

Next day Kutjek took us first to the Baffin coast to collect a boat he wanted. He was not feeling well so we camped an hour or so later. In the morning Mino, Panikpakuttuk, and I went seal hunting, leaving Kutjek in bed. We killed a seal and gave the dogs a feed before Kutjek got up, saying he felt rather better.

We set out for Igloolik shortly before midnight, met rough ice just to the north of the island, but found a good way through it and crossed the isthmus to reach Ikpiakjuk and the mission late in the afternoon. It was 16 May; the journey from Arctic Bay, which I had hoped would last little more than a week, had taken twenty-five days, and I had only *War and Peace* left for summer reading.

A new island

16 May – 8 June 1939

Father Trébaol met us outside the mission and after a cup of tea Kutjek, Panikpakuttuk, and Mino left for Akudneq, where Kutjek's wife was living. The father was alone and, seeing how tired I was, suggested I have a good sleep. I woke up at noon the next day, fifteen hours later, much the better for it. Father Bazin, who had been at Igloolik Point, returned during the day with four dog teams to carry lumber for a small cabin he was intending to build there. The three of us spent a happy evening talking together in a mixture of English, Inuktitut, and French. They brought me up to date with events at Igloolik during the winter and I told them about those I had met on my travels and what I had learned. I also added my latest news, only a month old, of the deteriorating situation in Europe.

The next day was Ascension Day when the mission followed a Sunday routine and a number of Inuit came in for the service. Among them was Aipilik, the first Iglulingmiut Reynold and I had met when he had crawled into our igloo on our journey to Igloolik. He was now a young man and said he would come and help me excavate during the summer.

Snow still lay on the land and the ground was hard frozen, so archaeological work would not be possible for two or three weeks at least. This might give me time to resolve a question that had been at the back of my mind. Most of our crossing of Baffin Island in the winter had been along a frozen river, but there had been a short stretch between two lakes where the river ran in a deep ravine, too rocky and steep for travel by komatik. We had had to make a long detour. My barometer had indicated that the upper lake was nearly four hundred feet higher than the

lower lake, and I thought there was probably an impressive waterfall in the few miles between them. I had already discussed
with Kutjek the possibility of making a quick journey to the river
and back. He said he would come with me but he wanted to take
his wife and family. I could understand this as he had not seen
them since January, but it would mean a much slower journey
and I did not have that much time. Eventually he agreed the two
of us would travel alone and I said I would then give him a rifle
he wanted.

Kutjek came back to the mission on 21 May, and we left early
the following afternoon. Conditions were good for travelling and
we camped on Siorarsuk at the entrance to Murray Maxwell Bay.
We continued to make very satisfactory progress in a strong wind
the next day, stopping sometimes to hunt if we saw a seal sleeping
on the ice conveniently close to us. Once I jumped off the komatik
to land right in a seal-hole. Fortunately I had a spare pair of sealskin boots. We camped at the east end of Jens Munk Island. In
the morning I shot four ptarmigan which arrived nicely in time
for breakfast.

We had not seen any Inuit as most people were away on their
long spring trading journeys to Pond Inlet or Arctic Bay but, soon
after passing Iglorsuit, a camp near Cape Thalbitzer, we met a
team and found the driver was a man to whom we had been
asked to deliver a large box. With a lighter load and no longer
obligated to visit his camp, we continued along much the same
route we had followed in February, camping on one of the small
islands in Kangirllukjuak, not far from the mouth of the river
that had led us across Baffin Island.

Next day was very warm, with standing water on the river ice.
We could not take the short cut we had followed in the winter
because the river terraces were now almost bare of snow so we
had to keep to the wet and meandering course of the river. When
we reached the lower lake Kutjek saw two caribou. Within a couple
of hours he had shot and skinned them, and we could continue.
As we had expected, we found too many rocks to proceed by komatik more than a few hundred yards along the narrow ravine
through which the river entered the lake, and I continued on foot
while Kutjek hunted.

The ravine became narrower and steeper as I made my way
very gingerly through the rocks that had fallen from the cliffs
that rose as high walls on both sides. My path was slow and

slippery and some of the rocks looked suspiciously like recent arrivals. It was not long before I heard rocks falling in the ravine ahead and I began to feel rather uncomfortable. The warmth of the day would certainly bring down many more rocks, and I did not like the thought of being even a random target. I checked my barometer which I had set at the bottom of the ravine and saw that I had climbed over two hundred feet. I found it easy to persuade myself that, if there were a waterfall, it would be much less impressive than I had hoped. The chances of being struck by a falling rock were probably low, but it seemed a silly and lonely place to be brave, so I retreated to where I had left the komatik. Kutjek soon joined me.

I considered going to the upper lake and following the river down from there, but I decided it would not be worth the time it would take. There was so little snow on the land that sledging would be slow and difficult. I thought we would instead go south to the island called Kagiuyak that Mathiassen had reported. He had named it Koch Island but had not been able to visit it. From there I thought I might be able to see the two large islands, both called Sadleq, that Reynold and I had first been told about in Qaunnaq's camp at Gore Bay. The more eastern Sadleq, which many years later was officially named Bray Island, had been visible across the sea ice on our journey to and from Piling. Our path had taken us too far north to see the western Sadleq.

We left the ravine, camped just outside it, and set out next evening. The sun was above the horizon all the time, but the nights were usually cooler, making for better sledging. In a strong wind we drove down the river on which the water had now frozen. Much longer distances could be covered at this time of year than during the winter. The komatik ran easily over the ice, there was no deep snow, and we did not have to stop to re-ice the runners. Our destination was Maniqtuuq, a small island where there was usually an Inuit camp. Here we hoped to find some seal or walrus to feed our dogs rather than the caribou meat, which Kutjek wanted to take back to his family. When we got there we found the Inuit had left a few days earlier. We had been travelling for well over twenty-four hours so we camped and slept throughout the day. We were very close to the much larger island of Kagiuyak.

It was still dark when we sledged the remaining seven miles to reach Kagiuyak. I did not then know the Inuit history of what had happened on that island some time in the eighteenth century. A large party of Inuit from Pond Inlet, wanting to avoid vengeance for a murder their leader had committed, travelled to Kangirl-lukjuak and on to Kagiuyak. Here they found game was plentiful in the summer, but more than thirty people starved in the winter. They had been used to hunting seal on the firm sea ice in the fiords, and they did not know the techniques of hunting evolved in Foxe Basin where strong currents broke off the sea ice soon after it had formed.

We drove the two miles on land to the highest point of the low limestone island, a small hill called Potonik, which I estimated to be about two hundred feet high and from which there was an unobstructed view. The weather was perfect – a beautiful morning, clear, and cloudless. I could see the northern part of

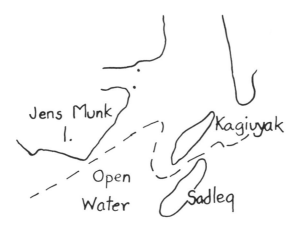

Map 10   Rough map drawn by author from the hill, Potonik, on Kagiuyak

Foxe Basin to the horizon and beyond because the land was loom-ing strongly. To the south was open water and across it, about ten miles away, lay a very large island, the western Sadleq, its coast running to the southwest as far as I could see. Its area is now known to be well over one thousand square kilometres. Like Kagiuyak it was of light grey limestone but rising rather higher. To the east I thought I could just make out the eastern Sadleq with dark sky above it. Far to the west Cape Konig, the south-ernmost point of Jens Munk Island, shone in the bright sun. I could not help feeling elated to be the first to share this magnificent prospect with the Inuit. Potonik was a splendid vantage point from which I recorded a round of compass bearings which included Cape Thalbitzer and the eastern entrance to Murray Maxwell Bay.

We continued southwest for what I estimated to be nine and a half miles to a point where I could take the bearing of Potonik and some of the same places as before. From this base line and my compass readings I could later make a rough estimate of their positions. Turning back, we checked the distance to Potonik and passed Maniqtuuq before we camped. It had been an exciting day and I would be able to add one more large island to the map of Canada. In fifteen years time DEW Line stations would be under construction on both it and the other Sadleq.

It was time to return to Igloolik. Our dogs were now too tired and hungry to work well, and we had to walk by the komatik most of the way. Kutjek hunted two or three seals but could not get near them. We went first to Iglorsuit, near Cape Thalbitzer, and then to a camp at the eastern end of Jens Munk Island where we spent the night. At both places the people were still away. Next day we met a man travelling with his family who had dog-food to spare and gave us all we needed. Nasook was the oldest son of the leading man at the Iglorsuit camp. Many years later he became a canon in the Anglican church and was appointed to the Order of Canada. He was the only Inuk I met in my travels who was a non-smoker and had no interest in tobacco. Fortunately we still had some tea and biscuits, and could also give him a few boxes of matches of which he had run short.

The dogs had a good feed when we camped and, after a sound sleep, we set off on the last stage of our journey. Travel was fast because most of the pools of water that form on the sea ice when the snow melts in the spring sun had drained through the seal holes. We stopped for a rest at Siorarsuk but did not camp. Soon after this break Kutjek shot a silverjar, a year-old ring seal which makes excellent clothing and is also good to eat. We reached Igloolik Point that evening, and Kutjek went on to rejoin his family at Akudneq. We had travelled a long distance but had been away only eleven nights.

Serious sledging was now over for me for the year. Things had turned out better than I could have hoped. We had however had one major failure. Mino's long journey had not found him a wife. We had been together so much that I could share his uncomplaining disappointment.

I arranged to stay the night with Arnatsiaq, another of Ituksarjuat's sons, and Ituksarjuat and Ataguttaaluk returned later that day from Arctic Bay with several other Inuit. They were in excellent spirits and very friendly, happy to be home after being away for over a month. In the morning I accompanied Arnatsiaq and his family to the mission and found both priests there. Two days later Father Trébaol and a son of Arnatsiaq were going to Abverdjar, and I went with them to look at the site. Some inches of snow covered where I wanted to excavate, but it was melting fast. As soon as I was back at the mission I began to get everything ready and when a team went to Abverdjar at the end of the week I took the opportunity to move there.

I had all I really needed for the summer though I was rather short of tobacco. I would have bought more at Arctic Bay but I had misunderstood how much Pat said he would leave for me of the excellent Barneys tobacco he and Reynold had been given.

28

Excavating at Abverdjar

8 June – 16 September 1939

Abverdjar is on the east coast of an island that lies west of the rather larger Igloolik Island and is separated from it by a strait less than two miles wide. The two islands are very different in character. Igloolik is formed of flat-bedded light grey limestone, its horizontal geometry accentuated by old beach lines rising like wide steps out of the sea, while Abverdjar is typical Canadian Shield of dark brown, weathered granite with steep shores and rocky knolls hiding small lakes. Whenever I moved from one to the other, I was struck by the contrast.

Father Bazin had built a small cabin at Abverdjar in which he or Father Trébaol would often stay when there were people at the camp there. With his customary kindness, he said I could use it throughout the summer. The cabin gave me a place to sort, study, and pack the artifacts I hoped to dig. Here I unloaded my possessions and shared a meal with Arnatsiaq's son before he returned to Igloolik. Left on my own I could examine my new surroundings.

To the east lay the low coast of Igloolik Island and to the north I could see across the sea ice of the eastern approaches to Fury and Hecla Strait. Behind me the rough ground rose steeply enough to cut off my view of the lake that lay behind the rise. The cabin was about twelve feet wide and ten feet long with a single glass window, a narrow wooden bed, a bench, and a table. It had been used frequently and had not yet had its spring cleaning but that would take only a day or two.

Outside were the turf walls of the houses where the Inuit lived in the fall, adding a roof of skins and canvas supported by wooden spars. I could see where they had been cutting turf, which was where Father Bazin said they had found the artifacts in the collection he had given me. It was a gradually sloping bank of turf rising from a height of about twenty-three feet to forty feet above high-water mark.

The Inuit had taken away the turf from part of the gradual slope near their fall houses, but much of it was undisturbed. A trial dig showed that below the turf a layer of soil lay directly on beach sand, and underneath that was a yielding white clay. The thickness of the turf and soil combined varied from about ten inches at the bottom of the bank to as little as two or three inches at the top. Apart from the recent Inuit sod houses, the only signs of dwellings on the surface were three or four scarcely visible circular hollows, up to four yards in diameter, near the top of the bank.

The land west of Hudson Bay was known to be rising, sometimes at the rate of about a metre a century, and the raised beaches on Igloolik Island showed a similar uplift, though the rate there was then unknown. As Inuit usually camp by the sea, it is often possible to estimate the age of a site by its height above sea level, but at Abverdjar the Dorset site was at much the same height as the present Inuit camp.

I was not alone for long because Abverdjar lay close to a route that many Igloolik hunters followed. Sledging on the sea ice remained possible until mid-July and I often had visitors. Abverdjar was a convenient place to stop to drink tea, but I think their real reason was concern for my well-being. They wanted to make sure that nothing had happened to me. The second day I was there Kutjek came to see me with Panikpakuttuk, who said he would like to help me excavate later in the summer.

Visitors were very welcome because the weather was terrible. Instead of the twenty-four hours of bright sunshine that is common in Igloolik in June, each day seemed to bring snow, hail, mist, rain, and wind, and I did not see the sun for days on end. I could only make test excavations, and each hole I dug quickly filled with water. A pond at a rather higher level than the cabin overflowed its banks and a small swift stream began to erode the turf that had been used to bank the cabin. My archaeological shovel came in useful for building small dams and cutting new channels.

I spent much of my time exploring the island, hunting, looking for nests, and cleaning the cabin. Less successful were my attempts to dry caribou meat by hanging thin strips on a line. Whenever I put some out to dry, the rain began, and each time I moved the meat I could not resist eating a little. The end of June brought a few dry and sunny days, but by then I had no caribou left to dry.

Despite the lack of sun, there was no doubt that summer was approaching. Snow buntings, immaculate in their black and white summer plumage, were everywhere, and a nest behind the cabin soon held five eggs. They were followed by lapland longspurs. Phalaropes swam in small circles in the ponds. Large flocks of eiders flew over the sea ice, always seeming in a desperate hurry. Choruses of oldsquaw, the shattering cries of passing red-throated loons, and the screams of gulls filled the air. Arctic terns, with energy undiminished by their long migration from the Antarctic, swooped on me if I approached any area they wanted to protect, and the predatory aerobatics of jaegers reminded me of the less pleasing side of bird life. The first purple saxifrages flowered, to be followed by the first mountain avens and the first arctic poppies. A few bumble-bees and butterflies seemed to add an exotic touch.

For over a week I had no visitors, probably because of the miserable weather, and I realized that before going to Abverdjar I had never in my life passed more than a few hours without seeing another soul. I was not lonely and I probably appreciated the advent of the northern spring more fully without the distractions of company. A thousand years earlier, solitary Celtic monks on isolated islands off the west coasts of Scotland and Ireland must have felt much the same.

I had no difficulty in finding enough to eat, though this could be time-consuming. Ptarmigan, ducks, eggs, and seal gave variety. If I had more than I needed I could give the surplus to visitors, who often supplemented what I had. I lent a pair of sunglasses to Amiimiarjuk, who was suffering from snow-blindness on his way fishing, and he returned them with a very welcome arctic char. On the last day of June Panikpakuttuk arrived with his grandfather, and stayed behind when his grandfather left a few hours later. I put up a tent to give us more room and we slept in it for a few nights, but another spell of wind and driving rain followed, and we retreated to the cabin from a tent that was always threatening to blow away.

A week later Aipilik came with a party who stopped overnight, and he too decided to remain. The stormy weather had reduced the flow of visitors and Panikpakuttuk was very pleased to have someone much nearer his own age to talk to and to keep him company. As well as helping me to excavate, Aipilik enjoyed hunting for our food and was much better at it than I.

Many years later I heard the story of Aipilik's birth, a story that is still told in Igloolik. He was a month premature and neither his mother nor a twin brother survived. The tiny baby was handed to his grandmother, who put him inside the wide sleeve of her caribou-skin atigi. Here, safe and warm in the fur, he was watched day and night in the igloo. From time to time she plucked a single caribou hair from her sleeve to hold near the baby's nostrils to see if he were alive and breathing. The Inuit say a month passed without her sleeping, and then she had slept for two days.

All our visitors were not welcome. I had already seen one or two mosquitoes, but now they arrived in numbers. I was spared them for the next three days because I developed very severe tonsilitis which kept me inside. I have no idea what caused it. Neither Aipilik nor Panikpakuttuk was affected and they spent the time hunting.

Before beginning the exciting adventure of excavating, I had photographed the site and laid out a baseline on the sloping bank from which to measure the position of every artifact we uncovered. We found little within the turf, but in the soil below it and on, but not in, the underlying sand there were artifacts scattered all over the bank. In some places a number of horizontal flat stones, apparently arranged as small, irregular, incomplete pavements lay on the sand. Some of these pavements were within and some outside the circles just visible on the surface, and I could determine no relationship between them. They might have been floors for some sort of shelter, but there were no stone tent rings and, while the faint circles were all near the top of the bank, artifacts were more plentiful lower down. The people who had made these artifacts probably lived in turf, snow, or skin shelters.

I soon became confident that this must be a pure Dorset culture site. Eventually we excavated some 1500 artifacts. Only one

showed any drilled holes and that was found partly within the
turf. Many had holes, from the eyes of tiny needles to holes for
binding ivory sledge runners, but they were all gouged. Most artifacts, including nearly one hundred harpoon heads, were of types
ascribed by Diamond Jenness to the Dorset culture; a few were
different from any found before and could well be Dorset. It was
also clear that the collection Father Bazin had given me was from
this site and this site alone.

Sometimes we dug at night when the mosquitoes were fewer.
I remember one day watching a snow bunting eating mosquitoes.
It seemed less active than most birds when feeding, and I realized
this was because it could catch all the mosquitoes it wanted without moving its feet. Around the middle of July the sea ice became
unsafe for sledging, though Aipilik would venture onto it to hunt
seals. By the end of the month there was enough water by the
beach for us to set a net. The next day the ice went out and
what had seemed a white desert to the horizon changed overnight
to blue sea. It was as if a curtain had been raised.

The first whaleboats arrived within a day and the cabin was
soon crowded with people drinking tea. The Iglulingmiut had several whaleboats, which were used to move camp and for hunting
walrus and seals. They were about the size of the *Polecat* and most
had reached Igloolik by being lashed to komatiks, and hauled from
Repulse Bay by dog team. The Inuit told us the date was 30 July.
I thought they were wrong because my diary made it 27 July.
I found out later that it was I who was wrong. The sky had been
overcast so much, the nights had been as light as the days, I had
gone to bed when I was tired, and I never knew how long I had
slept. Early in the summer I had broken my watch, and tides were
not so obvious when the sea was covered in ice. Somewhere I
had lost three days.

The Inuit were now starting to hunt caribou on Melville Peninsula, and we became a port of call on the way there and back.
The whaleboats depended on sail so we could see them coming
and have a kettle boiling before their crews landed. In one boat
I saw a large loon they had shot. That evening I was looking in
Taverner's *Birds of Canada* and realized that it could only have been
a yellow-billed loon, which was supposed to be a Western Arctic
bird and had never been reported in the east. The boat had already
sailed so I told those in the next boat bound in the same direction

that I would have liked the skin. Skins of loons were used as towels, so it had not been thrown away, and a week or two later another boat brought it back to me. I learned that these loons often bred on Melville Peninsula. The skin provided Dr Taverner with evidence for extending the range of the yellow-billed loon by several hundred miles.

We had been having little luck with our fishing because the shore sloped too steeply for us to wade out to the full length of the net to set and check it. For this we needed a boat. We found three empty ten-gallon oil drums by the side of the cabin and were able to lash them to three pieces of wood to form a triangle. Aipilik sat in the centre with a rope round his waist and we pushed him out to set the net, and to check it once or twice a day. From then on we caught more char than we could eat.

Meanwhile our excavating continued. Though we did not know what the Dorset people at Abverdjar had used as shelter from the weather, hardly a day passed without our learning something new about them. We collected the bones we dug up and older hunters would help us identify them, which they could usually do without hesitation. The Dorset people had hunted walrus, ring and bearded seal, polar bear, caribou, and fox, the fox bones being surprisingly numerous. They also killed some birds. From the fish spears we excavated we knew they caught fish, but fish bones had not survived. There were no bones of bowhead whale, white whale, and narwhal, nor of dog. We excavated no human bones and I could find no old graves anywhere near Abverdjar.

Our growing collection showed that the Dorset people had a rich material culture. The chert points and tools were carefully flaked and sometimes ground, as were the few slate blades. There were two new types of stone tools, burin-like chert tools that were both flaked and ground, and quartz crystals with one end sharpened to a chisel-like edge. Ivory, bone, and antler artifacts were small and usually beautifully finished. Soapstone had been used for oval-shaped lamps and pots, with both inside and outside often coloured with red ochre; soapstone was not used for carvings. Some of the bone tools were of new types, such as a small, barbed, antler trident, pieces of caribou leg bones sharpened to a chisel edge, and straight pieces of hard bone roughened to use as flint flakers. We found only two scraps of metal, a short length of copper wire used as a binding and a very small copper point.

In Father Bazin's collection, a fragment of iron, probably meteoric, had been used as a knife blade.

The Dorset people did not leave only tools, weapons, and bones. Among them there were artists of superb skill and our greatest excitements came when one of us shouted that he was finding something unusually good. Sometimes we had to wait for hours or even overnight before the ground had thawed enough for it to be removed safely for us to admire. The most beautiful were ivory carvings an inch or two long of bears, walrus, seals, caribou, and birds, or parts of these animals, carved with amazing precision, and each with a little hole for suspension. One carving was a man with a child on his shoulders. A very unusual piece was a section of antler about eight inches long on which twenty-eight human faces had been carved, each different and one indicating tattoo markings. It was as if the Dorset people were leaving us their record of what they wanted and how they looked.

Two other types of artifacts were particularly intriguing. One consisted of paddle-shaped ivory pendants about three inches long, often with incised lines and dots in patterns that must have had some special significance, because some of the patterns are repeated exactly on similar pendants found elsewhere in the north. The other consisted of thin strips of antler and oval pieces of caribou scapula, which had been tied together to form small boxes. Both the ends and the sides sometimes bore complicated, often tree-like, incised patterns.

Almost as interesting as what we found was what we did not find. The well-worn sledge runners but no dog bones or trace toggles suggested their sledges were probably drawn by hand. There were no ulus, the curved knives that played so large a part in the lives of Thule women and are still used today. We found no evidence for bows, nor for kayaks or umiaks though the Dorset people must have had some sort of boat. They seemed not to have hunted any whales. Negative evidence is not as convincing as archaeological finds, but the Dorset people appeared to have lived very different lives from the Thule.

The elevation of the site above sea level indicated an earliest date of about AD 1000. The method of dating archaelogical material by carbon-14 analysis was not known when I was digging at Abverdjar. Ivory from the site has since been dated in this way, however, and suggests a probable occupation date of AD 900 to 1000.

Walking by the sea one morning I found a long piece of driftwood, brought thousands of miles by the vagaries of wind and current probably from Siberia. I thought what such a find must have meant in Dorset times, when the people knew nothing straight and strong in their country, except the tusk of a narwhal, an animal they seldom if ever killed here. Wood could be used for poles, shafts, sledges, bows, arrows, and boats; it could be shaped and carved much more easily than bone, ivory, or antler. As a rare chance gift from an unknown world it must have seemed a treasure; in quantity it would have transformed their material culture.

Inuit continued to arrive in their whaleboats, one of which took Panikpakuttuk back to his family who were hunting caribou. One man told me that he and another man still sometimes used a bow and arrow, partly because they were quieter than guns and did not frighten the caribou, and partly because of the cost of ammunition. Unfortunately he did not have his bow with him.

Inuit often brought me artifacts they had found in old houses. They were usually Thule specimens because the Thule stone houses were so conspicuous. One small collection was wrapped up in a birdskin, which I could not recognize or find in *Birds of Canada*. I asked if it were a common bird. They said it was not, adding that they knew Reynold had been interested in birds and so they had kept it. I wrapped the specimens again in the birdskin and packed them away.

By early August the mosquitoes were past their worst and I could swim in the nearby lake. Aipilik said he would like to be able to swim and so I taught him. I was surprised and pleased at how quickly he learned. The water was much too cold for protracted lessons. He became the only Iglulingmiut who could swim, and I have been told that, many years later, he was able to rescue two children who were being carried out to sea on a piece of ice.

As August wore on, my time grew shorter. The previous year I had heard on 26 August that the *Thérèse* was having trouble with ice in Foxe Basin. If ice conditions were easier this year, she could reach Igloolik by the end of the month. A whaleboat arrived on 27 August by my diary and I decided it was time to return to the mission on Igloolik Island. Three days earlier there had been ice on pools in the rocks. When I remembered I might have lost three days and it could be 30 August, I packed up quickly.

The next day Kutjek's boat arrived. He had Mino with him, and I heard for the first time that Mino's search had reached a very happy conclusion. During the summer he had married a most capable widow who had brought three sons and a daughter with her. They formed a contented family and Mino was cheerful and relaxed with an air of accomplishment. I could share his satisfaction just as I had shared his earlier disappointment.

We were delayed another day by a storm and drifting snow, but the weather cleared and we had a quick sail to the mission, where I learned that it was really 2 September. There was no sign of the ship. I spent two days packing to be ready if the *Thérèse* should arrive.

The arctic summer is too short for an archaeologist to waste, so I decided to investigate a site on Igloolik Island that was little more than an hour's walk from the mission. By this date the previous year the *Thérèse* had decided not to make another attempt to reach Igloolik and was unloading the Igloolik mission freight at Repulse. It seemed history was repeating itself, and I would learn nothing by waiting at the mission. I was not in the least worried that I would probably not be able to sail for the south. I was very happy at Igloolik and I would have a perfect excuse for staying there.

Kutjek loaded his boat with our camping things and we sailed to Arnaquaksaat, at the southwest corner of Igloolik Island where there were a number of well-preserved Thule stone houses. They did not appear old and the stones of the bed platforms and kudliq stands had been little disturbed in some of them. Both Kutjek and Mino brought their families. It was a good place for seals, and Kutjek and Mino spent the days hunting in the boat while Aipilik and I excavated and the women looked after the children, cooked, sewed, and cleaned the skins of the seals the hunters killed.

The ground was beginning to freeze and we had the first heavy snowfall on 7 September. In the short time we had for excavation the site proved interesting because I soon found the Thule houses were built where Dorset people had lived before. The large stone and whalebone houses emphasized the contrast with the Dorset people, who had left little trace of where they had lived. I wished I had more time to explore whether the two cultures were related in any way.

I walked over to the mission once or twice. The fathers were no longer expecting the *Thérèse* and were as unconcerned as I. Father Bazin would still be much better off than he had been for most of the time he had lived at Igloolik, and he and Father Trébaol had already shared the experience of waiting for a ship that did not arrive. It came therefore as a surprise when, walking to the mission on 14 September, I saw the *Thérèse* approaching the bay under a leaden sky.

Hurrying down the hill to the shore I did not know whether to be pleased or sorry, or whether I would go south in the ship or stay in the north. I had completed what I had set out to do, though in fact it was the Inuit who were responsible for any success I had had, together with good luck. The arrival of the ship had destroyed my excuse for staying in the north. Now that I would be able to leave I realized more fully the extent to which I had become attached to the land and the people.

The fathers and I rowed out to the *Thérèse* as soon as she anchored. We found that as well as the mission's supplies she was carrying everything for a Hudson's Bay Company post at Igloolik, including the manager, John Stanners, who had been in charge of the Pond Inlet post when I had first arrived there with Jack Turner. We asked what was happening outside and learned that Germany had invaded France, and war had been declared ten days before. There was now no thought of my staying at Igloolik.

We had little time to hear about the war or even to listen to the reports on the ship's radio. The supplies for both the mission and the HBC had to be unloaded, as well as lumber for the HBC buildings, and the *Thérèse* did not have the comparatively large crew of the *Nascopie* to discharge cargo and assist with construction. I had to arrange payment of the Inuit who had helped me and to distribute possessions I now no longer needed, including two tents, two rifles, a down sleeping bag, and some duffle. Nothing else was pleasant about departing.

The *Thérèse* was at Igloolik for less than two days. I went round the tents to say goodbye to everybody. One old man I particularly liked could speak a little English and I remember what he said as we shook hands:

"War again?" "Yes."

"Germans again?" "Yes."

"You go fight war?" "Probably."

"Damn fool. You stay here."

His words came back to me as we sailed. Igloolik faded into the distance and I realized how much I hated to leave and that I was closing a chapter of my life.

29

South to the war

16 September – December 1939

The *Thérèse* had other calls to make before she headed for the south. The next place on her itinerary had been Cape Dorset, but the calm in which we had sailed from Igloolik changed later in the day to storm and mist, making conditions too risky for her to try to enter the harbour there. Instead we went first to Southampton Island. Here we anchored well out from Coral Harbour, giving us a five-hour row to the post. I spent a short night ashore talking to the HBC post manager, who was from New Zealand, before we rowed back to the ship early in the morning.

Not until 22 September did we get in to Cape Dorset, where the *Thérèse* had established a Catholic mission earlier that summer. Cape Dorset had two trading posts because the Baffin Trading Company had set up there in opposition to the HBC. The Baffin manager was Felix Conrad, who had spent many years at Repulse Bay with the Revillon company.

Crossing Hudson Strait to the bold coast marked by Cape Wolstenholme, we visited the post where Jimmy Thom, the HBC manager, met us. He too had a Repulse background, and had been the clerk who had tried to persuade Captain Cleveland to install the windows the correct way round. He took us to the Catholic mission at Ivugivik and back before we sailed for Wakeham Bay, where there was another mission the *Thérèse* had supplied earlier that year. Here we were delayed, ostensibly by a gale at the entrance to Hudson Strait, but I suspect because this was the last port of call, and there was a celebration to mark the completion of the summer's work. The crew had to have time to recover before we could sail. Out in Hudson Strait the weather was fine with little wind, and it remained beautiful as we rounded Cape Chidley for an uneventful run down the Labrador coast. The *Thérèse* was diesel-powered but she set sails, which increased her speed and held her steady despite her shallow draft.

We saw no other ships until we were in the Gulf of St Lawrence. We heard later that the German pocket battleship *Deutschland* was off Labrador at the time. Even had she seen us she would probably have decided we were not worth sinking because this would give away her position. The weather was clear and sunny and the leaves were beginning to turn as we sailed along the North Shore to dock in Quebec City on 3 October.

I took the train to Montreal to thank Bishop Turquetil for the hospitality I had enjoyed at his missions and on board the *Thérèse*, and to pay the very small charge they had made for my transportation. From there I went to Ottawa to stay with Dr Dave Nichols of the Geological Survey of Canada, whom I had met on board the *Nascopie* in 1937.

I had no doubt that the war would last a long time, and that I would become involved in it though I did not know how. There seemed to be no chance of joining the Canadian forces. A friend of Dave, John FitzRandolph, came round one evening. Some years earlier he had been an RCMP constable in Baffin Island but he was now the adjutant of a unit in the Canadian army. He told me that a number of units, including his, were being brought up to war strength. The vacancies were however being filled by the many thousands of volunteers from those units of the Non-Permanent Active Militia that had not been mobilized.

I heard that Pat Baird had reached Pond Inlet and had gone on to Bylot Island. In June he had sledged into the interior of the island, but had gashed his left hand badly and could do little during the rest of the summer. The *Nascopie* had brought him south with Jack Ford from Pond Inlet and Bill Ford from Arctic Bay, and all three had joined the army together in Montreal. Tom and Jackie Manning were thought to be in Foxe Basin; they did not learn we were at war until they visited Cape Dorset in January 1940. I decided I would return to England, but I thought I should first record what I had discovered in the north.

Dr Diamond Jenness examined the material I had excavated at Abverdjar. It fully supported the theories he had advanced, and he pointed out to me features I had not noticed. There were some new types of artifacts and he was particularly interested in what he identified as an ice-creeper, a strip of ivory that was tied under the foot to prevent slipping on glare ice. Identical ice-creepers had been found in Alaska. I was particularly grateful to Dr Jenness for the help he gave me in writing an account of my work, together with a résumé of what was then known about the Dorset culture, for publication in the *American Anthropologist*.

I went to see those in the surveyor-general's office who were responsible for northern mapping to tell them what I had discovered about the route across Baffin Island and the islands in northern Foxe Basin and to give them the maps I had made. I thought there might be a need for maps of the Arctic before the war was over. Years later I was told that my discoveries were included in the new maps of the north that Canada compiled for the us Army Air Force when it first began to fly over Baffin Island during the war.

While unpacking my specimens I came across the birdskin in which some of them had been wrapped. I took it to Dr Percy Taverner, along with the skin of the yellow-billed loon, and asked him what it was. He looked excited as well as puzzled, and said he could not be sure and would have to send it to a specialist in Toronto for confirmation, but he believed it could only be a fieldfare. This bird, well known in Europe, had never before been found in either Canada or the United States. His identification proved correct and the fieldfare became a new addition to the lists of Canadian and North American birds.

As soon as I could see an end to my work in Ottawa, I booked a passage to England early in December. I had actually telephoned for a taxi to take me to the station to catch the boat train, when Dave Nichols came in to say goodbye. He had by chance that morning met John FitzRandolph, who had asked about me. The taxi had not yet arrived so I telephoned John. He mentioned he had been notified that morning of an increase in the authorized size of his unit and asked if I was still thinking of joining the Canadian army. I replied that I had telephoned to say goodbye because I was just about to return to England.

I took my baggage downstairs to the now-waiting taxi and asked to be driven to the station. In the taxi I could arrange my thoughts. I realized I was following a course of action only because all arrangements had been made. I knew the time the train left and the ship would sail a few hours later, but there was no real reason why I should be tied to this chain of events. I had learned in the north to avoid rigid plans. As we reached the end of the road I asked the driver not to turn left to the station but right to the temporary barracks where FitzRandolph's unit was being mobilized. Before the end of the day I was in the Canadian army and within a month I was again on my way to England, as assistant adjutant on the *Empress of Australia*, an old German liner that had become part of the Canadian Pacific fleet as reparations after the First World War, and was now a trooper. I would not return to Canada and the Arctic until the war in Europe was over.

Ataguttaaluk

The cold seeped through the wall and turned to stone
  All she'd held warm and dear. The bed she shared
  With death she stripped of sleeping skins, and bared
Their shrivelled bodies, skin drawn tight on bone,
Their spirits could endure through her alone,
  Her will to live, which flickered, faded, flared.
  Only her dead were left as she prepared
To end her hopeless struggle to postpone
The ease of death. Cold, comatose, and blind,
  Light yields to darkness. Silence, the absolute pall,
Covers the igloo, spreads within her mind.
  Faint in space-time she hears a snowbird call,
Singing of spring, and steeling her to find
  Courage to face the cruellest test of all.

Igloolik, 1993

Game

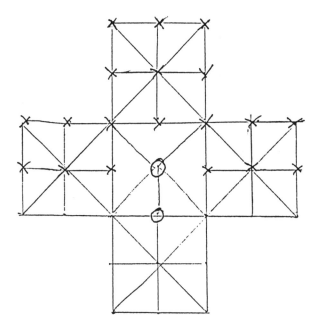

A has 19 men placed as shown – X. He is the attacker.
B has 2 men placed as shown – O. He is the defender.
Moves are made along the lines.
Only B can take men and does so as in checkers or draughts –
by jumping over an opponent's man into an unoccupied space.
A tries to confine B's men so they cannot move.
B starts.

Life histories

AIPILIK   Aipilik remained in the Igloolik area and was employed for some years at the scientific laboratory there. After he retired he was always busy hunting, fishing, or carving ivory until he died in 1995. Two or three years ago he had gone to hunt ptarmigan with a .22 rifle and brought home a polar bear. Once when I visited Igloolik I asked a daughter of his if there was anything he would like. She replied, "You know my father. He is a very simple man. All he wants is to have many children, and for them to love him." He must have died content knowing that he had some hundred descendants and that he was loved by everybody at Igloolik.

PAT BAIRD   Pat Baird went overseas in the First Division of the Canadian Army. He was soon commissioned, trained as a commando, and became involved in mountain and arctic warfare training in the United Kingdom, Iceland, and Canada. He commanded the moving force of Exercise Musk-Ox, which carried out a journey of over three thousand miles in northern Canada in the winter and spring of 1946. He directed the Montreal office of the Arctic Institute of North America for some years and led the institute's summer expeditions to the Barnes Ice Cap and Penny Highland in Baffin Island. Later he taught at the University of Aberdeen. In 1960 McGill University asked him to return to Canada to lecture and direct the university's field station at Mont Saint-Hilaire. After retiring he led several climbing parties in Baffin Island. He died on New Year's Day 1984.

FATHER ÉTIENNE BAZIN   Poor health forced Father Bazin to leave Igloolik and to return in 1948 to Burgundy where he was a parish priest for over twenty years. He died in 1972.

PETER BENNETT   Soon after returning to England, Peter was posted to India and seconded to the Madras Sappers and Miners. In the Second World War he served with them in Iraq and later in Burma throughout the Burmese War. In 1947 he returned to Canada to lead a group of British Army officers studying winter warfare in the Canadian Arctic and spent another year there. He served with the British airborne forces before retiring as a colonel. Peter then lived in Devon and Northumberland, dying at Hexham in 1993.

SAM FORD   After Clyde River, Sam Ford became post manager at Cape Smith and then Povungnituk, before retiring from the Hudson's Bay Company in 1945 to live in St John's, Newfoundland. In the summer of 1950 he joined the Eastern Arctic Patrol as an interpreter on the C.D. Howe. He was killed that year when the ship's helicopter crashed into the sea at the mouth of the Koksoak River shortly after taking off from the ship's deck.

ITUKSARJUAT and ATAGUTTAALUK   Ituksarjuat died towards the end of the war, and the camp at Abverdjar was then abandoned because he had said people had lived there too long and the land should rest. Ataguttaaluk was the dominant personality in Igloolik until she died of influenza in July 1948. The school at Igloolik was named after her at the request of those living there.

DICK KEELING   Dick Keeling left us to become the doctor on the Eastern Arctic Patrol in the Nascopie for the northern part of her voyage in 1936. After she docked in Halifax he returned to England to specialize in gynaecology, but with the outbreak of war he joined the Royal Army Medical Corps, going to France in 1939. He was evacuated from the Dunkirk beaches the following June and was then posted to command a field ambulance in North Africa. From there he went to Sicily and Italy and was at the battle of Monte Cassino. After six years in the army he decided it was too late to specialize in gynaecology and turned to general practice in Reading until he retired to Somerset. He died during a visit to Kenya early in 1990.

KUTJEK and PANIKPAKUTTUK   Kutjek remained a successful, reliable, and responsible hunter. Panikpakuttuk became leader of the camp at Usuarjuk for several years and then worked on the Distant Early Warning (DEW) Line. He now lives and hunts at Hall Beach. I last saw him in 1993, and we agreed that we would no longer be able to fit into the same sleeping bag.

TOM MANNING   Tom did not hear about the war until he visited Cape Dorset in January 1940, and another year passed before he and Jackie could reach Churchill and the south. He then joined the Royal Canadian Navy, spending much of the war assisting the US Armed Services in the Arctic in such ways as siting the airfield they built on Southampton Island. He also advised on and tested arctic equipment and worked on other defence-related activities in the north. After the war he completed a number of difficult but invariably successful arctic journeys when working for the Defence Research Board, the Geodetic Survey of Canada, the Geographical Branch, and the National Museum of Canada in many parts of the north, while continuing his own zoological research. Few, if any, have equalled him as an arctic traveller. He now lives near Burritts Rapids, Ontario.

MINO   The improvement in Mino's fortunes continued until his death late in 1953 in hospital in Montreal. He had become a successful hunter and family man, and is fondly remembered in Igloolik.

ALEX STEVENSON   In 1937 Alex was transferred to Ungava Bay and was in charge of the post at Port Burwell in 1940 when he went on furlough and joined the Royal Canadian Air Force. He was shot down near Bremen in 1942 and spent most of the rest of the war in a prisoner of war camp in Silesia. In January 1945 his group of prisoners was forced to march west ahead of the advancing Russians who liberated them in May. Returning to Canada that July, he rejoined the Hudson's Bay Company, but after a few months he took a position in the Department of Resources

and Development because he thought he could do more there
to help the Inuit. He developed a great interest in arctic history,
and had become administrator of the Eastern Arctic before retiring
in 1975. He died seven years later.

CANON JACK TURNER   Jack continued his long pastoral journeys
each winter. In 1944 his fiancée arrived from England in the
Nascopie to join him, and they were married at Pond Inlet, moving
later to Moffet Inlet. In late September 1947, when he was returning from hunting, he slipped and his gun discharged wound-
ing him in the head. It was the period of freeze-up, making it
impossible for an aircraft to land. A Canadian Army team including a doctor was dropped by parachute to help his wife look
after him. Ice conditions forced them to abandon an attempt to
sail to Arctic Bay. On 21 November the ice on a lake twenty-
three miles away had become thick enough for an RCAF Dakota
to land and pick up the party who had managed to sledge there.
Jack was taken to hospital in Winnipeg where he died that
December.

Publications from the expedition

Bennett, P.M. "The British Canadian Arctic Expedition."
Geographical Journal 95 (1940): 109-20
Bray, R.J.O. "Notes on the Birds of Southampton Island, Baffin
Island and Melville Peninsula (with Comments by T.H. Man-
ning)." *Auk* 60 (1943): 504-36
Bray, R.J.O., and G.W. Rowley. "A Winter in Foxe Basin." *Times*
(London), 16 May 1938
Manning, E.W. *Igloo for the Night*. London: Hodder and Stoughton
1943
Manning, T.H. "Blue and Lesser Snow Geese on Southampton
and Baffin Islands." *Auk* 59 (1942): 158-75
- "Eskimo Stone Houses in Foxe Basin." *Arctic* 3, no. 2 (1950):
108-12
- "Hunting Implements and Methods of the Present-Day Eski-
mos of North-west Hudson Bay, Melville Peninsula, and
South-west Baffin Island." *Geographical Journal* 103 (1944): 137-
52
- "Notes on the Coastal District of the eastern Barren Grounds
and Melville Peninsula from Igloolik to Cape Fullerton."
Canadian Geographical Journal 26 (1943): 84-105
- "Notes on Some Fish of the Eastern Canadian Arctic." *Canadian
Field-Naturalist* 56 (1942): 128-29
- "Notes on the Mammals of South and Central West Baffin Is-
land." *Journal of Mammalogy* 24 (1943): 47-59
- "Remarks on the Physiography, Eskimos, and Mammals of
Southampton Island." *Canadian Geographical Journal* 24 (1942): 17-
38

- "The Foxe Basin Coasts of Baffin Island." *Geographical Journal*
  101 (1943): 225-51
Manning, T.H., and E.W. Manning. "The Preparation of Skins
  and Clothing in the Eastern Canadian Arctic." *Polar Record* 4, no.
  28 (1944): 156-69
Rowley, G.W. "Snow-house Building." *Polar Record* 2, no. 16
  (1938): 109-16
- "The Dorset Culture of the Eastern Arctic." *American Anthropologist, New Series* 42 (1940): 490-9
Taverner, P.A. "Fieldfare, an Addition to the American List and
  Some Arctic Notes." *Auk* 57 (1940): 119

Index